Disability and Medieval Law

Disability and Medieval Law: History, Literature, Society

Edited by

Cory James Rushton

CAMBRIDGE SCHOLARS

PUBLISHING

Disability and Medieval Law: History, Literature, Society
Edited by Cory James Rushton

This book first published 2013

Cambridge Scholars Publishing

12 Back Chapman Street, Newcastle upon Tyne, NE6 2XX, UK

British Library Cataloguing in Publication Data
A catalogue record for this book is available from the British Library

ISBN (10): 1-4438-4973-1, ISBN (13): 978-1-4438-4973-9

TABLE OF CONTENTS

PREFACE

This book began as a series of round table papers at the annual medieval conference held in Leeds. During the book's long journey to completion, the study of medieval disability has gone from a slightly suspicious fringe activity to an increasingly central, vibrant field. It has also become a strangely fractured field, prone to producing studies that always feel like the first study. In one way, this should be expected: disability theory itself has long argued that the field has an interesting, even dynamic, tension between the study of disability as an idea and as a social group, and disability as a category composed of different, sometimes radically different, lived experiences. Attempts to create social or legal policy on a one-size-fits-all model are doomed to failure, just as any grand narrative of the history of medieval disability in the west must be doomed to fail. To that end, a book like this one seems timely: a series of case studies united only by the question of how the Middle Ages dealt with the conflict between personal impairment and the law, case studies which might help colour in some of the many blank areas in our understanding.

Some thanks yous are in order. First, to St Francis Xavier University, who subsidized a trip to the Wellcome Trust in London, where much of the introduction was written. Second, to Carol Koulikourdi of Cambridge Scholars Press, who solicited the manuscriot many years ago and has been a model of patience through many delays. I am also grateful to the contributors, who have waited to see this book reach print. Third, I would thank Michael O'Rourke, who first organized the disability sessions at the Internation Medieval Congress in Leeds, at a time when few took seriously the possibility of working on medieval disability across disciplines. Last and certainly not least, thank you to my wife Susan Hawkes, who intervened to format the manuscript at the last minute, on account of my being utterly useless when it comes to that kind of thing.

INTRODUCTION: PUNISHMENT AND PITY

CORY JAMES RUSHTON

The English chronicler Matthew Paris tells the story of an assassination attempt aimed at King Henry III, taking place at Woodstock. One detail of the plot concerns us:

> On the morrow of the nativity of the Blessed Mary, a certain man at arms, a man of some education, came to the king's court at Woodstock. Pretending to be mad, he said to the king: "Resign to me the kingdom which you have unjustly usurped and long detained." And he added that he had the mark of royalty on his shoulder. When the king's servants ran upon him, intending to beat him and drive him from the king's presence, the king checked them, saying "Let him alone in his folly." But in the middle of the night, the madman climbed into the king's sleeping chamber by the window, a naked knife in his hand, and he came to the king's bed.[1]

Fortunately, "by the providence of God the king was with the queen" and the assassination attempt failed; it seems that God does indeed move in mysterious ways. Under torture, the would-be assassin confessed that he was an agent of the de Marisco family of Lundy Island, who were in a land dispute with the king. Here, madness does not play the problematic role it does in legal cases today, as a defence which ameliorates or excuses what would otherwise be a crime. Instead, the assassin feigns madness to gain access to the castle at Woodstock, a heavily protected space. That madness further gains him a privileged proximity to the body of the sovereign, his target. Further the text adopts the man's own position in its vocabulary: when he sneaks into the king's private room, he is not "man at arms" (what we might see as his reality) but "madman" (his pretence). Perhaps the text does confirm a kind of madness, linked to the insane act of trying to kill a monarch placed on his throne by God. To perform or attempt to perform madness is to actually be mad, whether we would read this as "madness" or not. Gerd Althoff argues that royal anger (*ira regis*), when it appears in medieval texts, is no sure indication of a king's actual state of mind. The monarch puts anger on like a cloak when it suits his purposes.[2]

It would seem possible, then, that the act is genuinely mad, but the individual (in this case, a would-be assassin) is "mad" only when committing that act.

On the other hand, there is love: which often appears in contemporary texts as an outside force, something which attacks the mind, soul, and body. Indeed, love could be considered madness or to at least prompt madness across a wide variety of texts ranging from medical tracts (the Viaticum of *Constantine Africanus*, a gloss on that work by Gerardus Biturcensis, and Avicenna's *Canon medicinae*) to vernacular romances. Far from being a metaphor for romantic feeling, lovesickness was considered a real medical problem for which real medical solutions were proposed: in most cases, sex with the beloved was best, but sex with someone else – even sex the sufferer paid to have – would do the trick. In other words, an emotion read as a temporary disability was to be cured by breaking social and ecclesiastical injunctions on non-marital sex. (Our more secular age has redefined lovesickness as a virtue, and in the west we still discuss love with the language of medieval medicine.) Henry's mercy towards an apparently insane attacker testifies to an understanding that madness could justify solutions which circumvent the normal working of the law, just as lovesickness could. Like a modern society, however, determining if a case of madness was real or feigned was very much a central concern for the law.

The would-be assassin's true position comes out only when the right questions are asked at the point where his body is being broken: where modern jurisprudence tends to see torture as illegitimate and ineffective, medieval criminal investigation sees it as partially restorative and partially demonstrative (in that it demonstrated the ways in which law was to be considered real). Torture breaks one body to heal the greater social body. This argument is a familiar one after the work of Elaine Scarry in *The Body in Pain*, subtitled "The making and unmaking of the world." Scarry writes that "Torture … consists of a primary physical act, the infliction of pain, and a primary verbal act, the interrogation." The world disappears for the victim of torture, replaced by the torturer's question.[3] This does not at first appear to sufficiently account for the public role of torture in pre-modern societies, as discussed by Michel Foucault, where it is linked to issues of sovereignty and the display of power, but also to the act of confession itself: "When it is not spontaneous or dictated by some internal imperative, the confession is wrung from a person by violence or threat; it is driven from its hiding place in the soul, or extracted from the body. Since the Middle Ages, torture has accompanied it like a shadow, and supported it when it could go no further: the dark twins".[4]

With both Foucault and Scarry in mind, Matthew Paris's story of the broken assassin is both public, in that it is communicated to the people through chronicle, and verbal, in that his identity (not-mad or no-longer-mad) is fixed by the act of torture.[5] In the sequel to these events, the leader of the de Mariscos is captured, put on trial, and publically tortured to death. An illustration in the manuscript shows this latter man being dragged by horse to his own execution, obviously a highly-public event which impressed itself on the maker of the manuscript as an important historical and social moment.

This preamble will not surprise many readers: the Middle Ages provide us with a record of many cruelties, enough that the era has become synonymous with barbarity in the public mind. At the same time, many medievalists will be alarmed or perhaps annoyed. The discipline has struggled, perhaps not universally, to change some of these negative perceptions of the various societies that comprised the medieval European world. To begin a discussion of medieval disability with a story in which one of the most successful monarchs of the age presides over the torture and execution of his enemies is to risk confirming a simplistic perception of the era, a perception which the study of historical disability has been largely content to absorb and continue. It is about to get worse before it gets better, though, for the other part of Paris's story worth attending is the casual acceptance of a small but crucial detail: when the assassin first approaches the king, his aggressive accusation of usurpation is met with a near-beating. Only the king's intervention saves the man – not only saves him, but leaves him within the walls of the royal residence, near to Henry's body. The king's pity for a perceived mental illness endangers his own life: the assassin relied upon the king's kindness to further his own goals. A king will feel pity: indeed, as Chaucer's narrators often say, "Pity runneth soon in gentle heart." The assassin has reason to expect that this feint would get him closer to his goal, because kings must appear merciful when the situation calls for it.

The standard reading of the medieval era is thus that it was cruel, but it was also Christian and subject to medieval Catholic doctrine concerning charity and pity. Disability, mental/intellectual or otherwise, would seem a likely target for the *caritas* or love enjoined on all members of the Church community at least as often as it was the result of medieval jurisprudence. The poor could expect hand-outs at the kitchen doors of both castle and monastery, and we can assume there were many disabled individuals within these ranks (although it is important to heed the warning of Henri-Jacques Stiker that the disabled would not "simply melt into the crowd of the poor", that they would have a presence in medieval society even if we have trouble delineating that presence as closely as we would like).[6] More than this, disability historiography has long considered the feudal era one in which the disabled could make a greater contribution to economic society than they have since the Industrial Revolution, with its specialized and increasingly complex jobs: as Michael Oliver influentially argues, medieval economics were agricultural and small scale-industrial and "did not preclude the great majority of disabled people from participating in the production process, and even where they could not participate fully, they were still able to make a contribution".[7] This is important, but it can also be overstated, as Winzer has argued: "In the thousands of years of human existence before 1800, life for most exceptional people seems to have been a series of unmitigated hardships. The great majority of disabled persons had no occupation, no source of income, limited social interaction, and little religious comfort... Their lives were severely limited by widely held beliefs and superstitions that justified the pervasive prejudice and callous treatment. Individuals seen as different were destroyed, exorcised, ignored, exiled, exploited—or set apart because some were even considered divine."[8] It is perhaps best to understand disability in the medieval period as being just as complex and variable as it is today.

The medieval impaired individual, then, was not universally marginalized nor permanently on the wrong side of an able-bodied/disabled line: the flexibility of medieval ideas of time and labour, limited only by the seasons and by the natural rhythms of the day, meant that in practical everyday terms "ability" was seen on a spectrum. The law, however, is a different story. In legal matters, ability – to understand the charges against one, to make rational decisions regarding one's goods, to control one's emotions – really did matter, and medieval authorities were not dissimilar from modern authorities when it comes to drawing a strict line between competence and incompetence in legal matters. In William Langland's fourteenth century social satire *Piers Plowman*, the issue of disability comes to the fore during an episode in which various allegorical figures represent society coming together to support itself. Among the individuals who try to take without giving are "faytours" (idlers), who pretend to be disabled: they "leyde here legges alery, as such lorelles conneth" and claim to be unable to work (VIII.128-29). The presiding allegorical figure, Piers the Plowman, claims that anyone who refuses to work will be forced to eat barley-bread and drink brook water (VIII.141-42). But he insists on a privileged space for those who really are "blynde or broke-legged or bolted with yren" (the last phrase meaning they wear leg-braces to help them walk) will have their physical needs met (VIII.143-48; he also places those who pray, friars and hermits, in the same category). This scene is an allegorical representation of the ideal earthly society, one in which the able-bodied have a social obligation to assist those who cannot fend for themselves. When this injunction does not work, Piers asks a knight to enforce – legally and through force of arms – the rule that only those who are willing to work will be allowed to eat (VIII.157-60).[9] The social becomes the legal very quickly, and the poem at least opens up the possibility that part of legal enforcement would be to differentiate and determine who is disabled and who is not.[10]

Indeed, "disability" and "disablement" have always been terms describing the legal as much as the social: Simi Linton reminds us that *Stedman's Medical Dictionary* defined disability in 1976 as a "medicolegal term signifying loss of function and earning power."[11] For the purposes of this introduction, I will begin with what is by now a key distinction, common enough across Disability Studies to be considered standard: *impairment* is any loss or abnormality of psychological, physiological, or anatomical structure or function; *disability* is any restriction or lack (resulting from an impairment) of ability to perform an activity in the manner or within the range considered normal for a human being; *handicap* is a disadvantage for a given individual, resulting from impairment or disability, that limits or prevents the fulfilment of a role that is normal, depending on age, sex, social and cultural factors, for that individual.[12] There are problems with these definitions, not least of which are the core concept of 'normality', and the further difficulty of determining the norms for medieval culture. Disability Theory's key distinction is between impairment ("the biological 'fact', the bodily manifestation", as Metzler puts it)[13] and disability, socially-constructed disadvantages justified by perceived insufficiency of body or mind, which will differ from society to society and change over time.[14] Metzler is helpful here: "Or to put it another way, a 'cripple' in the thirteenth century could share the same physiological condition with a 'cripple' in the later twentieth century, yet the scientific, medical or biological discourse of each time would already describe each body, though outwardly manifesting the same symptoms, in different ways."[15] A volume such as the present one, concerned with the law's relationship with impairment, is almost by definition deeply concerned with the social model of disability. The law, rooted in large questions about society and sovereignty and in concerns about who has access to authority and in what measure, both runs up against and potentially braces itself in notions of normality/normativity and abnormality. While law is always admittedly ideological, it is at least at some basic level concerned with the actual physical bodies and minds of actual physical people.

In the first issue of the theory/medieval culture journal *postmedieval*, dedicated to the posthuman, Julie Singer wonders whether there can be a "premodern posthuman", whether Disability Studies could help "take us from the sub- to the posthuman".[16] She acknowledges that the "activist strain" is reluctant to see itself as a "critical movement that interrogates the fringes and limits of human experience" given its "commitment to the destigmatization of disability" – in other words, their reluctance to declare disability one of the fringes of human experience, instead pursuing accessibility of various kinds. Borrowing from Donna Haraway, Singer argues for an opening of the boundaries, a push to extend the human beyond the traditional idea of the normal, organized around a series of dichotomies: male/female, able-bodied/disabled, etc. Singer's impulse – that the medieval disabled were "neither post-, para- nor subhuman", that they are something both "undeniably human" and "*something else*" – is exciting and attractive. However, some caution is required. Tobin Siebers explains the limits of Haraway's "justly famous theory of the cyborg vis-à-vis actual impaired bodies", and is worth quoting here at length:

> Haraway's cyborgs are spunky, irreverent, and sexy; they accept with glee the ability to transgress old boundaries between machine and animal, male and female, and mind and body. They supposedly make up a future, fortunate race, but in fact they exist everywhere today. Our cyborgs are people with disabilities, and Haraway does not shy away from the comparison. Severe disability is her strongest example of complex hybridization … Moreover, she views the prosthetic device as a fundamental category for preparing the self and body to meet the demands of the information age. "Prosthesis is semiosis," she explains, "the making of meanings and bodies, not for transcendence but for power-charged communication" (244). Haraway is so preoccupied with power and ability that she forgets what disability is. Prostheses always increase the cyborg's abilities; they are a source only of new powers, never of problems. The cyborg is always more than human – and never risks to be seen as subhuman. To put it simply, the cyborg is not disabled.[17]

In other words, for Haraway and Singer the disabled body or mind is full of potential, each unique individual pointing to a society in which difference is the norm. There would be no "able" to be troubled. The law, however, starts to look like a polar opposite, dedicated as it is to strict definitions and a firm binary of legal/illegal. A completely flexible law would be no law at all: it would be anarchy. Medieval thinkers knew this. Psalm 85 suggests through prophecy the difficulties of reconciling mercy and truth, righteousness and peace (Ps 85:10), a paradox that manifests itself in the dance of the daughters of God in texts like *Piers Plowman*

(XX:459-68), a dance predicated on the mystery of Christ's incarnation and sacrifice. The irreconcilable conflict God's perfect justice (we all deserve our doom) and God's perfect mercy (we can all be rescued) could only be solved through metaphor in this world. Medieval law struggles with precisely this conflict, but disability troubles this by calling for more mercy (or pity) than most might deserve, even as individual actions remain fully punishable.

The connection between disability and law/politics is explicit in the Middle Ages, and in subsequent eras, in the metaphor of the body politic. The best early formulation of this idea comes in the *Policraticus* of John of Salisbury (who claims to derive it from Plutarch: "For the republic is, just as Plutarch declares, a sort of body which is animated by the grant of divine reward and which is driven by the command of the highest equity and ruled by a sort of rational management."[18] The body metaphor is quite explicit:

> The position of the head in the republic is occupied, however, by a prince subject only to God and to those who act in His place on earth, inasmuch as in the human body the head is stimulated and ruled by the soul. The place of the heart is occupied by the senate, from which proceeds the beginning of good and bad works. The duties of the ears, eyes and mouth are claimed by the judges and governors of provinces. The hands coincide with officials and soldiers. Those who always assist the prince are comparable to the flanks. Treasurers and record keepers (I speak not of those who supervise prisoners, but of the counts of the Exchequer) resemble the shape of the stomach and intestines; these, if they accumulate with great avidity and tenaciously preserve their accumulation, engender innumerable and incurable diseases so that their infection threatens to ruin thre whole body. Furthermore, the feet coincide with peasants perpetually bound to the soil, for whom it is all the more necessary that the head take precautions, in that they more often meet with accidents while they walk the earth in bodily subservience; and those who erect, sustain and move forward the mass of the whole body are justly owed shelter and support. Remove from the fittest body the aid of the feet; it does not proceed under its own power, but either crawls shamefully, uselessly and offensively on its hands or else is moved with the assistance of brute animals.[19]

This so-called organic metaphor is an argument for cohesion and, perhaps strangely given the importance of the head, an argument against hierarchy as society's only organizing principle, as Cary Nederman suggests: "At the center of this analogy is an attempt to construct civil order on the principle of the social division of labor while rejecting the strictly hierarchical values of the Platonic *polis*."[20] Despite the apparently independent wills of the various parts of the body, the physical whole is governed by rationality and self-interest; if any part is removed, the social body is effectively disabled. Christine de Pizan makes this clear in her early 15th-century *Book of the Body Politic*, where she describes society as "one living body, perfect and healthy": "For just as the human body is not whole, but defective and deformed when it lacks any of its members, so the body politic cannot be perfect, whole, nor healthy if all the estates of which we speak are not well joined and united together."[21] A society so deeply invested in the body as metaphor for the human world cannot help but be similarly obsessed with bodily perfection, with the individual bodies which make up the social classes which in turn make up the whole social body. The centrality of the Aristotelian ideal of the mean ensured that normality was the centerpoint between extremes of deficiency and excess at the macro and micro levels.

Our understanding of the medieval social model of disability thus must also cope with the all-consuming popularity of the ubiquitous 'Monster Theory', popularized by the work of Jerome Jeffrey Cohen.[22] Monster Theory purports to examine the human and the marginal in medieval culture by focusing critical attention on the monsters found in medieval travel narrative and romance: these include the dog-headed people, giants, and so on. According to David Williams, for Isidore of Seville "monstrosity is constituted in one of the following ways: (1) hypertrophy of the body, (2) atrophy of the body, (3) excrescence of bodily parts, (4) superfluity of bodily parts, (5) deprivation of parts, (6) mixture of human and animal parts, (7) animal births by human women, (8) mislocation of organs or parts in the body, (9) disturbed growth (being born old), (10) composite beings, (11) hermaphrodites, (12) monstrous races".[23] Most of these categories could encompass modern notions of disability: the loss or abnormal size of bodily parts, birth defects which result in premature aging, or even physical features which might be interpreted as 'animal'. In effect, the monstrous races of medieval manuscript tradition help bolster Singer's call for the posthuman: if medieval thinkers could handle the idea of radical variability among sentient populations, why can't we?

While Monster Theory points to an essential dichotomy between the human and the monster, arguing that the latter polices the boundaries of the former, Disability Theory has been to make inroads by pointing to a spectrum in which the disabled were seen to exist somewhere between the fully human and the fully monstrous. The dog-headed men had souls which could be saved; so could Jewish men, but they menstruated as a sign of their monstrous difference (at least as early as Jacques de Vitry). The medieval human was partially conceived as being on a scale, albeit one complicated by the one-sex model which postulated that women were simply imperfect manifestations of maleness.[24] It is as though Erving Goffman's three stigma types – physical deformities, character traits that a society considers problematic (which might include homosexuality in many historical contexts), and the "tribal" troika of race, ethnicity, and religion[25] – do not fully obtain in the medieval period, when the first and third types are so elided as to be indistinguishable. Further, gender would almost certainly count as a potential stigma for medieval law, as women lacked a number of key legal rights. The question of what constitutes either a disability or an impairment is difficult enough in our own culture, especially given a wide variation in what is considered problematic across both time and cultures.

A prime example of the less-than-humanness of women under medieval law comes from the Old French romance *Silence*, in which an English king has banned women from inheriting land; a couple who have only a daughter conspire to get around a law which the text itself seems to suggest is unjust. With their daughter, Nature has created the perfect girl. Nature's arch-rival Nurture is credited, allegorically, with some success: the girl is raised as a boy by her parents, largely so she can inherit their property. But Nurture herself seems to know she has pulled something off: "I have succeeded very well / in turning a noble child into a defective male."[26] Silence him/herself echoes this later, debating whether to continue as a male or not: "I don't want to lose my high position; / I don't want to exchange it for a lesser …"[27] The tension between defectiveness on the one hand (she is not really male) and being lesser (the appearance itself is more powerful than her actual reality) speaks to disability directly: *Silence* effectively mines this territory by suggesting that male clothes are what Mitchell and Snyder call "narrative prosthesis", defined as the way in which deviant bodies become that on which "literary narratives lean for their representational power, disruptive potentiality, and analytical insight. Bodies show up in stories as dynamic entities that resist or refuse the cultural scripts assigned to them." Silence complicates this because his body is in one sense not deviant at all: Nature made her perfect, albeit a perfect specimen of the female, but Silence continues to make himself through the adoption of male clothing and behaviors: in other words, through the prosthetic, correcting as much as possible those physical aspects which threaten to undermine the behavioural aspects of Silence. What makes *Silence* so powerful in modern culture is that it flirts with refusing to accept easy categorization of either gender hierarchy or deviance, which is not the same thing as saying it does not ultimately embrace those categories: Silence clearly seems to raise questions in the expectation of shutting them down, but this closure seems impossible to achieve in the 21st century. Indeed, we rightly delight in those questions. The text uses male and female pronouns to describe Silence as Silence imagines him/herself at any given time. Just as Matthew Paris' would-be assassin "is" a madman while he feigns madness, so Silence is whichever gender he or she claims at any given textual moment, the performance trumping essentialism, if only temporarily. It is of some interest that at one point, Silence is in double-disguise, first as a boy and then as a peasant; at that point, "Nature's color becomes apparent" and the peasant disguise fails in a way that the gender disguise does not.[28] Peasants, too, are socially and legally disabled, but (and?) may actually be closer to the monstrous somehow.

Once physical difference, wherever it is located, is admitted as making one less-than-human, disability pushes one closer to the monstrous and away from the human. This does not mean that medieval society was not capable of assisting disabled people or feeling sympathy, but it does sound a warning that, at the very least, disabled persons in the Middle Ages could expect to lose access to many things their still-fully human contemporaries expected as a matter of course (what we would call basic human rights). If medieval law helped to form the modern individual – and increasingly most studies claim that it did – then how the law defined madness, or the human, or social responsibility, would seem to matter. As Rosemary Garland Thomson writes, "Disability is the unorthodox made flesh, refusing to be normalized, neutralized, or homogenized."[29] The law is intended to protect the political and the social, to maintain some ideal society: "For the national body to become increasingly 'coherent,' citizens must begin to recognize themselves as either contributors to or detractors from the overall health of the body politic."[30] This could happen even to high-ranking individuals: a strong case can be made that the Wars of the Roses are essentially a response to the disabling catatonia suffered by King Henry VI, a case in which society had to accommodate not the individual but a serious challenge to its norms. It was better to have a usurping monarch than to continue forward with a sharp absence at the centre of society, a political body without a functioning head. [31]

Medieval law would agree that the disabled are not simply human but something else: they are metaphor, in large part because their full humanity is itself in question. As Titchkosky says, "One meaning constituted today is that disability is the metaphor of choice to express problems, while often disappearing from the social landscape as a form of human existence."[32] Susan Sontag's insistence that "illness is *not* a metaphor, and that the most truthful way of regarding illness – and the healthiest way of being ill – is one most purified of, most resistant to, metaphoric thinking", has only been fitfully heeded; witness the controversy around, and even the need for, Barbara Ehrenreich's *Bright-Sided: How Positive Thinking is Undermining America*, an investigation that confirms, through a look at modern America, that Sontag was right to note how happiness was and still is seen to be an effective ward against illness (and was even as far back as the sixteenth century).[33]

One of the most challenging recent developments in medieval disability studies therefore concerns what to do with the old notion that disability and illness were written on the human body so that they could be read, with obvious implications for the law: leprosy for lust, madness for pride. Tory Vandeventer Pearman's *Women and Disability in Medieval Literature* notes that Edward Wheatley "finds that medieval notions of disability were tied to the linking of inward sin with outward appearance" (which should surprise nobody) but that recent scholarship has often tried to "'rescue' the Middle Ages from assumptions that construe medieval society as intolerant of and even cruel toward people with physical and mental impairment."[34] No lesser a light than the Venerable Bede would appear to disagree with Wheatley, but actually seems to confirm the point. Speaking of the blind patriarch Tobit in the apocryphal book named for him, Bede says this of his blindness:

> Do not be surprised, reader, that sometimes, typologically speaking, men's good deeds have a bad meaning and their bad deeds a good meaning; that *God is light* would never have been written in black ink but always in bright gold if this were not permissible; but even should you write the name of the devil in pure white chalk, it still means deep darkness.[35]

If bodies are to be read for the meanings of their illnesses and pain, then they are read typologically just as Tobit is to be read; and that meaning will not always be the obvious one. In fact Metzler notes that Bede believed that illness could have a variety of meanings, one of which is that an illness might not have a meaning at all.[36]

Augustine noted that infants could be differently-abled than their parents: "But who could enumerate all the human births that have widely differed from their ascertained parents?" His conclusion is that all such babies, whether they have "one eye in the middle of their forehead" or have "their eyes in their shoulders", they remain rational and mortal descendants of a single ancestor: therefore, human. Even here, though, there's a lesson to be learned from the oddness of individual disabilities: that Adam is our mutual ancestor, and the account of human creation in *Genesis* is true. Human diversity of ability is a celebration and confirmation of God's ability to see and account for "the similarities and diversities which can contribute to the whole."[37] Tim Stainton argues further that Augustine's influential thinking does suggest that particular disabilities could be interpreted in a variety of ways:

> The ideas of grace and the 'divine plan', while opening up a limited space for acceptance and broad equality in the eyes of God, also reinforced and legitimated an inferior and despised position in this world, leaving those who were considered to have an intellectual disability on the margin of social life and subject to a charity ultimately undertaken for the salvation of the giver, rather than for the welfare of the recipient.[38]

Still, the default position appears to have been the legibility of illness and injury, the commonly understood metaphor provided by the physical body which pointed to interior or divine truths. Metzler discusses the important example of Gospel of John 9, in which a man blind from birth is healed by Christ's miraculous intervention. Asked which was the sinning party – the man or his parents – Christ says it was neither. The man was blind for the purposes of the public healing itself, exactly to make explicit the greatness of God. Even if a disability said nothing about the person, it still said something about the natural and supernatural worlds. Indeed, disability was a place in which the two levels of existence met and interacted in telling and sometimes spectacular ways.

V. A. Kolve noted how the shepherd's talk of sheep diseases, in the Chester cycle of biblical plays, functioned as metaphors for the soul, and were not simply "a comic exploration of the obsessive way un which simple men talk about the thing they know best." Rather, the shepherds set up a metaphor in which they provide healing for their flocks just as Christ provides spiritual healing for his flock (which includes the shepherds themselves).[39] This healing, Jeremy J. Citrome argues, is of a higher order than human healing, particularly as the latter is manifested in invasive surgical practice. Surgery was seen ambivalently through much of the Middle Ages, "the last possible resort in a threefold hierarchy of healing strategies": diet/regimen, medicine, and then surgery.[40] Citrome notes that to "a medieval patient, illness and its subsequent treatment must have seemed like a microcosm of Original Sin and its treatment through the intervention of Christ. At the simplest level, successful surgery depended on the presence of divine grace".[41] Further and significantly, "With the coming of Christ, sickness can be healed without the violence of surgery. Where God before had severed putrefied members of humanity, such putrefaction can be transformed with Christ."[42] In other words, surgery was an imperfect course of action both within the medical world and insofar as it could only imperfectly approximate complete healing.

Further, surgery (as practiced in the Middle Ages) tended towards the expulsion of parts (putrefied limbs, excess blood), as opposed to the body of the Church which was capable of healing its parts in a new way in contrast to God's severing of whole populations in events like the Flood (although the Church, too, expelled diseased parts). Medicine was not a way of perfecting the world, but an accidental symbol of how far it was fallen.

What seems clear is that the Middle Ages had the same confusing and sometimes contradictory approaches to physical difference and disability as modern societies, albeit with the tensions located in sometimes very different places. Medical practitioners had a strong tendency in the medieval period to promise full cures, not simply treatment of any given condition, raising at least one question for Sara Butler: "It is difficult to understand why medical professionals undermined their own credibility and risked losing their wages by making everything contingent on a cure."[43] Part of the answer might be that the medieval attitude to illness was itself all or nothing: imperfect was imperfect, and the restoration of health was so closely linked to restoring something in the world as to be invisible to the medieval mind. (And besides, the maircalous was always a possibility). To look as specific examples of medieval law as a cultural space which must make precise and specific decisions governing who can or cannot make oaths or testify, how a legal sentence should be written on the body and to what extent, will help sort out these areas of confusion. For Augustine, all political power was flawed in a similar way: "…political structures of power are wholly a postlapsarian and not a prelapsarian development, and since they rely on coercive measure to meet their goal, they are especially vulnerable to the divisiveness and inequities resulting from the fall."[44] The law was prosthetic, restoring or attempting to restore a fallen world, a world that was once perfect (and would one day be remade perfectly): "God did not create out of any need, nor to perfect any deficiency in himself (*Conf.* 13.4.5)."[45] The law is both practical and limited, very much of the world *sub aeternitas*. Medieval society sometimes understood disability to be symbolic, and I argue here that in some fundamental way, medieval society knew that its law was also symbolic: punishment and restitution do not actually restore anything, but instead temporarily recreate a vision of social stability or justice (the sense of qualification here is intentional). Law shares this with medicine: the human body is inherently flawed across class, gender and race; so too is the damaged world in which that body finds itself. The world was disabled by an apple, and law must deal with the various disabilities that arise as a result of that great crippling act.

About the volume

To conclude, Disability Theory has been making its presence known in traditional disciplines for several years; Medieval Studies is no exception. While it is possible to find and explicate instances of disability in medieval literary texts and historical chronicles, these findings often seem isolated and thin: like the literature of all ages, medieval literature often turns away from physical imperfection except to make moralistic judgment or engage in sentimental paternalization. Medieval legislation and jurisprudence, however, had to engage with the reality of disability: how variations from the physical norm affected the regular unfolding of the law, how disabilities resulting from violence could or should be compensated, which "imperfections" could bar a person from particular professions (or, sometimes, open some professions to that person). This collection draws on scholars from a variety of disciplines to delineate the relationship between law, government and society on the one hand, and the able-bodied and disabled individuals within society on the other. Any collection of this kind risks appearing diffuse, but the other side of this risk is to seem to reinvent the wheel: the work of Metzler, Turner, Wheatley, Josh Eylar and others has effectively laid the groundwork and set out the controversies. The work at this moment is to collect examples of historical cases, literary figures, and theological debates which will help elucidate and modify that groundwork, and contribute to answering those controversies. The current volume does not aspire to be a full discussion of the links between medieval law and medieval understanding of disability, but rather aspires to advancing the conversation(s).

The volume is intended to be accessible to specialists in a number of fields, drawing on the interdisciplinary nature of Medieval Studies to provide a comprehensive view of its subject; it is not intended as a complete overview of the complicated issues of disability and law in the Middle Ages. This volume is best seen as comprised of case studies: models for how the field might go about looking at both new issues raised by Disability Studies (Philomela's muteness and Chaucer's pity) and old issues newly problematized (the last days of Francis of Assisi, Margery Kempe's roaring). The volume is divided into two equal parts, reflecting the major ways in which law dealt with issues of disability: Punishment and Pity.

The collection begins with Metzler's examination of disability as it appears in the legal codes formative early medieval period, down to roughly 1300. Metzler finds that these early texts are concerned with "three aspects of physical disability": the restriction of impaired persons from public life, the extension of certain rights to impaired persons which able-bodied persons do not have, and the issue of compensation for impairment. Metzler confirms that disability had a wider social definition in the period: women, in a fundamental way, could not be legally impaired because they could not lose rights they never had; Visigothic law seems to confirm that to be asleep was to be "temporarily incapacitated." Dwarfs and the mobility-impaired could not inherit because they could not fulfil the military obligations which came with land. What emerges from Metzler's careful work, and the charts which accompany the chapter, is the lack of any "umbrella notion such as our modern term 'disability'", although she does find a significant difference between the exclusionary character of Roman law and the compensation model of the Germanic law codes.

Amanda Hopkins explores the deliberately-disabling policy of physical mutilation, noting that mutilating someone rather than imprisoning or executing them could "preserve some measure of the offender's economic value to society." Hopkins emphasizes the textual quality of penal mutilation, the way that it wrote the crime on the body; using Philippe de Rémi's *La Manekine* as a case study, Hopkins reads the heroine's self-inflicted loss of her hand and its eventual miraculous restoration as paradoxically liberating. Manekine's negotiation of physical, legal, and identity problems reveals her to be a model for the disabled, capable of circumventing pity and embracing at least a sense of self-sufficiency.

Marian Lupo follows with a theologically informed discussion of Margery Kempe, whose Middle English autobiography has seemed to record a form of mental disability for many critics; Lupo argues that this ignores the contemporary understanding of the issues involved, and that Disability Theory can help us understand Margery even as Margery helps us understand disability and its social formation.

Donna Trembinski turns our attention to the Franciscan order, and the questions surrounding the illnesses which Francis suffered towards the end of his life. She delineates the way in which the fledgling Franciscan order had to decide what to do with a leader who was experiencing a variety of ailments, and also refusing to seek treatment. Traditionally, the disabled have been marginalized by their societies in various ways; this was very difficult to do with Francis.

The collection continues with Wendy J. Turner's discussion of mental disability among the merchant class in the medieval English city, drawing on documentary evidence. Turner turns to the way in which English administrators wrestled with mental incapacitation in both criminal and inheritance cases, drawing on and modifying a well-developed Roman terminology to create a sometimes very precise English set of terms. Turner traces changes to this terminology which testify to the careful and sophisticated approach taken by English law.

Finally, Cory James Rushton provides a look at Chaucer's Philomela, the victim of a bloody assault which leaves her unable to speak, making her a litmus test for the problem of legal accommodation for both women and the mute at precisely the historical moment when the oral oath and spoken proofs are giving way to written evidence. Rushton suggests that Chaucer testifies to a number of social and legal anxieties, even unconsciously. The conflict between pitying the disabled and the victimized, and actually being able to accommodate their differences, is still with us today.

Notes

[1] Matthew Paris, qtd. in F. M. Powicke, "The Murder of Henry Clement and the Pirates of Lundy Island," *History* 25 (1941): 285-310.

[2] Gerd Althoff, "*Ira Regis*: Prolegomena to a History of Royal Anger," in *Anger's Past: The social uses of an emotion in the Middle Ages*, edited by Barbara Rosenwein (Ithaca and London: Cornell University Press), 59-74.

[3] Elaine Scarry, *The Body in Pain* (New York and Oxford: Oxford University Press, 1985), 27-59.

[4] Michel Foucault, *The History of Sexuality: An Introduction*, trans. by Robert Hurley (New York: Vintage Books, 1990), 59.

[5] Michel Foucault, *Discipline and Punish*, trans. Alan Sheridan (New York: Vintage, 1977).

[6] Henri-Jacques Stiker, *A History of Disability*, trans. W. Sayers (Ann Arbor: University of Michigan, 1999), 66.

[7] Michael Oliver, *The Politics of Disablement* (Basingstoke: Palgrave MacMillan, 1990), p. 27. See also Brendan Gleeson, *Geographies of Disability* (London: Routledge, 1999).

[8] Margaret A. Winzer, "Disability and Society Before the Eighteenth Century," in Davis 1997, 76.

[9] William Langland, *Piers Plowman: A New Annotated Edition of the C-Text*, ed. Derek Pearsall (Exeter: University of Exeter Press, 2008). In fact, the knight's intervention does not work, and Piers turns to Hunger itself, who literally beats the idlers. One could say law fails here, but in the process it also normalized: the law exists, perversely, to protect even the lazy from themselves.

[10] This may sound perilously close to the argument made by Deborah A. Stone in her 1984 book *The Disabled State*: "In this she posits the historical existence of dual 'distributive systems' in societies: one involving the activities of those producing sufficient value to meet their own needs and more; and the other, what may be described as a 'social circuit of dependency' which includes those who

cannot maintain self-sufficiency. From this dualism a basic 'redistributive dilemma' is held to arise, presenting an enduring socio-political problem for states. The tension between the two systems based on work and need is the *fundamental distributive dilemma* (Stone, 1984:17) (emphasis added). For her, disability is explained as a juridical and administrative construct of state policy which is aimed at resolving this supposed redistributive predicament" (Gleeson, 64). Gleeson rightly notes that Stone's model only obtains for a much more recent period in which individual achievement and individual reward are fully linked, but the *Piers Plowman* scene could be an interesting early version of this idea. Gleeson's second objection to Stone is that her model "can only reveal the meaning of disability *to the state;* it cannot adequately claim to capture the concrete reality of impairment within social relations generally" (Gleeson, 65). For my purposes, this is precisely right: disability becomes disability when society, notably the law, begins to take account of and to define it.

[11] Simi Linton, "Reassigning Meaning," in Davis 2006, 162.

[12] Metzler, p. 3. Her discussion is central, carefully negotiating the differences in modern terminology and the differences in medieval terminology.

[13] Metzler, 20-21.

[14] The classic discussion is in Oliver, 1990.

[15] Metzler, 21.

[16] Julie Singer, "Toward a transhuman model of medieval disability." *postmedieval* (2010): 1-7.

[17] Tobin Siebers, "Disability in Theory," in Davis 2006, 178.

[18] John of Salisbury, *Policraticus*, ed. and trans. by Cary J. Nederman. Cambridge Texts in the History of Political Thought (Cambridge: Cambridge University Press, 1990), 66.

[19] John of Salisbury, 67.

[20] Cary J. Nederman, *Lineages of European Political Thought* (Washington, DC: Catholic University Press of America, 2009), 70.

[21] Christine de Pizan, *The Book of the Body Politic*, ed. by Kate Langdon Forhan (Cambridge: Cambridge University Press, 1994), 90.

[22] Particularly in *Of Giants* (Minneapolis: University of Minnesota Press, 1999) and *Monster Theory* (Minneapolis: University of Minnesota Press, 1997), an edited collection.

[23] David Williams, *Deformed Discourse* (Exeter: University of Exeter Press, 1996), 107.

[24] See Thomas W. Laqueur, *Making Sex: Body and Gender from the Greeks to Freud* (Harvard University Press, 1990). The one-sex model is not universally considered the only gender model available to the Middle Ages: see also Joan Cadden, *The Meanings of Sex Difference in the Middle Ages: Medicine, Science, and Culture* (Cambridge: Cambridge University Press, 1995).

[25] Erving Goffman, *Stigma* (London: Penguin, 1968/1990), 14-15.

[26] *Silence*, ed. Sarah Roche-Mahdi, ll. 2601-2.

[27] *Silence*, ll. 2651-52.

[28] Silence, ll. 2921-75.

[29] Thomson qtd in Siebers, 23.
[30] Sharon L. Snyder and David T. Mitchell, *Cultural Locations of Disability* (Chicago, 2006), 23-4.
[31] Cory James Rushton, "The King's Stupor: Dealing with Royal Paralysis in Late Medieval England," in Wendy J. Turner, *Madness in Medieval Law and Custom* (Leiden and Boston: Brill, 2010): 147-76.
[32] Titchkosky, 6-7.
[33] Susan Sontag, *Illness as Metaphor and AIDS and Its Metaphors* (New York: Picador, 1988), 3, 55; Barbara Ehrenreich, *Bright-Sided: How Positive Thinking is Undermining America* (New York: Picador, 2010).
[34] Tory Vandeventer Pearman, *Women and Disability in Medieval Literature* (New York: Palgrave MacMillan, 2010).
[35] Seán Connolly, ed., *Bede: On Tobit and on the Canticle of Habakkuk.* (Dublin: Four Courts Press, 1997), 41-2.
[36] Metzler, 46.
[37] From *Civitate* 16.8, qtd. in Tim Stainton, "Reason, grace and charity: Augustine and the impact of church doctrine on the construction of intellectual disability," *Disability and Society* 23:5 (2008): 485-96.
[38] Stainton, p. 494.
[39] V. A. Kolve, *The Play Called Corpus Christi* (Stanford: Stanford University Press, 1966), 151-55.
[40] Jeremy J. Citrome, *The Surgeon in Medieval English Literature* (New York: Palgrave, 2006), 2.
[41] Citrome, 5.
[42] Citrome, 31.
[43] Sara M. Butler, "Medicine on Trial: Regulating the Health Professions in Later Medieval England," *Florilegium* 28 (2011), 73-4.
[44] J. Joyce Schuld, "Augustine, Foucault, and the Politics of Imperfection," *Journal of Religion* 80.1 (2000): 1-22, p. 11; see also R. A. Markus, "Two Conceptions of Political Authority: Augustine, *De Civitate Dei*, 19.14-15 and Some Thirteenth Century Interpretations," *Journal of Theological Studies*, n.s., 16 (1965): 68-100.
[45] William E. Mann, "Augustine on evil and original sin," in Eleonore Stump and Norman Kretzmann, *The Cambridge Companion to Augustine* (Cambridge, 2001): 40-48 (p. 43).

REFLECTIONS ON DISABILITY IN MEDIEVAL LEGAL TEXTS: EXCLUSION – PROTECTION – COMPENSATION

IRINA METZLER

Notions and perceptions of physically impaired people as presented in legal texts can tell us about the status, social position and rights (or restrictions) impaired people may have had. Similarly, the 'evaluation' of impairments in legal discourse can illuminate societal attitudes. What degree of legal differentiation was made? Were all impairments simply bundled together as so-called disabilities, or were physical impairments hierarchised (e.g. was sensory impairment regarded as worse than orthopedic impairment; was blindness regarded as worse than the loss of one hand)? Throughout I speak in terms of impairment when describing an anatomical, biological, material condition, rather than disability which as a term is reserved for the social and culturally-specific construct superimposed on impairment. In this distinction I am following the discipline of present-day disability studies.[1]

I deliberately will disregard the issue of judicial maiming, i.e. the question of whether or not, and if so how frequently, people were physically impaired through punishments and judicial torture. Nevertheless there is some controversy as to the extent of these practices which cannot be answered in a short article such as this. However, two examples of mutilating punishments may serve as illustration of the problem. In the Laws of Cnut (compiled 1020-23) there seemed to be a reluctance to execute criminals outright, instead there was a sliding scale of judicial mutilation. This followed a principle similar to the modern notion of 'three strikes and you're out'. An accused man, who could be accused of any criminal act although the majority mainly related to theft, had three chances of conviction, with a harsher penalty in each instance: the first conviction could still be resolved by a compensation payment and through wergild, but the second and third instances required corporal punishments:

> [30.4.] And on the second occasion there is to be no other compensation, if he is convicted, but that his hands, or feet, or both, in proportion to the deed, are to be cut off. [30.5] And if, however, he has committed still further crimes, his eyes are to be put out and his nose and ears and upper lip cut off, or his scalp removed, whichever of these is then decreed by those with whom the decision rests; thus one can punish and at the same time preserve the soul.[2]

Note that in terms of impairments, the second level of punishment caused the convicted criminal to have an orthopedic impairment, while the third level inflicted sensory impairments. Note also the clause denying legal responsibility, in that although it was likely that the third degree punishments would lead to the death of the convicted man, his death would not have been directly caused by capital punishment, which the laws of Cnut expressly tried to avoid for the sake of "preserv[ing] the soul". Just over 200 years later, on the 30 August 1255, the council of Siena, the Consiglio della Campana, discussed the methods of punishment to be used against the occupants of the castle of Torniella in Val di Merse, who had rebelled against Siena. Some councillors wanted to blind the inhabitants, others to put out one eye of each, some to cut off their hands and feet, others to cut off just one hand and foot each, others still to hang them all.[3] What this catalogue of potentially impairing mutilations demonstrates is, firstly, the readiness of contemporaries to apply penal mutilations, and secondly, the continuity with earlier judicial practices or traditions.

By the early Thirteenth Century the church was becoming more concerned about its clergy being involved in the shedding of blood (i.e. through warfare, practising surgery or by being present at judicial ordeals).

> This insistence [at the council of 1215] that clerics should have no blood on their hands occurred at a time when secular justice was becoming increasingly bloody. As execution and mutilation grew in importance, edging out earlier systems based on compensation, the priest and the clerk found that the rules of their order and the practices of the secular courts were increasingly discordant.[4]

Whereas the older legal systems, both secular and clerical, had tried to avoid bloodshed and mutilation, by the thirteenth century secular legal proceedings began to deviate more strongly from such sentiments which canon law nevertheless still entailed. One important question for further research therefore might surround the apparent increase in judicial corporal punishments during the later middle ages.

However, in terms of sources for this present study, the focus is on secular texts from the period up to around 1300. This article will therefore not be covering canon law, or later medieval civil or secular law at any great length, but will focus mainly on the so-called *Leges Barbarorum* of the earlier medieval period, but also on some redactions of Roman law, which form the two key types of sources for the period 400-1200. Here the two main texts of Roman law were the Theodosian[5] and Justinian Codes: the former compiled in 438, and confirmed to be the authoritative collection of Roman law in the western empire and subsequently under the barbarian rulers; in the eastern empire the Justinian code, completed in 534, became the main source. Western medieval Europe re-discovered the Justinian Code's *Digest* first in Italy from around 1050 onwards, spreading widely to the rest of western Europe during the twelfth century,[6] which means that subsequent codifications of earlier, perhaps orally transmitted laws, became much more influenced by Roman law.

The Germanic tribes moving into the regions formerly ruled by Rome had also codified their laws, to some extent amalgamating Germanic and Roman customs.[7] The laws of the Visigoths, especially the *Breviarium Alaricianum* compiled in the early sixth century, formed the foundation of many other collections, such as the laws of the Bavarians and of the Lombards; the text known as the Visigothic Code was itself compiled in the mid-seventh century; the laws of the Lombards were put together between 643 (the date associated with an important text known as Rothair's Edict) and 755; not forgetting the influential laws of the Salian and Ripuarian Franks.[8] Furthermore, a multitude of Anglo-Saxon laws existed, for example the collection put together under the supervision of archbishop Wulfstan of York (died 1023) known as the laws of Ethelred, as well as laws of king Alfred, a translation into Latin and compendium or summary of the earlier Anglo-Saxon laws known as the *Quadripartitus* (1114), and finally the *Leges Henrici Primi* as a last collection that still shows the influence of the barbarian codes (made under Henry I some time between 1110 and 1120, with surviving manuscripts dating from c. 1201 and the early fourteenth century). To provide a southern European perspective, but also to highlight continuity with the earlier Visigothic code, some mention is made of the *Usatges* of Barcelona, issued in the mid-twelfth century within the court of count Ramon Berenguer IV of Barcelona (1131-62). Lastly, reference is also made to the *Sachsenspiegel* of the early thirteenth century, for reasons that this particular text still includes many of the kinds of attitudes encountered in the earlier barbarian codes, and can be located at the interstices of barbarian and later medieval legal codes.

The early legal texts are primarily concerned with three aspects of physical disability, which will therefore constitute the three focal points of this article:

1. The restriction, and thereby exclusion, of impaired persons to participate in public life, e.g. to inherit under certain conditions, to hold certain offices, to marry.
2. The protection of impaired persons in law, e.g. certain rights are accorded the physically disabled that the able-bodied do not have under similar circumstances.
3. Compensation law, with a multitude of examples (see table 1) to draw from during the earlier medieval period on monetary payments to injured parties in the event of loss of physical function of specific body parts.

Exclusion

Exclusion relates to the restriction imposed on impaired persons to participate fully in public life. Roman law in the case of the Justinian codes was particularly concerned about impaired people and their ability to make property transactions of various kinds (be it wills, stipulations, promises). Distinctions were made between congenital and acquired impairments, in that people who had been born with conditions such as deafness, blindness or muteness, were excluded from certain legal transactions or their transactions were regarded as not valid. For example, a blind man could not make a will (*Institutes* 2.12.4). The particular provisions made in the Justinian codes for persons with speech and/or hearing impairments will be considered below in a special section on the legal status of deaf and mute people. In general, sensorily impaired people could not be legal guardians of minors or of other legally incapable people, although the blind could appoint their own procurator. However, all groups of sensorily impaired – blind, deaf and mute – could inherit (*Institutes* 2.19.4).

Similar sentiments were carried forward into northern Europe. Infantilisation and abrogation of the legal rights normally accorded to non-impaired adults were the main restrictive aspects of Roman and some 'barbarian' laws. Nordic law codes, too, had sections excluding the physically impaired from certain legal rights or duties. In an Icelandic law code relating to jury service, those people who cannot walk fast enough are excluded from jury service.[9] This begs the question why ability to walk fast mattered in relation to sitting on a jury. Was this a form of excluding the elderly and senile as well as the young(er) physically impaired? This is found, too, in *Britton*, an Anglo-Norman law book of the late thirteenth century, where the following kinds of people are forbidden from making appearance by attorney: "no child under-age, no-one deaf, mute, nor natural fool, no purely demented man, nor anyone else without discretion [i.e. rational sense], nor anyone accused of a felony ... nor lepers ousted from the community of men"[10] It is noteworthy that as recently as 1999 British law would not allow a deaf person to sit on a jury (since the deaf person would require an interpreter, which would mean *de facto* a thirteenth juror, according to the official reason given), whereas by that time in the US seven states had allowed deaf jurors to serve.[11]

According to German legal texts from the second half of the thirteenth century, too, blind people could become neither judges nor members of the town council.[12] The well-known German *Sachsenspiegel*, compiled by Eike von Repgow around 1230, also has sections dealing with the legal exclusion of physically (and mentally) impaired persons. Most of these relate to the rights to inherit property or make property transactions, similar to the stipulations already found in Roman law. So, certain categories of impaired persons may not inherit:

> Neither tenancy nor hereditary property can devolve upon the feebleminded, dwarfs, or cripples. The actual heirs and their next of kin are, however, responsible for their care.
> (Uf altvile unde uf getwerge erstirbit weder len noch erbe, noch uf kropels kint. Wer denne ir nehisten magen und erben sint, die enphan ir erbe und sollen si halden in ire phlage.)[13]

In a manuscript of the *Sachsenspiegel* at Oldenburg, made around 1336, an illustration accompanies this section of the text: figures of a leper, a blind man carrying a cane, and a cripple without arms and just one leg are shown in the margin of the page.[14]

Also similar to Roman law is the qualification the *Sachsenspiegel* placed on someone's ability to transact business with regard to their property, although again the qualification here is no longer to do with sensory impairments, but much more literally physical:

> A man may transfer all movable property without consent of the heirs as long as he can climb on a horse by himself, with sword buckled on and shield in hand, using a wooden block or stone an ell high without help from anyone except the person who holds the horse and stirrup for him. But if he (fol. 22r) cannot execute this, he may not give away movable property nor transfer nor lend it in order to deprive the person who has claim to it upon his death.

> (Alle varende habe gibit der man ane erben gelob in allen steten unde lezit unde liet gut de wile her sich vermag, daz her begort mit eime swerte unde mit eime schilde uf ein ros komen mag von eime steine adir stocke einir dummellen ho, sunder mannes hulfe, daz man im daz ros unde den stegereif halde. Wenne her des nicht geton mag, so en mag her geben noch lien noch lazen, daz herz ieneme mite entpherne, der ez wartende iz nach sime tode.)[15]

This precise description and requirement of physical skills could also exclude the elderly, and it is worth noting that occasionally in the *Sachsenspiegel* old men are described as feeble and decrepit. Interestingly, even the very local *Stadtrecht* (municipal law) of the city of Münster, which was transferred to the nearby town of Bielefeld between 1209 and 1214, expressed similar sentiments about the ability of a person to transmit property, stating: "8. While he is still capable of raising his hand, a sick burgess may bequeath his property if he wishes... (*Ein kranker Bürger darf, solange er noch die Hand erheben kann, seinen Besitz vermachen, wenn er will ...*)."[16] Although primarily this regulation referred to persons on their death-bed, who needed to be just capable enough of raising their hand, by inference this could relate to the severely disabled, too.

The physically impaired could be quite excluded from legal rights given to able-bodied people. This becomes evident from the low position the impaired held in the ranking order of those people who are allowed to transact certain legal business. There is a section in the Theodosian code dealing with who can be appointed tutor for under-age children (Bk. III, title 17: *De tutoribus et curatoribus creandis*). In cases where the husband of the mother had died (section 4.3) the widowed mother was permitted to apply for guardianship of her under-age children herself (in contrast to other cases where a male tutor is appointed), but only in those circumstances where "a statutory tutor is lacking or when ... he is found to be incapable of managing even his own property because of mental or physical infirmity".[17] This complex legal stipulation means that ideally under-age children have a male and able-bodied tutor appointed for them, but if the only male tutor available happens to be mentally or physically impaired, then it is preferable, in the view of the law, to have the mother appointed tutor or guardian, whereas a woman would not normally have held such legal rights. Physical impairment in a male therefore becomes a disability in the modern sense, in that the male person is excluded from rights and activities otherwise associated with the masculine. For women, physical condition, whether impaired or able-bodied, is pretty much irrelevant in legal terms, since they were generally excluded from exercising legal rights anyway – that is why this section of the Theodosian code is so interesting, because of the 'last resort' status of the widowed mother.

That women were *a priori* disadvantaged in a legal sense is evidenced in an example from one of the barbarian codes. In the Lombard laws of Rothair, duke of Brescia, a stipulation was made regarding exemption from normal marital agreements if the wife is or becomes impaired in some way.

> Concerning the girl who becomes a leper after her betrothal. If it happens that after a girl or woman has been betrothed she becomes leprous or mad or blind in both eyes, then her betrothed husband shall receive back his property and he shall not be required to take her to wife against his will. And he shall not be guilty in this event because it did not occur on account of his neglect but on account of her weighty sins and resulting illness.[18]

It is therefore only the woman's physical or mental condition that matters, while there is no equivalent section in the code that allows a woman to return her betrothed husband as quasi 'damaged goods'.

Protection

Protection relates to certain rights or prerogatives of impaired persons that under similar circumstances the able-bodied do not hold. Ironically, the very exclusion of certain categories of physically impaired in some aspects of the law could sometimes accord them protection in other ones. In the *Sachsenspiegel* there is some evidence for a kind of 'protection' of the impaired and other people requiring special treatment in the law. So for example:

> [a] woman with child may not be given a sentence more severe than flogging and the cutting of her hair. Neither shall fools nor the feebleminded be sentenced to punishment. If they cause harm to someone, their guardian shall pay compensation.
> (Man en sal obir kein wip richten, de lebende kint treit, hochir den zu hut unde zu hare. Ubir rechte thoren unde sinnelosen man en sal man ouch nicht richten. Wenne se abir schaden thon, ir vormunde sal ez gelden.)[19]

In this sense the *Sachsenspiegel* is echoing earlier Roman law (appointment of guardians) and barbarian codes (in Anglo-Saxon law the congenitally deaf-mute are exempt from punishment). In all probability the dividing line between people with a sensory physical impairment such as speech or hearing difficulties, and people with a mental impairment (the ‘feebleminded’) was not very clearly drawn.

Legal protection could also mean exemption from some of the more risky aspects of thirteenth-century justice: trial by combat. An illustration at the bottom of the page in one of the manuscripts of the *Sachsenspiegel* depicts a physically impaired (crippled) man who, like a woman, has a guardian performing trial by combat on his behalf. According to the text, lame men were allowed to represent their own legal interests, unless proceedings moved to trial by combat, in which case a lame man could allocate a guardian (from among one of his male relatives) who was of similar rank (*ebenbortig*), or offer to pay someone unrelated to fight for him.[20] In using a substitute for trial by combat, thirteenth-century law is recognising the decreased physical ability of someone impaired. The twelfth-century *usatges* of Barcelona already exempted elderly knights from trial by battle and allowed them instead to swear an oath: “Let an old knight who cannot defend himself on his own or a poor one who cannot equip himself for judicial battle be believed on oath”.[21] It is interesting to observe that those incapacitated by old age and those incapacitated by poverty were lumped together into a similar category (see below the respective chapters on ageing and charity for the associations between disability and each of these categories). And the thirteenth-century Laws of Alfonso X of Castile and Léon allowed sick and elderly persons who were witnesses to be questioned before the actual trial took place, on account of the distinct possibility that they might die before the trial proper took place.[22]

In this, high medieval legal thinking demonstrated a greater awareness of people’s physical differences than earlier Roman laws, where the only ‘protection’ related to being excused from certain public duties, such as tutelage or curatorship (*Codex Justinianus* 5.68.1 and 10.51.1); such Roman laws were motivated more from considerations for protecting the perceived decorum of legal proceedings and for maintaining standards of public participation than concern for physically impaired persons and their abilities.

One of the thirteenth-century secular jurists asserted that legal aid must be given to those persons who were incapable of presenting their case or of defending themselves, due to alleged mental feebleness to which category he reckoned women, children and the aged (the latter presumably because the mental rather than the physical deteriorations of ageing could render them disabled in this context). Canon law also recognised a group of people termed ‘the miserables’ (*miserabiles personae*), better described as ‘the needy’, who, in a tradition going back to biblical texts, due to their condition were deserving of assistance. Such assistance could be in the form of general charity (on the subject of the needy here see chapter 5) but more specifically in the context of law could relate to legal assistance. During the pontificate of Innocent IV (1244-54) canon law began to refine the categories of people who were entitled to legal assistance, so that poor widows, orphans, cripples, lepers, prisoners and poor old people could henceforth bring their cases directly to the ecclesiastical courts. There was however no *a priori* assumption that all such people who were technically *miserabiles* will in economic reality have needed the legal support, so in effect a kind of means testing ruled that those people with enough financial resources (regardless of the fact that technically they were among the *miserabiles*) had to turn to secular courts first and only then were permitted access to the ecclesiastical courts.[23]

Compensation

Compensation covers by far the largest section concerning disability in medieval legal sources, with a multitude of examples in the barbarian codes of monetary payments to injured parties in the event of the loss of sensory or motor function pertaining to specific body parts. Some laws were quite detailed, distinguishing individual segments of digits, such as in the Frisian laws, while others outlined more general tariffs.[24] Physical injury was differentiated in the law codes between *vulnera* (wounding) and *debilitates* (maiming, impairing, laming). For example, the Burgundian laws differentiated between a broken arm or tibia that healed without certain impairment (*sine certa debilitate*) and one that does become affected by a visible debility (*evidenti fuerint debilitate damnatae*).[25] Both types of injury are categorised according to a hierarchy of the limbs, e.g. at severest level loss of the entire arm, then one hand, then individual fingers.[26] Most European law codes dating from between the fifth and the tenth centuries contained provisions for wergild, the financial compensation for injuries according to their severity. Even injuries to animals could be compensated for by making wergild payments to the owner, as in the cases of laming cattle or dogs cited in the *Sachsenspiegel*.[27]

An interesting observation has been made recently by Lisi Oliver concerning the relationship of these texts with medical texts of the same period. While the latter describe thaumaturgic procedures that involve a *physicus*, “a specialist in herbal medication”, the former

> consider injuries which can only be cured by surgical intervention. While the medical treatises address infection and cure, the legal stipulations pertain to fractures of the skeletal system ... The first cases involve

> disability caused by nature; the second wounds caused by human aggression.[28]

Some of the law codes implied the use of experts to classify injuries. For example, the laws of the Salian Franks required that wounds be assessed by “men of proven skill”.[29] Measuring of wounds for compensation among ancient Germanic and Slavonic peoples was already mentioned by Jacob Grimm: “in our oldest laws the worth of all bodily injuries is carefully discerned according to the individual limbs, the size of the wound and other evaluations”.[30] The Old Frisian laws extended the criteria for measurement to include a strong concept of ‘honour’: wounds were not to be compensated for simply according to how deep they were, or how much pain or impairment they caused, but according to how much they damaged the honour of a person, so that actions like pulling or cutting someone's hair was deemed just as much an injury as a flesh wound.[31] Nevertheless, the oldest Germanic laws contain methods for evaluating all physical injuries or woundings according to individual limbs, the size of the wound and other measurables. By the later Middle Ages such concepts were still around. A municipal record book of Göttingen dating from the early fifteenth century contains a drawing of an instrument for measuring the depth of wounds, with markers on the instrument called ‘S’ and ‘H’ (for *Stichwunden* = stab wounds and *Hiebwunden* = cut/ slash wounds) to indicate if the wound was of the required depth to warrant compensation.[32] The idea was to establish if the wound was deep and therefore severe enough to legally qualify for compensation or as an offence. There was a legal case in Göttingen in 1430 with respect to a headwound, where it was not deemed necessary for the depth of the wound to reach the measure on the instrument,[33] presumably because alone by being a headwound it was a serious enough injury to warrant compensation. The incidence of violence that could lead to impairment of the victims was such within later medieval towns and cities that some authorities passed special laws to prevent the carrying of weapons. For example, this fifteenth-century policing regulation from Nuremberg draws attention to wounds and lameness as a consequence of violent actions:

> In consideration of the killings, lamings, woundings and the uproar which have occurred the honourable council has decided to order seriously and resolutely that in future nobody, be they burgher, inhabitant or guest, may be permitted here in the city neither by day nor by night to carry on them any kind of weapon, with the exception of simple harmless breadknives.
>
> (Angesichts der Totschläge, Lähmungen, Verwundungen und des Aufruhrs, die sich ereigneten, hat sich der ehrbare Rat entschlossen, ernst

und entschieden zu befehlen, dass in Zukunft niemand, er sei Bürger, Einwohner oder Gast, hier in der Stadt weder bei Tage noch bei Nacht irgendeine Waffe, ausgenommen einfache ungefährliche Brotmesser, bei sich tragen soll.)[34]

For the scheme of compensation for wounding people the most notable feature is the hierarchy of compensation in the early medieval law codes. Simple wounding by blows carried less compensation than injury involving the drawing of blood,[35] while finally wounds that caused the loss of the function of a bodily part carried the highest levels of compensation. The description of wounds and their compensation tended to follow the schema already established in medical texts, of a head to toe, *a capite ad calcem*, listing of body parts and what injuries they might sustain. With regard to sensory impairments, the Ripuarian, Alamannic, Bavarian and Saxon laws all distinguish between loss of the organ (eye, ear) but retention of sensory perception, and damage to the sensory perception but remaining organ.

For example, if the eye remains in situ, but has been blinded, the fine is half the amount it would be if the eye has been struck out. ... The regulation of the ear presents the converse to that for the eye: if the ear has been struck off but hearing is not damaged, the fine is half what it would be for striking off the ear and causing deafness.[36]

In addition, compensation payments were tied to a person's social and legal position: nobles, clerics, freemen, and serfs were compensated for and fined different payments according to their rank. However, one should note that the compensation tariffs were primarily drawn up with free men (and to a lesser extent free women) in mind, hence "like gender, rank and status are of secondary interest in the personal injury schedules".[37]

The comparative ranking of the different injuries and compensations taken from the *Lex Saxonum* (c. 802) has already been alluded to. This tariff scheme in the *Lex Saxonum* combines a carefully thought out hierarchy of what the injury or loss of a specific body part means, in terms of its impact on the overall physiological functioning of a person – losing the thumb impairs ability to grip and is therefore rated higher than loss of a finger; similarly loss of the big toe impairs balance and walking ability and is also rated higher than loss of any other toes – with a more abstract and symbolic method of allocating the various compensation rates – in multiples of 12, or as fractions of the full wergild – that provides us with some interesting examples of the culturally-specific perception of physical impairment. Bilateral loss of a body part, as in both hands or both feet, was also rated at the full wergild, while loss of one limb alone equated to exactly half the compensation. It is interesting to compare such an earlier medieval scheme of compensation with modern rates, as has been done for German law in relation to reduced working ability (*Minderung der Erwerbsfähigkeit*), a concept originating with late-nineteenth century developments in social security and employment law.[38]

In Anglo-Saxon England the earliest legal text, Ethelbert of Kent's code, probably compiled around 602, stated: "If a servant's eye or foot is destroyed, the full value is to be paid for him" (article 87 of the law).[39] This of course means payment to the lord, not to the servant! The eleventh-century laws of Cnut state the hierarchical system most clearly, in that distinction is to be made according to "age and youth, wealth and poverty, freedom and slavery, health and sickness".[40] One may note, however, that in the *Introduction* to the *Laws* of Alfred, the compensation for loss of an eye or a tooth in a (male or female) serf is in fact the liberation of that serf.[41] This passage is rendered in Latin in the *Quadripartitus* compilation, and is based on Exodus 21:26: "And if a man smite the eye of his servant, or the eye of his maid, that it perish; he shall let him go free for his eye's sake. And if he smite out his manservant's tooth, or his maidservant's tooth; he shall let him go free for his tooth's sake." The biblical 'eye for an eye, tooth for a tooth', which formed the conceptual basis for the subsequent *lex talionis*, here cannot allow the taking of an eye/tooth, since the culprit is the master himself. A more cynical interpretation would say that the manumission of the thus disabled servant reflects the notion of the servant as useless and damaged goods with a reduced working ability, for whom the master has no need for any longer; setting free a slave or serf is therefore also an economic liberation for the master who no longer has to feed and sustain a now useless slave.[42]

Over time there was a change from the earlier Middle Ages, where most regions and ethnic groups of western Europe had some form of wergild and compensation law element in their legal codification, to a gradual diminishing of compensation laws in the later Middle Ages. In England, wergild and compensation law made an early and almost total disappearance during the twelfth century – one should however note cap. 59,21 of the *Leges Henrici Primi* which allows for either mutilation or compensation in cases of theft – although in parts of Europe wergild-type compensation continued to be payable for various kinds of homicide (accidental killing, killing in self-defense, and even for manslaughter) until the seventeenth century.[43] So for example the thirteenth-century *Sachsenspiegel* still contained a section on compensation payments for wounding mouth, nose, eyes, tongue, or ears, and laming hands or feet of another (for which half a wergild was deemed sufficient),[44] while the same section also specifies the mutilating punishment of hand-amputation for laming and wounding[45] – a case of both the older wergild and the more recent mutilating punishments being combined in one normative text. In southern Europe, the *usatges* of Barcelona provided compensation for striking "a knight in his limbs so he appears incapacitated" (*usatge* 5) at the same level as for the death of a knight (twelve ounces of seared gold – I 4), but furthermore descended down the social scale to peasants "or any other man who holds no rank besides being a Christian" whose "incapacitation and beating" (*usatge* 11) was to be compensated in copper sous.[46] Incapacitation may here be equated with 'disability'.

Compensation for injuries, whether sustained accidentally or deliberately, continued to be a feature of later medieval legal practice, regardless of the demise of wergild. For example, in Ghent in 1374 one Annin Arents had to pay 72 Parisian pounds in compensation to Annin Masins for shooting him in the eye with an arrow, an injury that would have left Masins blind in that eye, hence the fairly high rate of payment.[47] Still in Ghent, in 1377 Colard Van den Gardine had to pay 150 Parisian pounds compensation because his son had accidentally blinded a boy named Gillekin Van der Meere by poking an object in his eye while both boys were at school.[48] Hence fines were also imposed in fourteenth-century Ghent on people who had been tasked with looking after children if these were injured, but even if such injuries resulted in permanent impairments, fines were set at a lower rate than the equivalent for adult injuries;[49] the 150 pounds paid to Gillekin may be an unusually high level of compensation. More typically, it seems, were the three Parisian pounds that had to be paid annually for 12 years as damages to the daughter of Jan Appelman for an accident (unfortunately for us this is not further detailed), or the same amount owed by Mergriet Van der Wostinen for her "carelessness" with the son of Jan Van Wachtebeke, who was so seriously injured that he would never have full use of his arm again.[50] Carers were held responsible for keeping children out of danger, for instance the nurse who was charged with looking after the infant daughter of Neeze Botermans but left the baby by the fire, so that she burned four fingers and was severely mutilated; in this case the magistrates (*scepenen*) of Ghent awarded 54 Parisian pounds in compensation.[51]

Having outlined some aspects of wergild and compensation law, and briefly traced the subsequent decline of this legal scheme, it is worth reminding ourselves of the origin of the key features of compensation law. Among the earliest of the barbarian codes was the Salic law, first codified under king Clovis (481-511), which in terms of compensation law set the marker that subsequent codifications were to follow. Some examples are given here:

Title XVII. Concerning Wounds ...

1. If any person strike another on the head so that the brain appears, and the three bones which lie above the brain shall project, he shall be sentenced to 1200 denars, which make 30 shillings.
2. But if it shall have been between the ribs or in the stomach, so that the wound appears and reaches to the entrails, he shall be sentenced to 1200 denars – which make 30 shillings – besides five shillings for the physician's pay.
3. If any one shall have struck a man so that blood falls to the floor, and it be proved on him, he shall be sentenced to 600 denars, which make 15 shillings.
4. But if a freeman strike a freeman with his fist so that blood does not flow, he shall be sentenced for each blow – up to 3 blows – to 120 denars, which make 3 shillings.[52]

What clearly emerges from this catalogue is that the rate of compensation given in the tariff reflects the perceived severity of the wound, and recognition that potentially impairing wounds (such as headwounds) warrant the highest compensation level. The mention of a physician is interesting, not least for the kind of wound that it is deemed appropriate to have professionally treated – perhaps less severe wounds do not require specialist medical attention.

Rothair, duke of Brescia, codified Germanic law for the Lombards in 643, resulting in 338 edicts, of which numbers 48 to 124 (i.e. a total of 76 edicts) relate to compensation law. They are concerned with the minutest detail of the location of an injury, for example:

(50) On cutting off lips [20 solidi fine]
(52) Concerning the molar teeth
(69) Concerning big toes
(70) Concerning second toes
(71) Concerning third toes
(92) Concerning fourth fingers[53]

And so on, always citing payments for damages to specific body parts, but in other respects are not very different from similar lists of tariffs. Several passages deal with the loss of an eye or the nose, which were to be compensated with half the wergild for a person, in the case of eyes being knocked out by a culprit making distinctions between the social rank of the victim (i.e. whether he is a *ministerialis* or a serf), but in many respects similar to other 'barbarian' laws.[54] Some similarities can be discerned, for instance, between injury tariffs in the edict of Rothair and the slightly earlier laws of Aethelbert of Kent.[55] The Kentish laws dating from the seventh century provide an interesting insight into the relative values attached to specific physical abilities, for instance the loss of a single eye (cap. 43) at 50 shillings was rated twice the worth at 25 shillings of losing hearing in one ear (cap. 39). The later laws of Alfred and the *Leges Henrici Primi* continued to follow the hierarchy of compensation set by Aethelbert's laws, in that loss of an eye was accorded the same value as loss of a foot,[56] but a lesser tariff was paid if the eye remained in the head rather than being lost completely and just vision was impaired.[57] Alfred's laws are unusual in that they form the only text which hints at the disabling effects of an injury, legislating one of the highest fines "for a wound to the *geweald* (literally 'power') resulting in laming".[58] The consequences of a wound are often taken into consideration by the tariff schemes, for example the "*Pactus Alamannorum* §11.3 lessens the fine for a leg wound if the victim can go about on *stelzia*",[59] that is on crutches, implying that the victim can be mobile with artificial support as opposed to being completely immobile or bed-ridden. The function of an injured limb is rarely considered specifically, however, so for example handedness, i.e. whether the victim was right- or left-handed, is not mentioned in a single of the law codes; the Frisian laws are the only ones to even come close to this concept by taking into account the occupation a wounded person had, so that "maiming the hand of a harpist or a goldsmith requires fourfold compensation"[60] above and beyond the hand of 'normal' person.

Legal compensation for conditions that could be impairing could, however, take a wider variety. An interesting example that places an alternative emphasis on what was deeming impairing stems from the *Laws* of King Alfred, prepared between 871 and 899:

> 35.3. If in insult he disfigures him [an innocent ceorl] by cutting his hair, he is to pay him 30 shillings compensation.
>
> 36. Moreover, it is established: if anyone has a spear over his shoulder, and a man is transfixed on it, the wergild is to be paid without the fine.
>
> 36.1 If he transfixed before his eyes, he is to pay the wergild; if anyone accuses him of intention in this act, he is clear himself in proportion to the fine, and by that [oath] do away with the fine ...[61]

These passages say several things in relation to impairment and disability. Firstly, disability need not be caused by an actual physical impairment, but can be a culturally-perceived disadvantage, as in the disfigurement caused by short-cut hair at the time of the 'long-haired kings'. Similar sentiments are found in the *Leges Henrici Primi* (cap. 93,1) where compensation scales are differentiated according to whether the injury is visible, concealed or temporary. As Lisi Oliver has observed, in general the Germanic laws had a propensity "to fine visible damage at a higher rate than hidden".[62]

Secondly, accidental injury, caused by someone negligently carrying a spear over their shoulder, can happen inadvertently and is to be compensated at a lower rate than maliciously intended injury. Another aspect of what the notion of disability might entail in legal terms is encountered in a section of the Visigothic Code (Bk. 8, title 3) on compensation to be paid to someone old, weak, or a sleeping person if they are crippled by a falling tree.[63] Here the types of people identified for compensation payment could all be categorised as vulnerable in one sense or another, either permanently (old or weak) or temporarily (the sleeper). One may regard this as a case of 'disability' in the modern sense being applied to people (such as the sleeper) whom we would not even necessarily regard as physically impaired. According to Visigothic thinking, by being asleep the sleeper is temporarily incapacitated, i.e. not aware of their surroundings, hence in a very loose sense the sleeper is already 'disabled' through sleep before perhaps in actuality being disabled by a falling tree.

The *Leges Henrici Primi* contained elements of Anglo-Saxon law that were carried over into the text, with detailed rules and schedules of compensation for injury, ranging from the loss of a fingernail at 4 shillings to the death of a thegn at 1200 shillings. Physical impairments are specifically singled out for higher compensation payments, e.g. loss of hearing warrants twice the compensation of loss of the ear itself (cap. 93,4), loss of eye, hand or foot are valued at a *triens* (a third of a 100 shilling wergild; cap. 93,31), and what probably equates to some form of paralysis due to a neck injury deserves a minimum of 100 shillings (cap. 93,37), in other words the full equivalent of wergild .

One of the most illuminating descriptions of what kind of injury warrants compensation payment is found in the Alamannic and Bavarian codes (Alam. 57.62 and Baiw. 4,28). Here the movement of a person who has sustained an orthopedic impairment is described as becoming a *tautragil*, called *Tauschlepper* in modern German (that is, someone who is dragging their lame foot through the dewy grass). This appears to be the only instance of a physical impairment in the catalogue of legal codes where a figurative metaphor is used to describe the condition of the afflicted person; although Oliver thinks the action of dragging one's limb through the dew is for curative purposes concerning an acute injury, rather than the permanent limping gait associated with impairment.[64] All the other compensation tariffs are mundanely and repetitively matter-of-fact in providing just the briefest of anatomical reference points.

In general, compensation laws recognised the greater damage done by an impairing injury and reflected this in the tariff. In Germany, bishop Bernhard of Hildesheim between 1133 and 1137 confirmed the rights of the peasants of Eschershausen, stating that in the event of one person injuring another in anger and drawing blood, he should pay three shillings to the steward, and two shillings to the injured person; but if the wound resulted in lameness, the culprit is again to pay three shillings to the steward, but in addition should humiliate himself in front of the lamed person and should show him through appropriate compensation how much he valued the reconciliation with him.[65] In the *Sachsenspiegel* compensation payments of half a wergild were to be made if someone injured another on mouth, nose and eyes, tongue and ears, or their genitals.[66] Interestingly enough, here one single point in the text cites four of the five sensory organs whose injury could lead to loss of the relevant physical faculty, i.e. speech, smell, sight, taste (or touch) and hearing. In another version of the text, injuries to hand, foot, arms or legs and subsequent impairment (that is lameness) of these body parts are also mentioned, again valued at half a person's wergild.[67] In general, one may deduce from the hierarchical treatment given to injuries to different body parts that, "unsurprisingly, wounds that may cause permanent incapacitation or disability are fined higher than those which may eventually heal."[68]

The early medieval compensation schemes have been criticised by modern scholarship. Stanley Rubin, in his book on the medical history of medieval England, had remarked that

> ... the laws show a lack of appreciation of the functional results of injuries, which points to a corresponding deficiency in the knowledge of surgical theory and practice. It seems evident that the higher ranks of society, for whom these laws were chiefly though not entirely composed, were more concerned with honour and appearance than with the more practical and mundane issues of physical disability.[69]

One may respond to this criticism by pointing out that modern compensation law is equally not very 'rational', since the whole area of evaluating human life and placing a pecuniary value on human body parts is problematic. Furthermore, the Anglo-Saxon (and other Germanic) elites, by virtue of their wealth and status, could afford to be more concerned with honour and their appearance than simply with the "mundane issues of physical disability"; also the stigma of disfigurement is a disability in itself, whereas the loss of a physical function may not necessarily be a stigma.

Different injuries may cause surprisingly differing levels of incapacity – surprising to the medical novice, that is. The functional rationale behind the compensation set in the legal tariffs is not as irrational as Rubin had accused it to be. For instance, head injuries causing damage to the skull are not always as dangerous as one might think, so that "even today, injury to the outer *tabulum* of the skull and loss of the great toe do not seem to be vastly inequivalent injuries."[70] One may recover from the skull injury without any lasting effects, but loss of the big toe causes a permanent limp. That (even) in early medieval Europe some people, at least, survived sometimes quite serious head wounds is attested by palaeopathological evidence.[71]

Overall, the earlier medieval legal codes reflect a loose recognition of the 'difference' of physically impaired persons, but there is no single dominating concept, no umbrella notion such as our modern umbrella term 'disability', and hence there is no special status *per se* outside of an individually negotiated position for each individual impaired person.[72] Simply giving equal compensation payment, like thirty shillings for the loss of a hand, to different people with the same injury does not guarantee equal treatment of these people outside of the narrow sphere of financial compensation. Nevertheless, the predominance of compensation laws in the barbarian legal codes over the exclusion laws in Roman codes marks a significant shift in legal attitude to and notion of impairment. There is far less legal exclusion in the barbarian codes, and not until the later twelfth and thirteenth centuries, with the greater re-use and re-working of Roman laws, do we find in texts such as the *Sachsenspiegel* the return to ideas of exclusion of some physically impaired people.

Finally, drawing on the distinction often made between impairment as the physical condition and disability as the social/ cultural superstructure, how can we interpret the treatment of physically impaired people in the eyes of the law? By themselves, the hypothetical person who has lost a hand and receives compensation for that loss is not necessarily disabled, just impaired. But if the loss of their hand subsequently means they cannot make property transactions or make a testament, then that is disabling them. Therefore, the earlier medieval law codes are not excluding people because of their disability, but they are disabling people because of their exclusion.

Notes

[1] For a fuller discussion of the appositeness of using the theories expounded by modern Disability Studies to aid understanding of medieval attitudes and mentalities cf. Metzler, 20-36.
[2] Whitelock, 459.
[3] Frugoni, 79. Frugoni notes, to our undoubted relief as modern readers, that "for once, the voice of moderation finally prevailed" (189 n. 66), but without informing us in what way: were the inhabitants spared, or simply killed quickly? Cf. L. Zdekauer, *La vita pubblica dei senesi nel Dugento*, Siena: L. Lazzeri, 1897, 98-9, the minutes of the council meeting are printed in appendix 4, 184-6.
[4] Robert Bartlett, *Trial by Fire and Water: The Medieval Judicial Ordeal* (Oxford: Clarendon Press, 1986), 98.
[5] On the Theodosian code see the recent collection of essays by Jill Harries and Ian Wood, eds, *The Theodosian Code: Studies in the Imperial Law of Late Antiquity* (London: Duckworth, 2nd edition 2010).
[6] Stefan Jurasinski, *Ancient Privileges: Beowulf, Law, and the Making of Germanic Antiquity* (Morgantown: West Virginia University Press, 2006), 25.
[7] Jurasinski, 93. For a summary discussion of the origin, adoption and regional spread of the Germanic laws, see the chapter "Barbarian Laws in Context," in Oliver, 8-25.
[8] Flint, 40-1, for summary of different barbarian legal codes.
[9] Peter Foot, at the University of Manitoba, has done an English translation of the first part of the Icelandic laws.
[10] "Chescun ne put mie fere attourné. Car enfaunt de eynz age, ne sourd, ne muet, ne fol nastre, ne homme purement aragé, ne autrement sauntz descrescioun, ne homme acusé de felonie, ne nul de qi nous le defendoms, ne mesel ousté de commune de gent, ne put mie fere attourné." *Britton*, Book VI, chap. X [CXXVI], 1, vol. II, 356, available at http://www.anglo-norman.net/texts/britton-contents.html (accessed 22 May 2012); in a similar list, given as "women ... serfs, and those under the age of twenty-one, open lepers, idiots, attorneys, lunatics, deaf mutes, those excommunicated by a bishop, criminal persons", certain people are forbidden from becoming judges (Peter Rushton, "Idiocy, the family and the community in early modern north-east England," in *From Idiocy to Mental Deficiency: Historical Perspectives on People with Learning Disabilities* (London and New York: Routledge, 1996), 47, refering to *Mirror of Justices*, ed. Whittaker). The reference to "open lepers" has similarities with the statement in Bracton that a leprous person with strikingly visible and severe (facial) deformities, appearing "so deformed that the sight of him cannot be endured (*si petens leprosus fuerit et tam deformis quod aspectus eum sustinere non possit*)", should be excluded from the right to plead in

court; *Bracton*, vol. IV, 30; Carol Rawcliffe, *Leprosy in Medieval England* (Woodbridge: D. S. Brewer, 2006), 194-5.

[11] Clare Dyer, "Deaf chief executive ruled out as juror," *The Guardian*, Wednesday 10 November 1999.

[12] Schleusener-Eichholz, vol. I, 495.

[13] *Saxon Mirror* Book I.3, 69-70 and *Sachsenspiegel* Landrecht 1.IV, 32.

[14] Depiction in exh. cat. *Der Sachsenspiegel*, 31.

[15] *Saxon Mirror* Book I.52, 83 and *Sachsenspiegel* Landrecht 1.LII.2, 58-9.

[16] Engel and Jacob, 35, citing *Urkundenbuch der Stadt und des Stiftes Bielefeld*, ed. Bernhard Vollmer (Bielefeld and Leipzig, 1937), document no. 4.

[17] Cited in Patrick Geary, *Readings in Medieval History, Vol 1: The Early Middle Ages* (Orchard Park, NY: Broadview Press, 1992), 24.

[18] In edict number 180, *Lombard Laws*, 84-5; Robinson, 51.

[19] *Saxon Mirror* Book III.3, 117 and *Sachsenspiegel* Landrecht 3.III, 118.

[20] *Sachsenspiegel* Landrecht, 1.XLVIII.2, 56: "Lame lute sollen ouch antwerten unde klagen ane vormunden, ez en si daz de klage zu kamphe ge, da si ir vormunde ein ir ebenbortige swertmag, wer her si, der ez ton wil. En mac der lame man, ab man in zu kamphe gruzit sines rechten vormunden nicht gehabin, unde tar her sin recht dar zu tun, her gewinnet zu vormunden, wer ez vor in tun wil, adir wen her mit phenningen dar zu gewinnen mag, aleine muge man sinen rechten vormunden bewisen."

[21] Ustage 51, *Usatges*, 76.

[22] Shulamith Shahar, "The Middle Ages and Renaissance," in *The Long History of Old Age*, edited by Pat Thane, 71-111. London: Thames and Hudson, 2005), 81, cf. G. Lopez, ed., *Las siete partidas del Rey Don Alfonso el Sabio* (Salamanca, 1555; reprint Madrid, 1974), Ley 2,74.

[23] Shahar, *Growing Old in the Middle Ages: 'Winter clothes us in shadows and pain.'* Translated by Yael Lotan. London and New York: Routledge, 1997), 165; cf. Tierney, 18-19.

[24] Michael Oliver, *The Politics of Disablement* (Basingstoke, UK: Palgrave Macmillan, 1990), 69.

[25] *Liber Const.* §§ XLVIII.1-3 in *Leges Burgundionum*, ed. Friedrich Bluhme, MGH Legum 3 (Hanover, 1898); Oliver, 169. In the case of the former non-debilitating injury, the fine was 10 per cent of wergild.

[26] The Salic, Alaman, Langobard, and Frisian laws are the most precise in this respect, what Jacob Grimm calls the nordic laws are less precise, and least of all the Burgundian or Visigothic law codes. Grimm, vol. II, 184.

[27] *Sachsenspiegel* Landrecht 3.XLVIII, p. 142: *Wer des anderen vie adir hunt totet oder lemet*, which passage runs through the hierarchical scheme of injuries in almost as much detail as the list given elsewhere for humans.

[28] Oliver, 24-5.

[29] Catherine Crawford, "Medicine and the Law," in *The Companion Encyclopedia of the History of Medicine*, edited by W. F. Bynum and Roy Porter (eds), 2 vols., 1619-40 (London and New York: Routledge, 1997), 1621; cf. Robert P. Brittain,

"Origins of legal medicine: *Leges Barbarorum*," *Medico-legal Journal* 34 (1966), 21-3.

[30]"In unseren ältesten Gesetzen wird der Werth aller leiblichen Verletzungen oder Verwundungen auf das Sorgfältigste nach den einzelnen Gliedern, nach der Größe der Wunde und nach anderen Bestimmungen ermittelt, ...", Grimm, vol. II, 130, cap. III.O.

[31] On the Old Frisian laws see Han Nijdam, *Licham, eer en recht in middeleeuws Friesland: Een studie naar de Oudfriese boeteregisters*. Middeleeuwse Studies en Bronnen CXIV (Hilversum: Verloren, 2008). Frisian law retained the earlier medieval compensation schemes for much longer than other European regions, and thereby escaped the later medieval trend towards more physical, that is mutilating punishments.

[32] "Dyt is de mate des peghels und is dar/umme hir gemalt: weret da de wunden peghel vorledit eder vorloren woerde, dat men denne nach dusseme gemalden eynen anderen machte maken [...], und myd deme ende, dar de boykstaf S geteykent steyt, pegelt men gesteken wunde mede, und myt deme anderen ende, dar dat H anne steyt, pegelt men de gehauen wunden." Cited by Boockman, 162. Cf. H. Boockmann, 'Das grausame Mittelalter', *Geschichte in Wissenschaft und Unterricht* 38 (1987).

[33] "Wiiwol de wunde nicht so deyp were, alse de pegel utwise...", cited by Boockman, 162, referring to *Göttinger Statuten*, ed. G. Freiherr von der Ropp ([Göttingen?], 1907), 145, note 1.

[34] *Nürnberger Polizeiordnungen aus dem XIII. bis XV. Jahrhundert*, ed. Joseph Baader (Stuttgart, 1861), 51, cited by Engel and Jacob, p. 74. That breadknives are not altogether harmless has regrettably been demonstrated all too often in contemporary times, with increasing knife crime in the UK (http://www.bbc.co.uk/news/uk-16626558, accessed 19 May 2012).

[35] On the drawing of blood cf. Bettina Bildhauer, *Medieval Blood* (Cardiff: University of Wales, 2006), 63-4, also *Lex Salica: 100 Titel-Text*, ed. Karl August Eckhardt, Germanenrechte Neue Folge. Abteilung Westgermanisches Recht (Weimar: Böhlau, 1953), pp. 138-40, and the *Schwabenspiegel* of c. 1275 in *Schwabenspiegel: Kurzform*, ed. K. A. Eckhardt, 2 vols, MGH Fontes iuris Germanici antiqui, NS 4-5 (Hanover: Hahn, 2nd ed. 1972-4), I, 388-9.

[36] Oliver, 93, also noting that since the site of a cut-off ear can be covered by hair, the loss is not immediately visible, whereas "there is no disguising the loss of an eye or the nose" (ibid., 95).

[37] Oliver, 203.

[38] See H. Feldmann, "Die forensische Bewertung von Körperschäden im frühen Mittelalter – ein Vergleich mit heutigen MdE-Sätzen." *Laryngo-Rhino-Otologie* 69 (1990), 166 on how legal and medical professionals over the last hundred years have framed the notion of disability as one of graded variation according to scientifically measured criteria. However, the metrification of a person has, as the barbarian compensation laws demonstrate, a much older pedigree.

[39] Cited in Geary, p. 237. Liebermann, vol. II, part II, pp. 292-3, comments that the culprit has to compensate the lord with the value of the full wergild for a serf since such an injury makes the serf unable to work usefully.
[40] English Historical Documents, 428.
[41] "Si percussit quispiam oculum serui sui aut ancillae et luscos eos fecerit, dimittet liberos pro oculo quem eruit. Dentem quoque si excusserit seruo uel ancillae suae, similiter dimittet eos liberos." *Aelfred Introduction* 20, given in Liebermann, vol. I, 33.
[42] See also Oliver, 174, who with regard to the Visigothic laws points out that the "law recognized and protected the full functional value of the working slave." Under Lombard law, "if the injured [freedman] is unable to work due to the nature of the injury, the perpetrator of the wound must also pay the doctor's fee and a further amount for the work the victim was unable to perform during recovery" (ibid., 210; see also 215, with allusion to compensation on account of the slave being a publicly visible status symbol for the master). According to such legal concepts, slaves, serfs and freedmen were valued purely for their output, like machinery in modern times, and not for any intrinsic value as a person.
[43] Naomi D. Hurnard, *The King's Pardon for Homocide before A.D. 1307* (Oxford: Clarendon Press, 1969), xi, for argument concerning total disappearance of wergild. But of course the demise of compensation law in England did not mean that either people stopped injuring one another, nor that they stopped asking for and receiving 'justice'. So the Lincolnshire assize rolls for 1202 mention the case of a man who pressed charges against another who had assaulted him and put one of his eyes out (Doris Stenton, ed., *Lincolnshire Record Society*, cited by James, 26).
[44] *Sachsenspiegel* Landrecht 2.XVI.5, p. 84; 2.XVI.6 specifies a tenth of a wergild for injured fingers and toes, while 2.XVI.7 specifies half a wergild in case of many acts of laming where the injured party does not die ("Die wile der man nicht en stirbit, we dicke man in lemet einer tat, man bessert in mit eime halben wergelde."), and repeated lamings of different limbs carry a fine of half a wergild for each instance (ibid.).
[45] *Sachsenspiegel* Landrecht 2.XVI.2, p. 83: "Wer den anderen lemet adir wundet, wirt her des verwunden, man slet im de hant abe."
[46] *Usatges*, 65-7.
[47] David Nicholas, *The Domestic Life of a Medieval City: Women, Children and the Family in Fourteenth-Century Ghent* (Lincoln: University of Nebraska Press, 1985), 146.
[48] Nicholas, 127; the source is Stadsarchief te Gent, ser. 330, *Zoendineboeken*, Z 6,2, f. 8v.
[49] Nicholas, 144 and n. 48.
[50] Ibid. This amount was less than half of what an adult master artisan might earn in a year.
[51] Ibid. and n. 49.
[52] Cited in Geary, 149-50.

[53] Daniel N. Robinson, *Wild Beasts and Idle Humours: The Insanity Defense from Antiquity to the Present* (Harvard University Press, 1996), 50.

[54] *Leges Langobardorum*, Cap. 48, 49: "De oculo evulso. Si quis alii oculum excusserit, pro mortuum adpretietur, qualiter in angargathungi (id est: secundum qualitatem personae); et medietas praetii ipsius conponatur ad ipsum, qui oculum excusserit. De naso absciso: Si quis alii nasum absciderit, medietatem pretii ipsius conponat, ut supra." Cap. 81: "De oculo evulso. Si quis haldium alienum aut servum ministerialem oculum excusserit, medietatem pretii ipsius quod adpretiatus fuerit, si eum occidisset, ei conponat." Cap. 105: "De oculo evulso. si quis servum alienum rusticanum oculum excusserit, medietatem praetii ipsius quod adpraetiatus fuerit, si eum occidisset, dominum eius conponat."

[55] Cf. Patrizia Lendinara, "The Kentish Laws," in *The Anglo-Saxons from the Migration Period to the Eighth Century: An Ethnographic Perspective*. Studies in Historical Archaeoethnology 2, ed. John Hines (San Marino and Woodbridge, 1997), pp. 21-42.

[56] At Alfred 71 and *Leges Henrici Primi* 93,31.

[57] At Alfred 47,1 and *Leges Henrici Primi* 93,5a.

[58] Oliver, 117, 134; refering to Alfred, 77. According to Liebermann, vol. III, p. 63, this means the top of the spinal column; spinal injuries are of course well-known for causing paralysis.

[59] Oliver, 120. The Alamann laws also go into most detail concerning the fines for injuries to the arms, differentiating between "striking arm off at the shoulder ([fine of] 40 per cent of wergild); striking arm off at elbow (20 per cent wergild); maiming the arm so it is useless (10 per cent wergild); maiming elbow so victim cannot lift hand or carry (6 per cent wergild)" (ibid., p. 124).

[60] Oliver, 141; *Lex Frisionum, Iudicia Wulemari* § 10, ed. Karl von Richthofen, MGH Legum III (Hanover, 1898).

[61] Cited in Geary, 253.

[62] Oliver, 142, although I do not concur with Oliver's distinction that a man without a hand is more visible than a man without a foot, so that therefore the laws should logically have awarded a higher valuation to the lost hand; furthermore, the argument that a "man without a hand may have suffered injury, but may conversely have been found guilty of perjury or theft" (ibid.) is one I would rather situate in the later medieval period, when mutilating punishments appeared to have been on the increase, than in the earlier Middle Ages, when judicial mutilation could often be converted into a monetary fine – an option only for those who could afford to pay it, of course. Furthermore, the "laws perhaps imply that for a freedman, [the loss of a foot] is restricted to the loss of functionality, whereas for a freeman, the visible fact of amputation additionally represents a loss of honour" (ibid., p. 209). Oliver (p. 165) reiterates the higher compensation for more visible wounds, adding that "if the fine for damage to a given body part is considerably greater than one might expect on the basis of functional worth, the additional fee is likely to be a surcharge for the embarrassment caused by visible disfigurement."

[63] Online Visigothic code, at http://www.libro.uca.edu/vcode/visigoths.htm (accessed November 2008).

[64] Oliver, 117.

[65] "Wer einem andern beim Streite im Zorne eine blutende Wunde beibringt, soll dem Vogte 3, dem Verletzten 2 Schillinge zur Sühne geben. Hat die Wunde aber eine Lähmung zur Folge, so soll der Täter an den Vogt zuvor gleichfalls 3 Schillinge bezahlen, vor dem Gelähmten aber sich demütigen und ihm durch angemessene Entschädigung zeigen, wie hoch er die Versöhnung mit ihm schätze." Günther Franz, ed., *Quellen zur Geschichte des deutschen Bauernstandes im Mittelalter* (Berlin, 1967), 183, Nr. 71 cited in Epperlein, 195.

[66] "Wird jemand an Mund, Nase und Augen, Zunge und Ohren oder seinen Geschlechtsteilen verletzt und muß man ihm dafür büßen, so muß man es ihm mit einem halben Manngeld vergelten". *Sachsenspiegel*, Oldenburger Kodex of early fourteenth century, fol. 45 verso, modern text following *Sachsenspiege*l Landrecht 2.XVI.5, p. 84; the illustration accompanying the text depicts a row of people receiving compensation payments, a man in the front row is shown with mutilated arms. See exhibition catalogue *Der Sachsenspiegel*, p. 40 for illustration, 41 for text.

[67] "Wird ein Mann an Mund, Nase und Augen, Zunge und Ohren oder am Geschlechtsglied, an Händen und Füßen oder an einem dieser Glieder verletzt und gelähmt, und soll man dafür Strafe zahlen, so muß es ihm mit einem halben Wergeld entgolten werden." *Sachsenspiegel* Landrecht, 2.XVI.5-9,p. 84, modern German rendition in Epperlein, 197.

[68] Oliver, 135.

[69] Stanley Rubin, *Medieval English Medicine* (New York: Barnes and Noble, 1974), 149.

[70] Oliver, 82.

[71] Oliver, 87, with examples at 76-87. Overall, the success rate for surgical interventions, such as trepanation, seems to have been quite high (Oliver, 92).

[72] I am in agreement here with the conclusion drawn by Oliver, 239-41, that the compensation tariffs do not really provide much more than a personal injury scheme, and can in no way be equated to our modern concept of 'disability'.

Appendix One

Disability in selections from Roman law and early medieval legal codes

Source	Modern English translation	Source text
Justinian's Institutes 1.23.4	Supervisors should also be appointed for the mentally afflicted, the deaf, the dumb, and the chronically ill, because such people cannot stand up for themselves.	Sed et mente captis et surdis et mutis et qui morbo perpetuo laborant, quia rebus suis superesse non possunt, curatores dandi sunt.
Justinian's Institutes 2.12.3	Again, the dumb and the deaf do not always have testamentary capacity. By deaf we mean completely unable to hear, not hard of hearing, and by dumb unable to speak at all, not having difficulty in speaking. Yet it often happens that educated and literate people lose their speech or hearing for one reason or another. To help them our pronouncement has provided certain ways and means for them to be able to make wills and perform other acts. If someone makes a will and is then struck deaf or dumb through illness or some other cause, his will remains valid.	Item mutus et surdus non semper facere testamentum possunt. utique autem de eo surdo loquimur, qui omnino non exaudit, non qui tarde exaudit: nam et mutus is intellegitur, qui eloqui nihil potest, non qui tarde loquitur. saepe autem etiam litterati et eruditi homines variis casibus et audiendi et loquendi facultatem amittunt: unde nostra constitutio etiam his subvenit, ut certis casibus et modis secundum normam eius possint testari aliaque facere quae eis permissa sunt. sed si quis post testamentum factum valetudine aut quodlibet alio casu mutus aut surdus esse coeperit, ratum nihilo minus eius remanet testamentum.
Justinian's Institutes 2.10	Neither a woman, nor youths below the age of puberty, nor a slave, nor a mute, nor a deaf person, nor a mad man, nor anyone forbidden from having property, nor one whom the laws declare worthless and incompetent to witness, can be witnesses.	Sed neque mulier neque impubens neque servus neque mutus neque surdus neque furiosus nec cui bonis interdictum est nec is, quem leges iubent improbum intestabilemque esse, possunt in numero testium adhiberi.
Justinian's Institutes 2.12.4	A blind man cannot make a will except under the scheme laid down by my father, the Emperor Justin.	Caecus autem non potest facere testamentum nisi per observationem, quam lex divi Iustini patris mei introduxit.
Justinian's Institutes 2.19.4	This requirement of testamentary capacity is satisfied not only in a person who can make a will but in one who can take for himself or another under a will but not make one of his own. A person qualifies even if insane, dumb, or posthumous; or a baby; or a dependant, free or unfree. Though these people cannot make wills, they can take by will, for themselves or for others.	testamenti autem factionem non solum is habere videtur, qui testamentum facere potest, sed etiam qui ex alieno testamento vel ipse capere potest vel alii adquirere, licet non potest facere testamentum. et ideo et furiosus et mutus et postumus et infans et filius familias et servus alienus testamenti factionem habere dicuntur: licet enim testamentum facere non possunt, attamen ex testamento vel sibi vel alii adquirere possunt.
Justinian's Institutes 3.19.7	It is obvious that a person who is dumb cannot stipulate or promise. The same has been accepted of the deaf. The stipulator must hear the words of the promissor, and the promissor must hear the words of the stipulator. Obviously we exclude only those who cannot hear at all, not those who have difficulty hearing	Mutum neque stipulari neque promittere posse palam est. quod et in surdo receptum est, quia et is qui stipulator verba promittentis et is qui promittit verba stipulantis audire debet. unde apparet non de eo nos loqui qui tardius exaudit, sed deo eo qui omnino non exaudit.
Codex Justinianus 5.34.3	That someone robbed of the light of their eyes may be appointed curator is a false opinion presented to you.	Luminibus captum curatorem habere falso tibi persuasum est.

Source	Modern English translation	Source text
Codex Justinianus 5.62.9	Your brother may not, because he has lost an eye, refuse a guardianship or cura; for this reason you will understand that he may not lay down the accepted office.	Frater tuus non ideo a tutela vel cura excusari debet, quod oculum amisit. proinde intellegis munus susceptum eum deserere non posse.
Codex Justinianus 5.68.1	Someone robbed of the light of his eyes, or a deaf person or a mute person [or insane person] or someone afflicted by chronic illness has an excuse concerning tutelage or curatorship.	Qui morbo Luminibus captus aut surdus aut mutus aut furiosus aut perpetua valitudine tentus tutelae seu curationis excusationem habent.
Codex Justinianus 6.22.8	After careful consideration we hereby prescribe that blind persons, whether they have become such through an illness or an injury or whether they have been born so, may only make their last will verbally, namely in the presence of seven witnesses, who also legally have to be present for other testaments, and the presence of one notary. Once these witnesses are all assembled, then the blind person has first of all to announce to them that they have been called to him because he wishes to testate verbally. Thereupon the same [blind person] has to specifically state the names of the inheritors and also their rank, so that doubt does not occur by the mention of the names alone. Then the same has to clearly and exactly say aloud the part or the parts to which they shall inherit, similarly what each legate or fidei commissioner shall have, and all that which the laws to decrees of last wills require. If all this has been discussed in one and the same location and at one and the same time and subsequently written down in the own hand of the notary in the presence of the previously mentioned witnesses, signed in their own hands by the witnesses, [and] sealed both by them and by the notary, then such a last will shall exist completely to rights ...	Hac consultissima lege sancimus, ut carentes oculis seu morbo vel ita nati per nuncupationem suae condant moderamina voluntatis, praesentibus septem testibus, quos aliis quoque testamentis interesse iuris est, tabulario etiam: ut cunctis ibidem collectis primum ad se convocatos omnes, ut sine scriptis testentur, edoceat, deinde exprimat nomina specialiter heredum et dignitates singulorum et indicia, ne sola nominum commemoratio quicquam ambiguitatis pariat, et ex quanta parte vel ex quotis unciis in successionem admitti debeant et quod unumquemque legatarium seu fideicommissarium adsequi velit: omnia denique palam edicat, quae ultimarum capit dispositionum series lege concessa.

Source	Modern English translation	Source text
Codex Justinianus 6.22.10	Since deaf and dumb is differentiated from one another in that both debilities are not always connected with one another, we therefore order that he who suffers both afflictions simultaneously and was born in that way may not have the right to make a will or a codicil, to leave a fideicommission[1], enact a gift because of death or manumit someone, whether by rod or by another method, and both men as well as women are subject to this law. If however a man or a woman have not been born with the misfortune of this debility, but they have lost their speech and their hearing through a later illness, we permit for the case that they have knowledge of writing that they may undertake what we have just forbidden, insofar they are able to write it in their own hand. But if both afflictions are separated from one another, which however is such rare a case, then we will hereby permit the deaf, even if by nature there are several degrees, to undertake both wills as well as codicils, gifts because of death, manumissions and other actions. Since if by nature he has only been lent an articulated voice, then there is no impediment for him to do everything according to his wishes. It is well known to us how some jurists very sharp-wittedly by cogitation elucidated and demonstrated, and how also Iuventius Celsus[2] assumed, that there may be nobody who should hear absolutely nothing when he is spoken into his ear from above, where the brain lies. In such cases, where someone has only been robbed of their hearing by a later illness, one may also not doubt the capability to conduct all affairs without impediment. If, however, he is capable to hear with his ears and he has only lost his speech, there is also no impediment for him to conduct all these affairs, although the older jurists hold very divergent opinions on this, if he is capable of writing, whether the affliction hit him from birth or as consequence of an illness. Also for this entire constitution there shall be no differentiation between men and women.	Discretis surdo et muto, quia non semper huiusmodi vitia sibi concurrunt, sancimus, si quis utroque morbo simul laborat, id est ut neque audire neque loqui possit, et hoc ex ipsa natura habeat, neque testamentum facere neque codicillos neque fideicommissum relinquere neque mortis causa donationem celebrare concedatur nec libertatem sive vindicta sive alio modo imponere: eidem legi tam masculos quam feminas oboedire imperantes. Ubi autem et in huiusmodi vitiis non naturalis sive masculo sive feminae accedit calamitas, sed morbus postea superveniens et vocem abstulit et aures conclusit, si ponamus huiusmodi personam litteras scientem, omnia, quae priori interdiximus, haec ei sua manu scribenti permittimus. Sin autem infortunium discretum est, quod ita raro contingit, et surdis, licet naturaliter huiusmodi sensus variatus est, tamen omnia facere et in testamentis et in codicillis et in mortis causa donationibus et in libertatibus et in aliis omnibus permittimus. Si enim vox articulata ei a natura concessa est, nihil prohibet eum omnia quae voluit facere, quia scimus quosdam iuris peritos et hoc subtilius cogitasse et nullum esse exposuisse, qui penitus non exaudit, si quis supra cerebrum illius loquatur, secundum quod iuventio celso placuit. In eo autem, cui morbus superveniens auditum tantummodo abstulit, nec dubitari potest, quin possit omnia sine aliquo obstaculo facere. In eo autem, cui morbus superveniens auditum tantummodo abstulit, nec dubitari potest, quin possit omnia sine aliquo obstaculo facere. Sin vero aures quidem apertae sint et vocem recipientes, lingua autem penitus praepedita, licet a veteribus auctoribus saepius de hoc variatum est, attamen si et hunc peritum litterarum esse proponamus, nihil prohibet et eum scribentem omnia facere, sive naturaliter sive per interventum morbi huiusmodi infortunium ei accessit. Nullo discrimine neque in masculis neque in feminis in omni ista constitutione servando.
Codex Justinianus 10.51.1	If your father suffers from blindness so much, that he has lost his sight in both eyes, he may obtain release from public duties.	Si ea caecitate pater tuus oppressus est, ut utriusque oculi aciem prorsus amiserit, levamentum personalium munerum sentiet.
Codex Justinianus 10.51.4	Physical debility of the father does not entitle the son to obtain release from public duties.	Casus patris corporis munerum personalium filio iure non praestat excusationem.

Source	Modern English translation	Source text
Laws of Aethelberht cap. 34-39	34. If a bone is laid bare, 3 shillings shall be paid as compensation. 35. If a bone is damaged, 4 shillings shall be paid as compensation. 36. If the outer covering of the skull is broken, 10 shillings shall be paid as compensation. 37. If both are broken, 20 shillings shall be paid as compensation. 38. If a shoulder is disabled [lamed], 30 shillings shall be paid as compensation. 39. If the hearing of either ear is destroyed, 25 shillings shall be paid as compensation.[3]	34. Gif banes blice weordey, III scillingum begete. 35. Gif banes bite weord, IIII scillingum gebete. 36. Gif seo uterre hion gebrocen wordey, X scillingum gebete. 37. Gif butu sien, XX scillingum gebete. 38. Gif eaxle gelæmed weoryed, XXX scill' gebete. 39. Gif oyer eare nowiht gehered, XXV scill' gebete.
Laws of Aethelberht cap. 43	43. If an eye is knocked out, 50 shillings shall be paid as compensation.	43. Gif eage of weord, L scillinga gebete.
Laws of Aethelberht cap. 52	52. If the power of speech is injured, 12 shillings [shall be paid as compensation].	52. Gif spræc awyrd weory, XII scillingas.
Laws of Aethelberht cap. 53 § 1	53 § 1. If an arm is broken, 6 shillings shall be paid as compensation.	53 § 1. Gif earm forbrocen weord, VI scill' gebete.
Laws of Aethelberht cap. 54	54. If a thumb is struck off, 20 shillings [shall be paid as compensation].	54. Gif yuman ofaslæhd, XX scill'.
Laws of Aethelberht cap. 56	56. For the slightest disfigurement, 3 shillings, and for a greater 6 shillings [shall be paid as compensation].	56. Æt yam lærestan wlitewamme III scillingas ond æt yam maran VI scill'.
Laws of Aethelberht cap. 65	65. If a thigh is broken, 12 shillings shall be paid as compensation. § 1. If he becomes lame, the settlement of the matter may be left to friends.	65. Gif yeoh gebrocen wedrdey, XII scillingum gebete. § 1. Gif he healt weord, yær motan freond seman.
Laws of Aethelberht cap. 67	67 § 1. For a stab [to the thigh] over an inch [deep], 1 shilling; for a stab between 2 and 3 inches [deep], 2 shillings; for a stab over 3 inches [deep], 3 shillings [shall be paid as compensation].	67 § 1. Gyfe ofer ynce scilling, æt twam yncum twegen, ofer yry III scll'.
Laws of Aethelberht cap. 69	69. If a foot is struck off, 50 shillings shall be paid for it.	69. Gif fot of weordey, L scillingum forgelde.
Laws of Aethelberht cap. 87	87. If the eye and foot of a servant are destroyed [by blows], his full value shall be paid.	87. Gif esnes eage 7 foot of weordey aslagen, ealne weorye hine forgelde.
Laws of Alfred cap. 14	If anyone is born dumb or deaf, so that he can neither deny nor confess his wrongdoings, his father shall pay compensation for his misdeeds.	[Be dumbra manna dædum.] Gif mon sie dumb odde déaf geboren, yæt he ne mæge [his] synna onsecggan ne geandettan, bete se fæder his misdæda.
Laws of Alfred cap. 44	30 shillings shall be given as compensation for a wound on the head, if both bones are pierced. § 1. If the outer bone [only] is pierced, 15 shillings shall be given as compensation.	[Be heafodwunde 7 odre liman.] Heafodwunde to bote gif da ban beod butu dyrel XXX scill. geselle him mon. § 1. Gif dæt uterre ban bid yyrel geselle XV scill. to bote.
Laws of Alfred cap. 46	If either ear is struck off, 30 shillings shall be given as compensation. § 1. If the hearing is stopped, so that he cannot hear, 60 shillings shall be given as compensation.	Gif him mon áslea oyer eare of, geselle XXX scill. to bote. § 1. Gif se hlyst o stande, yæt he ne mæge gehieran, geselle LX scill. to bote.

Source	Modern English translation	Source text
Laws of Alfred cap. 47	If anyone knocks out a man's eye, he shall give him 66 shillings, 6 pence and the third part of a penny[4] as compensation. § 1. If it remains in the head, but he can see nothing with it, one-third of the compensation shall be withheld.	Gif mon men eage ofáslea, geselle him mon LX scill' 7 VI scill' 7 VI pæningas 7 driddan dæl pæninges to bote. § 1. Gif hit in dam heafde sie, 7 he noht geseon ne mæge mid, stande driddan dæl yære bote inne.
Laws of Alfred cap. 48	If anyone strikes off another's nose, he shall pay him 60 shillings compensation.	Gif mon odrum yæt neb ófaslea, gebete him mid LX scill'.
Laws of Alfred cap. 52	If, as the result of another's actions, a man's tongue is torn from his mouth, the compensation [to be paid] shall be the same as that for an eye.	Gif monnes tunge bid of heafde odres monnes dædum dón, yæt bid gelic 7 eagan bot.
Laws of Alfred cap. 66	If a man's arm, with the hand and all below the elbow, is cut off, 80 shillings shall be paid as compensation for it.	Gif men sie se earm mid honda mid ealle ofácorfen beforan elmbogan, gebete dæt mid LXXX scill.
Laws of Alfred cap. 69	If a man maims another's hand outwardly, 20 shillings shall be given to him as compensation, if he can be cured. § 1. If half of it comes off, then 40 shillings must be paid as compensation.	Gif mon odrum da hond utan forslea, geselle him XX scill. to bote, gif hine mon gelacnian mæge. § 1. Gif hio healf onweg fleoge, yonne sceal XL scill. to bote.
Laws of Alfred cap. 71	If a man's eye is knocked out, or if his hand or foot is struck off, the same compensation shall follow them all – 6 pennies, 66 shillings and the third part of a penny.	Gif monnes eage him mon ófaslea odde his hand odde his fot, dær gæd gelic bot to eallum: VI pæningas 7 VI scill. 7 LX scill. 7 driddan dæl pæninges.
Laws of Alfred cap. 72	If a man's shin is struck off at the knee, 80 shillings must be paid as compensation for it.	Gif monnes sconca bid ófaslegen wid dæt cneou, dær sceal LXXX scill. to bote.
Laws of Alfred cap. 75	If the large sinew is damaged, and if it can be treated medically so as to make it sound, 12 shillings shall be given as compensation. § 1. If the man becomes lame as a result of the damage to the sinew, and if he cannot be cured, 30 shillings shall be given [to him] as compensation.	Gif mon da greatan sinwe forslea, gif hie mon gelacnian mæge, yæt hio hal sie, geselle XII scill. to bote. § 1. Gif se mon healt sie for yære sinwe wunde, 7 hine mon gelacnian ne mæge, geselle XXX scill. to bote.
Laws of Alfred cap. 77	If one man damages the tendons in another's neck, and wounds him so severely that he has no control over them, but [if] nevertheless he continues to live so wounded, 100 shillings shall be given to him as compensation, unless the councillors award him a juster and a greater sum.[5]	Gif mon odrum da geweald forslea uppe on yam sweoran 7 forwundie to yam swide, yæt he nage yære geweald, 7 hwædre lifie swa gescended, geselle him mon C scill. to bote, buton him witan ryhtre 7 mare gereccan.
Leges Henrici Primi c. 59, 21	Every theft, whether of livestock or other chattels, whether of one thing or of several, may be amended by making compensation or may not; of the ones which may be compensated for, some are satisfied by the loss of a limb, others by the payment of money.	Omne autem furtum mobile uel immobile, simplex aut multiplex, redimendum [uel] non est, redimendorum alia membris alia peccunia.
Leges Henrici Primi c. 71, 2	If the bewitched person does not die, but suffers some change of the skin or demonstrable physical sickness, compensation shall be paid as prescribed by the ancient provisions of wise men, in accordance with the circumstances.	Si autem insortiatus non fuerit mortuus, set cutis uariationem uel probabilem corporis contrahat egritudinem, emendetur sapientum antiquis diffinitionibus sicut acciderit.

Source	Modern English translation	Source text
Leges Henrici Primi c. 78, 6	If anyone is deaf and dumb from birth, so that he cannot confess to the charges laid against him or against anyone else, his father shall pay compensation for his misdeeds.	Si quis a natiuitate surdus et mutus sit ut sua uel alterius nequeat irrogata confiteri, emendet pater eius forisfacta sua.
Leges Henrici Primi c. 93, 1	If anyone suffers a wound, not involving the cutting off or maiming or breaking of a limb, on an uncovered and visible place (for example, in front of the hair or below the sleeve or beneath the knees), the compensation to be paid shall be double what would be due in the case of a wound inflicted on the head under the hair or on the limbs beneath clothes, that is, on a concealed place.[6]	Si uulnus eueniat alicui sine menbri truncatione uel debilitatione uel diffractione, in nudo et manifesto (ut ante capillos, ante manicam, sub genibus), duppliciter emendandum est supra id quod in capite sub capillis uel in menbris sub uestibus, in occulto, fieret.
Leges Henrici Primi c. 93, 4	If anyone's ear is cut off, compensation of thirty shillings shall be paid to him; if thereby he loses his hearing, the compensation paid shall be sixty shillings.	Si auris amputetur alicui, XXX solidis emendetur ei; si auditum inde perdat, LX solidis emendetur.
Leges Henrici Primi c. 93, 5	If anyone knocks out another's eye, he shall pay him sixty-six shillings, six pence, and a third of a penny.	Si quis alii crepet oculum, soluat ei LXVI solidos et VI denarios et trientem unius denarii.
Leges Henrici Primi c. 93, 5a	If the eye remains in the head, but so that the man can see nothing with it, a third part of the compensation otherwise payable shall be withheld.	Si oculus in capite remaneat ut tamen homo nichil inde uideat, tertia pars in eo emendationis consistat.
Leges Henrici Primi c. 93, 11	The same compensation shall be paid for the tongue as for an eye.	De lingua sicut de oculo componatur.
Leges Henrici Primi c. 93, 14	If both bones in the arm are broken, compensation of thirty shillings shall be paid.	Si utrumque os brachii fractum sit, emendetur XXX solidis.
Leges Henrici Primi c. 93, 25	If a man's arm along with the hand is completely cut off below the elbow, compensation of eighty shillings shall be paid.	Si homini sit brachium cum manu penitus amputatum sub cubito LXXX solidis emendetur.
Leges Henrici Primi c. 93, 29	If anyone causes an external injury to another's hand, he shall pay compensation of twenty shillings; if half the hand flies off, sixty shillings shall be paid for it.	Si quis alteri manum extra plagiauerit, XX solidis emendet; si dimidia manus auolauerit, reddantur inde LX solidi.
Leges Henrici Primi c. 93, 31	If anyone causes the loss of another's eye or hand or foot, he shall pay the same compensation for each of them, that is, sixty-six shillings and six pence and a third of a penny, which is a triens.	Si quis oculum uel manum uel pedem excutiat alicui, parem emendationem faciat de singulis, id est LXVI solidos et VI denarios et tertiam partem unius denarii, que est triens.
Leges Henrici Primi c. 93, 32	If anyone's shin is struck off below the knee, the penalty for the injury shall be assessed at eighty shillings.	Si crus alicui excussum sit sub genu, LXXX solidorum culpa iudicetur.
Leges Henrici Primi c. 93, 35	Anyone who injures the great sinews of another's lower legs shall, if they recover through response to medical treatment, pay twelve shillings as compensation.	Qui grossos tibiarum neruos truncauerit alicui, si medicamentum sanitatis admittant, XII solidis emendabit.
Leges Henrici Primi c. 93, 35a	If the man is lame because of the injuries to his sinews and cannot be healed, compensation of thirty shillings shall be paid.	Si homo claudicet pro uulneribus neruorum et sanari non possit, XXX solidis emendetur.

Source	Modern English translation	Source text
Leges Henrici Primi c. 93, 37	If anyone injures another on the neck so that he suffers a curvature or stiffness or a lasting disability from it, and yet remains alive though thus incapacitated[7], compensation of one hundred shillings shall be paid and also whatever has been paid out for medical treatment, unless the calculation of the judges prescribes a larger award.	Qui aliquem in collo plagiauerit ut incuruationem uel inflexibilitatem uel inde perpetuam contrahat egritudinem, et tamen uiuat ita contumeliatus, C solidis emendetur et quicquid in medicatura fuerit erogatum, nisi sapientum estimatio amplius iudicauerit.
Leges Henrici Primi c. 94, 2	Anyone who does an injury to another and draws blood shall pay compensation for this by the inch; for each inch five pence, when the injury is in a concealed place, and for each inch ten pence, when the injury is in a visible place; and no compensation shall be payable for wounds without blood and closed up.	Qui uulnus alicui faciet ac sanguinem, emendet hoc per uncias; ad singulas V denariis in cooperto, in nudo pro singulis unciis X denariis; et remaneat de cecis ictibus et belidentibus.
Leges Burgundionum 48	on infliction of wounds: (3) Also if someone breaks the arm or the leg of someone in the above mentioned manner and they will evidently be punished by debility, to them shall compensation be given in such form as the aforementioned law has decreed.	de inflictis vulneribus: (3) Ceterum si aut brachium cuiuscumque aut tibia supradicto ordine fractae et evidenti fuerint debilitate damnatae, ea compositionis forma servabitur, quae antedatis legibus[8] legitur fuisse decreta
Leges Burgundionum 49.2	on animals straying and being the cause of death or debilitating people	et dum intra clusuram retinentur casum mortis aut debilitatis incurrerint
Lex Ribuaria 3	breaking of bones[9]	
Lex Ribuaria 4	cutting through a limb (arm, leg, bone) through to the marrow of the bone[10]	
Lex Ribuaria 5	mutilation, with loss of function of limbs or sensory organs 5.1 If a freeman cuts off the ear of a freeman, so that he cannot hear, 100 shillings... If however he does not lose his hearing, 50 shillings.... 5.2 If he cuts off the nose, so that he cannot blow his nose, 100 shillings ... if he can still blow his nose, 50 shillings compensation. 5.3 If a freeman cuts out the eye of a freeman, 100 shillings ... If vision is restored in the eye and seeing is not fully mastered, 50 shillings ... 5.4 If a hand ... 100 shillings ... If the hand is hanging down lamed, ... 50 shillings 5.5 thumb 5.7 index finger 5.8 foot 5.9 toes[11]	De debilitatibus 1. Si quis ingenuus ingenuo auriculam excusserit, ut audire non possit, centum solid. culpabilis iudicetur. Si autem auditum non perdiderit, quinquaginta solid. componatur. 2. Si nasum excusserit, ut muccare non possit, 100 sol. culpabilis iudicetur; si muccare prevalet, 50 sol. componat. 3. Si quis ingenuus ingenuo oculum excusserit, centum solid. culpabilis iudicetur. Si visus in oculo restiterit et videre non potuerit, 50 solid. culpabilis iudicetur. 4. Si manum ... 100 solid. ... Si manus ibidem manca pependerit, ... 50 sol.
Lex Ribuaria 22	breaking of bones of an unfree man a) by a free man b) by a king's man or cleric	
Lex Ribuaria 23	unfree man breaks bones of a) a free man b) a king's man or cleric	
Lex Ribuaria 26	unfree man breaks the bones of another unfree person	

Source	Modern English translation	Source text
Lex Ribuaria 27	Of the mutilation of serfs by another unfree man If someone cuts off the eye, ear, nose, hand or foot, twice nine shillings shall be paid to his lord...	De debilitatibus servorum Quod si oculum, auriculam, nasum, manum, pedem excusserit, bis novenos solid. dominus eius culpabilis iudicetur
Lex Ribuaria 86	death or lameness brought about by magic 86.2 failed attempt at murder that brings on deformation or lameness: If however he is not dead but will probably have a deformation (=disfigurement) or lameness from that in his body, 100 shillings ...	Sin autem mortuus non fuerit, et varietatem seu debilitatem[12] probabile ex hoc in corpus habuerit, 100 sol. culpabilis iudicetur, aut cum sex iuret.
Leges Alamannorum 57. 62	If however one strikes another in the knee, so that he shall remain lame, and that his foot touches the dew, what the Alemanni call tautragil[13], he shall be compensated with 12 shillings.	Si quis autem alium in genuculo placaverit, ita ut claudus permaneat, ut pes eius ros tangat, quod Alamanni 'tautragil' dicunt, cum 12 solidis conponat.
Lex Baiwariorum 4, 28	on striking someone lame If one strikes another, so that afterwards he shall be lame, in that his foot touches the dew, what they call tautragil, he shall be compensated with 12 shillings.[14]	de plaga claudicationis Si quis aliquem plagaverit, ut exinde claudus fiat, sic ut pes eius ros tangat, quod tautragil vocant, cum XII sold conponat.
Lex Baiwariorum 6, 11	[If someone cuts off the ear and throws him in the water] If someone cuts off his ear, he shall be compensated with a shilling and a half. If he pierces his ear, he shall be compensated with one shilling. If he deafens him or strikes him in such a way, that he shall remain lame, what they call tautragil, and if he throws him in the water from the shore or from a bridge, in these cases he shall always be compensated with 4 shillings.	[Si aurem absciderit et eum in aquam impinxerit] Si aurem eius absciderit, cum solido et semi conponat. Si aurem eius transpunxerit, cum I solido conponat. Si eum surdaverit vel sic eum plagaverit, ut claudus permaneat, quod tautragil vocant, et si in aquam inpinxerit de ripa vel de ponte, in istis causis semper IIII sold conponat.
Pactus Legis Salicae 17, 4	He who strikes another man on the head so that the brain shows, and it is proved against him (called chiesiofrit in the Malberg gloss)[15], shall be liable to pay six hundred denarii (i.e., fifteen solidi).	
Pactus Legis Salicae 17, 5	If the three bones that lie over the brain protrude (called chicsiofrit in the Malberg gloss), he shall be liable to pay twelve hundred denarii (i.e., thirty solidi).	
Pactus Legis Salicae 29, 1	He who maims another man's hand or foot or gouges out or strikes out his eye or cuts off his ear or nose and it is proved against him (called sicti in the Malberg gloss) shall be liable to pay four thousand denarii (i.e., one hundred solidi).[16]	
Pactus Legis Salicae 29, 11	If the foot has been struck off (called chuldachina sichte in the Malberg gloss), he who did this shall be liable to pay twenty-five hundred denarii (i.e., sixty-two and one-half solidi).	

Source	Modern English translation	Source text
Pactus Legis Salicae 29, 12	He who puts out another man's eye (called lichauina in the Malberg gloss) shall be liable to pay twenty-five hundred denarii (i.e., sixty-two and one-half solidi).	
Pactus Legis Salicae 29, 13	He who cuts off another man's nose (called frasito in the Malberg gloss) shall be liable to pay eighteen hundred denarii (i.e., forty-five solidi).[17]	
Pactus Legis Salicae 29, 14	He who cuts off another man's ear (called channichleora in the Malberg gloss) shall be liable to pay six hundred denarii (i.e., fifteen solidi).[18]	
Pactus Legis Salicae 29, 15	He who cuts out another man's tongue so that he is not able to speak (called alchaltea in the Malberg gloss) shall be liable to pay four thousand denarii (i.e., one hundred solidi).[19]	

[1] Last wish of testator that the heirs have to honour.
[2] Jurist at the time of Trajan and Hadrian.
[3] For comparison: wergild for an ordinary freeman is 100 shillings.
[4] That is, a third of the wergeld at 200 shillings.
[5] Possibly reference to spinal injury. Some MSS of *Quadripartitus* add that full compensation is to be paid for a free man, half for a serf.
[6] Cf. c. 93, 26 where the subject is repeated in less detail.
[7] This clearly points out the limbo status of a person such impaired: between life and death.
[8] "antedatis legibus" refers to title 11.1 on wounds.
[9] Cf. Lex Burgundionum 48.
[10] Cf. Lex Baiwariorum IV.6.
[11] This passage follows Lex Salica 29.
[12] *varietas* meaning deformation of body, *debilitas* meaning lameness.
[13] *tautragil* = modern German: *Tauzieher*, *Tauschlepper* = dew-puller, so a metaphor for someone dragging their lame leg through the dew on the ground.
[14] Cf. Lex Alamannorum 57. 62. Also a similar law at Lex Baiwariorum Bk 5, 8.
[15] "The Malberg glosses (contained in some manuscripts) are thought to be Frankish words or the remnants of Frankish words for which no exact equivalent in Latin was found", Drew, *Laws of the Salian Franks*, 232 n.5.
[16] For cutting another man's hand so that it hangs crippled the fine is sixty-two and one-half solidi in Capitulary VI (thought to be of Childebert II, king of Austrasia 575-95 and king of Burgundy 592-5), case IV, 5, while in case V, 5 the fine for striking off a hand, cutting out the tongue, or castrating or otherwise incapacitating the penis is set at one hundred solidi.
[17] Same penalty in Capitulary VI, case III, 6.
[18] The penalty for cutting off the ear of a Frank is increased to thirty-five solidi in Capitulary VI, case II, 6.
[19] *Pactus Legis Salica*e 29,1 and 11-15 are repeated verbatim by *Lex Salica Karolin*a 16 (31), 1 and 12-16.

Appendix Two

Evaluation of bodily harm according to the *Leges Saxonum*, with percentage value in relation to the manslaughter fine of 1440 shilling[1]

Type of physical injury	Compensation in shilling	% of 1440 shilling
Beating	30	2
Bruising, swelling	60	4
Beating with bleeding	120	8.3
Bone emerges	180	12.5
Bone fracture	240	16.6
Facial disfigurement	240	16.6
Perforating wound – torso	240	16.6
Perforating wound – hip	240	16.6
Perforating wound – arm	250	16.6
One eye knocked out	720	50
Both eyes knocked out	1440	100
One ear deafened	720	50
Both ears deafened	1440	100
Nose cut off	720	50
One hand cut off	720	50
One foot cut off	720	50
One testicle cut off	720	50
Both hands cut off	1440	100
Both feet cut off	1440	100
Both testicles cut off	1440	100
Outer ear mutilated	360	25
One hand mutilated and lamed	360	25
One hand mutilated still actively mobile	180	12.5
One foot mutilated and lamed	360	25
One foot mutilated still actively mobile	180	12.5
Nose mutilated	360	25
Thumb entirely	360	25
Thumb half	180	12.5
Little finger entirely	240	16.6
One finger-joint	80	5.5

Type of physical injury	Compensation in shilling	% of 1440 shilling
Two finger-joints	160	11.1
Index finger entirely	180	12.5
One joint of index finger	60	4
Two joints of index finger	120	8.3
Middle finger	120	8.3
Ring finger	120	8.3
Individual joints of middle and ring finger each	40	2.7
One large toe	180	12.5
The three middle toes each	60	4
Together	180	12.5
Little toe	30	2
Manslaughter of a nobleman	1560	108.3
Manslaughter of a noblewoman	1440	100
Manslaughter of an unmarried woman/virgin	2880	200
Manslaughter of a semi-free man	120	8.3
Manslaughter of an unfree man	36	2.6

[1] After table 1 in Feldmann, "Die forensische Bewertung," 168.

PENAL AMPUTATION AND THE MUTILATED HEROINE IN *LA MANEKINE*

AMANDA HOPKINS

Disability is not strictly a term or classification applicable to the Middle Ages. Irina Metzler, in her exploration of medieval attitudes towards impairment in a wide range of material, follows the practice of disability studies in distinguishing between the terms *disability* and *impairment*, and she convincingly argues that the concept of disability—a term representing the negative social attitudes and disadvantages attendant upon impairment, which refers to the strictly physical condition—is largely absent from her theological, legal and literary sources.[1] Metzler concludes that while the status, meaning and implications of impairments are debated in both practical and moral terms in non-fictional medieval texts, the impaired themselves seem most usually to have been treated with sympathy.

Metzler addresses a variety of naturally occurring states of impairment: congenital, spontaneous, incidental and accidental. Yet it should not be forgotten that the deliberate infliction of a state of impairment, what might be termed *disablement*, forms part of the penal armoury of the Middle Ages. In various times and places, and for a variety of offences, medieval criminal law prescribed severe penalties, which included mutilation and amputation. Although secular and religious authorities tried to control the impulse towards vendetta by imposing often minutely detailed schemes of financial compensation (*compositio* or *wergeld*) and penances for criminal offences, the Mosaic principle of *talio* (an eye for an eye) proved a strong influence on the Christian world and was frequently taken literally in the enactment of legislation in early medieval European states.[2]

The Church also had a voice in matters relating to legislation and penalties. From the early Christian period, heresy had been considered a heinous sin, for which the Church demanded from the state, and received, the right to impose severe penalties.[3] In return, the Church often supported state legislation and indeed "found later no difficulty, when its interests seemed to demand, in demonstrating its sympathy with harsh penalties in other cases ... in spite of the fact that ... it had in the beginning announced its abhorrence of punishments of life or blood".[4] The connection between the Christian Church and modes of suffering, most strongly symbolized in Christ's Passion and Crucifixion, is echoed in much medieval cultural production, which is often concerned with the infliction of pain through scourging, torture and mutilation. In particular, hagiographical material frequently includes detailed verbal descriptions and visual images of torture, and the Church seems to have promoted depictions of suffering to its own ends: as Robert Mills observes, in early Christian representations, the virgin martyr, withstanding abuse, torture and mutilation, functions as "an icon of impregnability and a symbolic stand-in for the beleaguered but ultimately invincible Church".[5]

Execution and mutilation were prescribed for the gravest offences.[6] Capital punishment, as Yehudi A. Cohen observes, "is a technique employed to declare or redefine a citizen as a nonperson"; "[i]t is imposed on individuals whose behavior is regarded as threatening to the integrity of the society's anchorage-providing boundary systems";[7] amputation and other mutilations also impose a new identity on the perpetrator, a disablement that visibly articulates social disapprobation. In the legislation of the Germanic kingdoms of early medieval Europe, the nature of mutilations and amputations was often specific to the crime perpetrated, and intended to remove the opportunity to repeat the offence;[8] for example, in the laws of the Merovingian king Childebert II (570–95), a perjurer would lose a hand;[9] in the earlier Carolingian capitularies the writer of a false document would forfeit his thumb, and in the later codes lost his right hand.[10] Other than for state or political prisoners, imprisonment for serious offences was rare in early medieval Europe; as Edward M. Peters observes, there are few references to prisons in Germanic law: "the Franks used fines, enslavement, mutilation, and capital punishment far more often than they used prisons".[11] For the authorities, the option to impose physical penalties may have had a practical value not achieved by capital punishment or incarceration: the enactment of a mutilation specific to the crime, whilst both preventing the felon from re-offending and acting as a public display of disapprobation and warning, could also preserve some measure of the offender's economic value to society.[12]

Both the capitulary and the customary laws of the Germanic peoples influenced medieval France; the penalty of mutilation, borrowed from Germanic custom,[13] was encoded in a variety of custumals,[14] such as the *Anciennes Coutumes d'Anjou et du Maine*.[15] Although there appears to have been no formal scheme of penalties, medieval French jurists seem to have been in agreement about the need to be seen to punish criminals, and the custumals agree on "[s]ociety's right to vengeance, and the necessity of intimidating through the dread of corporal punishments".[16] A penal amputation would clearly signal an individual's criminal history to anyone who encountered him, identifying him as having been convicted of a serious misdemeanour and thus acting as warning both to those with similar criminal inclinations and to the law-abiding.[17]

One medieval French jurist whose work has survived was Philippe de Remi or Rémi, sire of Beaumanoir, to whom scholars for some time also attributed various literary works, including the romance *La Manekine*, before discovering that there were, in fact, two Philippes, *père et fils*. It was the son, now known as Philippe de Beaumanoir, who wrote on legal matters, while his father, distinguished as Philippe de Remi, composed various romances and poetic works.[18] Yet the focus on certain legislative matters presented in *La Manekine* makes it easy to understand how the romance might convincingly have been attributed to the jurist.[19] *La Manekine*, probably written in the second quarter of the thirteenth century,[20] is a variant of the folk-tale known as the Girl without Hands,[21] a widespread and enduring tale found all over Europe, in the Near East, Japan, parts of Africa, and both North and South America.[22] In *La Manekine*, the heroine, Joïe, cuts off her left hand to prevent her father, the King of Hungary, taking her in marriage, and flees his order of execution.[23] Having fled Hungary, she arrives in Scotland, where she refuses to identify herself and is given the nickname 'Manekine' by the king, whom she later marries. Joïe bears a son while her husband is absent, and her mother-in-law falsifies letters in an attempt to bring about Joïe's death.[24] Joïe escapes with her son and eventually arrives in Rome, where she is taken in by a senator. Eventually her father and her husband, who have been independently searching for Joïe, reach Rome and a series of recognition scenes takes place, culminating in a joyous reunion and the miraculous return and reattachment of Joïe's hand.[25]

The poem explicitly begins to address the twin issues of legality and impairment at the moment of Joïe's absolute defiance, when she removes her hand rather than be married to her father.[26] Both barons and clergy have willingly lent their support to the marriage—indeed the former have proposed it rather than have a unmarried king with no male heir[27]—leaving the heroine sole opponent of the union. Having ineffectually protested that marriage to her father would break God's laws (601–2), and learning that the king plans to force her to marry him, Joïe cuts off her hand and enters the court, declaring,

"… roïne ne doi pas estre,
Car je n'ai point de main senestre,
Et rois ne doit pas penre fame
Qui n'ait tous ses membres…" (795–8)
["I may not be queen, because I have no left hand, and a king may not take a wife who does not possess all her members."]

In M. Shepherd's gloss, the heroine's amputation thus "makes her unworthy—physically impaired as she is now—to be the mother of kings".[28] This reasoning has parallels in the analogues,[29] but Archibald views the core logic as problematic since the king who later marries the heroine is not repelled by her deformity.[30] Joïe's statement here indeed passes without challenge or question; yet Remi's choice of a Hungarian setting may itself counter potential disruption to the plot's logic by referring to the existence of a law relating to the unfitness of the impaired to rule.[31] Citing a late-thirteenth century example, Sedlar notes that physical disability sometimes led to disqualification from the throne in Hungary;[32] it is possible that a ruling relating to impairment as a basis for disqualification was in existence prior to the date of Sedlar's example, perhaps demonstrating Byzantine influence. Manuel I Komnenos had invaded Hungary in 1150–1 and subdued the country in 1167,[33] and, as Plinio Prioreschi observes, in the Byzantine Empire "[m]utilation, including blinding, was used not only to punish common crimes, but very often to prevent anybody, often a member of the imperial family, from claiming the throne. According to Byzantine constitutional theory, only a 'perfect' man could occupy the throne, and therefore the integrity of the body was necessary to become emperor".[34] However, Joïe's disqualification on the basis of impairment seems less clear-cut, since the primary marital duty of the royal female is to produce an heir and her one-handedness (as the text later demonstrates) cannot interfere with that function. John Haldon offers one possible solution, in suggesting that the debarment from kingship might have been due to the view of deformity as "laughable or ridiculous";[35] thus impairments may have been considered to compromise royal dignity in the eyes of peers and commoners.[36]

In Joïe's case, however, the king's response implies that a more serious issue is at stake, although a sense of injured dignity may also be in play. By removing her hand, Joïe repositions herself in others' eyes, not only willingly becoming physically impaired rather than break God's laws,[37] but also recasting herself as socially disruptive.[38] In determining her course of action, Joïe is aware of her father's likely response:

> "Car se jou ai ma main colpée,
> De moi nule pitié n'aura
> Li rois, car vraiement saura
> Que colpée l'arai pour lui
> Escondire. Lasse! mar fui!
> Bien sai qu'il me fera ardoir..." (696–701)
> ["For if I have cut off my hand, the king will have no pity for me, for he will truly know that I shall have cut it off to defy him. Alas! How unlucky I am! I well know that he will have me burned."]

By her own evaluation, she knowingly offers a grave, public, implacable challenge to the king's authority, and the text indicates that his anger is provoked by Joïe's deliberate and irrevocable act of disobedience (811–17). The horrified court offers no resistence to the king's sentence, which is indeed that Joïe should be burned at the stake (829),[39] since he threatens the same penalty to any who dare oppose him (830–4), underlining the fact that Joïe's action is more serious than mere filial disobedience; as the daughter of a king, her act is treason.

Wherever Joïe goes after removing her hand, the impairment has the potential to compromise her social integrity, a point addressed numerous times by the text.[40] At her arrival in Scotland, Joïe is taken in by the provost who takes her to the royal house. The provost tells the king that she is '"un biau gaaig"' (1253: 'a good find'), '"mout courtoise et sage"' (1260: "very well-mannered and wise"), so that he believes her to be '"de hau[t] parage"' (1259: "of noble birth"). Yet, in describing her impairment—'"Mais ele a une main colpée/ Dont ele est belement sanée"' (1261–2: "but she has one hand cut off, from which she has healed completely")[41]—an element of doubt arises.[42] The word *Mais* prepares the way for contradiction or compromise of the stranger's apparent nobility of blood and character, and it leads directly to the description of her impairment, offering the amputation as the primary reason for doubt. The provost states unequivocally that the hand has been cut off: its absence is expressed not in a general reference to loss, but in a term, *colpée*, which relates to a specific method of removal, and thus carries the implication that it has been removed by an external agency and for a specific, and perhaps justified, reason. The possibility of accident or self-mutilation is not considered by the provost.[43] Joïe's insistence on concealing her identity and history strongly suggests the possibility that, despite the noble and virtuous nature she demonstrates, the impairment is due not to accident, but to legal penalty; similarly, her status as stranger, together with her refusal to identify herself, evokes another, even more serious penalty: banishment.[44]

Joïe is, however, welcomed into the royal household and it not until she and the king eventually fall in love that the problem of her amputation, identity and status arises in earnest. In Hungary, the broad issue of the impossibility of a taking a deformed woman as queen was central; in Scotland the problem centres on Joïe's mutilation and her apparent exile,[45] which Joïe explicitly identifies as problematic as she considers her feelings for the king:

> "Quidé-je pour çou qu'il se donte
> A çou que aint une esgarée
> Et qui a une main colpée?" (1704–6)
>
> ["Can I believe for this reason that he might give himself to one who is a wanderer and who has one hand cut off?"]

The king also muses on the matter at length, recognizing possible causes of his beloved's amputation, and rejecting them:

> "Espoir qu'ele a la main colpée,
> Par son mesfait est envoïe
> Seule par mer sans compaignie.
> Par son mesfet! ce ne puet estre;
> Jà le fist Dix de sa main destre:
> Voir, à çou que je voi en li,
> Çou c'on li fist ne desservi;
> Mais il avient en mainte court
> Que tex ne peche, qui encourt.
> Or soit ensi, riens n'ait mesfet,
> Si ne sa-ge pas qui ele est.
> Ele est née, espoir, de vilains.
> De vilains! voir, ce ne fu ains…" (1550–62)
>
> ["It's possible that she had her hand cut off, because of her own transgression was sent alone on the sea without company. Through her own transgression!—that cannot be; surely God made her with his own right hand: truly, from what I see in her, she did not deserve what was done to her; but it happens in many courts that such a one who has not transgressed is punished. Now it must be thus, that she has not transgressed, if I do not know who she is. She is perhaps of low birth. Low birth! truly, this wasn't so."][46]

Joïe's impairment becomes highly problematic. This is not simply because Joïe, in continuing to conceal her identity and history, leaves herself open to suspicion that her mutilation and apparent exile may have been a judicial penalty, but because the poet, having placed his heroine in a position where she will automatically be viewed with suspicion, and indeed having defined the suspicions, must needs create an antagonist whose grounds for opposition must be appreciated by the audience and simultaneously received as unjustified, conforming with the practice of sympathy for the hero of a romance. In opposing her son's chosen bride, however, the queen mother is not without justification.[47] Although Remi attempts to attribute her hatred to innate wickedness (1804–11) or ill-will—

> … la vielle dame remet
> De la grant envie qu'ele a
> De chou que roïne sera,
> Non pas por mesfait qu'ele i voie,
> Fors pour envie qui la proie. (2130–4)

> [the old lady boils with the great resentment she has that that one will be queen, not because of any transgression that she sees in her, but only through the ill-will that preys upon her]

—her own words earlier when she refuses to attend the marriage feast suggest that her opposition is based on sound political reasoning:

> "Honis soit-il quant prise l'a,
> Ne qui le tenra mais pour roi!
> Or a-il fait trop grant desroy,
> Qui a ci prise une esgarée,
> Une chaitive, une avolée,
> Une femme o tout une main…" (2056–61)

> ["Shame on him for marrying her, and on anyone who ever again shall consider him king! Now he has acted with too great rashness, who has married here a vagrant, a wretch, a deceiver, a woman with just one hand."]

It is, in fact, the queen's intervention that has precipitated the marriage; having noted their affection for each other, the queen forbids Joïe the king's company (1816–21), threatening her with death should she disobey (1822–30, 1843–4). Whilst Remi again stresses the queen's wickedness in this episode (1803–4), and attempts to frame her threats as inappropriate by connecting the method stated—"'Vous en serés arse en un four'" (1828: "You shall be burned for it in a fire")—with the King of Hungary's sentence on his daughter, the queen's intervention is not unreasonable or inappropriate. Given the medieval obsession with bloodlines, inheritance and succession,[48] the problem of Joïe's origins is paramount, and, as the queen mother suggests, a king who marries an unknown woman, and moreover one with a mutilation which looks like a legal penalty, is open at best to ridicule, at worst to accusations of unfitness to rule.

The fact that the marriage has been carried out quickly and in secrecy emphasizes the issue. Where the barons at the Hungarian court are vocal in suggesting the marriage (if not in reasoning with the king in his anger), in Scotland not only are the king's vassals not asked for an opinion, but they are neither present at or aware of the wedding:[49] having decided to marry, the king has the ceremony take place at once, while his mother is asleep (2017–28). Only members of the household are present, and the event is later notified to the wider baronial population as a *fait accompli*.[50] Nor are the clergy invited to comment, although the ceremony is conducted by a priest:

> Li prestres refuser n'osa
> Sa volenté; ançois posa
> Maintenant leur .ij. mains ensamble,
> Et par parole les assamble:
> Plevie l'a et espousée;
> Tantost fu la messe cantée.
> Ce fu fait si privéement,
> Fors sa maisnie seulement
> N'avoit; mais si menant i erent… (2035–43)

> [The priest does not dare deny his wish; but immediately places together their two hands and joins them by word: he has made his pledge and married her; at once the mass was sung. This was done so privately that there was no-one present other than his household; but his own retainers were there…]

The astonishment of the household at these events is expressed by the narrator (2044, cf. 2016). Protocol and custom have clearly been broken. In marrying a *belle inconnue*—never mind one with a suspect impairment—and failing to consult his barons or seek clerical advice, the king ignores his dynastic responsibilities, marrying not as king and lord, but for himself, as an individual.[51] Marriage to Joïe can bring no political or economical benefits: no dowry, no estates, no prospect of powerful alliances;[52] indeed, the king's appreciation that his beloved may even be of low birth demonstrates that he understands the difficulties raised (1561–2, quoted above), for, as R. Howard Bloch observes, in aristocratic dynastic marriage, "[s]ocial movement is reduced a minimum, and nobility, not mobility, is the defining social rule".[53]

Despite Joïe's unknown identity and social status, this is a valid marriage, celebrated as a sacrament, not concubinage; and it is not to be a morganatic marriage. The King of Scotland quickly publicizes his intention to crown Joïe queen, this time in a ceremony to be attended by his lords and barons. The news is greeted with happiness by those who know Joïe, but causes some consternation amongst those who do not (2093–100). Although this is quickly dispelled by the new queen during the feast, and eventually all agree that the king has done the right thing (2333–44), misgivings persist:

> Se ne fust, sans plus, le mehain
> Que la roïne a de sa main,
> Autre cose en li ne set dire
> Nus hom qui sa biauté remire;
> Mais de ce durement anoie
> Tous ciaus qui de s'oneur ont joie. (2327–32)
>
> [If it were not for the damage, nothing more, that the queen has to her hand, no man who looks upon her beauty can find anything to say about her; but this greatly troubles all those who take joy in her position.] Marriage and coronation notwithstanding, Joïe's one-handedness remains problematic.

The dowager queen leaves the court, withdrawing to her own household; but when the king goes tourneying, leaving his pregnant wife behind, she finds an opportunity to do damage to Joïe, in an episode which again evokes the connection between impairment and legality. When Joïe bears a son, her mother-in-law intercepts the message sent to the king, sending instead news that the offspring '".iiij. piés a et s'est velue,/ Ex enfossés et grosse teste"' (3118–19: 'has four feet and is hairy, [with] hollow eyes and enormous head'). The fraudulent letters describe a monstrous being, a '"laide beste"' (3120: "an ugly beast"), a '"hideuse creature"' (3121: "a hideous creature"), which seems to have been engendered by the devil (3122).[54] The description offers an inversion of Joïe's physical condition, since, as Emily C. Francomano observes, "[i]ronically, the handless queen is accused of producing a beast with a superabundance of extremities".[55]

Here, Remi draws on a common medieval tradition that imputes the deformity of offspring to dubious morality or sinful conception;[56] yet the king reacts humanely, insisting that such an offspring is not the fault of his wife (3269–71), although again he resorts to secrecy, ordering that the matter be concealed (3283–6). The queen mother substitutes a letter requiring the death of Joïe and her child, making it appear as if the king

> … a oïes noveles
> De la Manequine peu beles,
> Bien set pour coi n'a c'une main:
> Pour noient n'eut pas ce mehain. (3453–6)
>
> [has heard news that speaks scant good about Manekine, and well knows the reason she has only one hand: not for nothing did she have this wound.]

This explicitly evokes the legal penalty of amputation, which is echoed again in the seneschal's reaction to the letter:

> "La raison mie ne savons
> Pour coi tel mandement nous fait;
> Espoir que on li a retrait
> Là où il est, dont ele est née
> Et pour coi eut la main colpée." (3534–8)
>
> ["We do not know at all the reason that he sends us this same order; perhaps there, where he is, someone has told him where she was born and why she had her hand cut off."]

Despite this command, the seneschal takes matters into his own hands, helping Joïe escape with her child and burning effigies in their place.

After another solitary sea-voyage, Joïe comes ashore in Italy, and again faces the problem of being a stranger with a missing hand. Yet here the issue is less critical. The amputation is still referred to—for example, when the fishermen who have taken her in discuss her with a curious senator (5078–84)—but poses no overt social problem. As the poem moves towards its dénouement, the handlessness is used as a recognition device, for example supporting the King of Scotland's discovery of Joïe's coronation ring, where the senator tells the king:

> "… pert sur li uns mehains,
> Qu'ele n'a point de main senestre,
> Et molt bien samble colpée estre." (6310–12)
>
> ["an impairment appears upon her, for she has no left hand at all and it very much looks like it has been cut off."]

The senator refers to his ignorance of the cause of the amputation, but by now Joïe has been living in the senator's household for seven years, demonstrating personal integrity in terms of austere living and religious fervour, so that the senator, from his own experience of her, does not hesitate to offer an interpretation upon the origin of the mutilation:

"Mout par fu plains de crualté
Par qui si grans maléurté
Li avint, comme du puing perdre." (6313–15)

["Completely filled with cruelty was he by whom such ill fortune happened to her as to lose her hand."]

Here, the senator explicitly articulates a matter that earlier has only been suggested privately, in thoughts: that the amputation of Joïe's hand was due to some form of injustice, although here any reference to a legal framework is omitted. The senator's words both recall the events leading up to the act of mutilation and lead into the *dénouement*, where the King of Hungary reveals in his confession that his daughter '"le mal ressoingna/ Tant que du puing se mehaigna"' (7117–18: 'dreaded evil so much that she cut off her hand').

Stiker observes that "the disabled person shares the status of the cared-for, integrated marginalised";[57] yet, while Joïe is often treated and spoken of with sympathy, she is never referred to or treated as inferior or incapable in any way, and the concept or construct of disability seems absent from this text. It is most notable that the impairment barely affects the Scottish king's, or others', perception of Joïe's beauty; indeed Sargent-Baur sees the mutilation as "set[ting] in relief her extraordinary charms of face, body, manners, and character, to the point where even a king can overlook her defect".[58] When she arrives in Scotland and is taken to Berwick, the focus is on her "bele faiture" (1225: beautiful form), despite the pallor brought on by her suffering (1226–7). After some time, the Scottish king begins to think about Joïe every night in meditations which alternately consider the problems raised by her amputated hand and unknown history and focus on a detailed appreciation of her physical beauty (1529–1676). Only once does the issue of her mutilation impinge on his impression of her attractiveness, when he contemplates the beauty of her remaining hand and wistfully wishes that she had two hands with which she might embrace him:

"Qui regarde sa biele main
Delie, blance; si doit
Sont blanc et delié et droit;
Car en éust-ele à un vol
Fait un dous las entor mon col,
Par si que l'autre main éust
Et .c. mil mars cousté m'éust!" (1614–20)

["Whoever looks at her beautiful, delicate, white hand; whose fingers are white and slender and straight: would that she had in one swoop made a sweet loop about my neck, provided that she had her other hand it would have been worth a hundred thousand marks to me!"]

Despite this wistfulness, Joïe's one-handedness is clearly no bar to sexual enjoyment, since their mutual pleasure once they are married is described in no little detail by Remi (2109–24).

The *dénouement* does not culminate in the reunion of the heroine with her husband and father, but with the restoration of her hand. This miraculous happening is the climax of a fairly complex sequence of events (7397-7579), in which two *clercs* find the hand in a pail of water drawn to fill the fonts of the church where the family reunion is taking place. Despite their attempts to dispose of it by emptying and refilling the pail, the hand persists in returning to the bucket so often that the *clercs* finally abandon their task and go to seek the advice of the pope, who quickly realises that the hand must be Joïe's and places it against her stump, at which the two join seamlessly. Surprisingly little is made of this event itself; instead of offering a depiction of the response of the heroine and the internal audience, the narrative at once continues to describe how a voice speaks from heaven, explaining that the hand had been swallowed and transported by a sturgeon, whose stomach has thus become a '"molt … biau saintuaire"' (7608: "very beautiful reliquary").[59]

The restoration of the hand has been read in various ways. Archibald, observing that "it is striking that it is only after the reunion with her father that Joie [*sic*] regains her hand", offers two possible interpretations. The first cites Fenster's suggestion "that the presence of the father is necessary for the establishing of her identity, which has been a mystery throughout her travels".[60] Although Archibald does not present a critique of Fenster's proposition, it seems untenable. In the father-daughter recognition, enacted and concluded more than four hundred lines before the restoration scene, when her father demands that she prove who she is, Joïe holds out her arm, paradoxically offering what is absent as the sole evidence of her identity:

„Vés ichi u brac le moignon
Dont je colpai le puig en son:
Si devés bien à ceste enseigne
De moi croire la vraie enseigne." (7169–72)

["See here on my arm the stump where I cut the hand from it: from this proof of mine you must indeed believe the true evidence."]

The king's response demonstrates unequivocally that he accepts the stump as proof—"Or ne se doute mais li rois" (7175: now the king no longer doubts)—so that, while it is clear that the king's presence is required to establish his daughter's identity, the restoration of the hand itself has no logical function as a recognition device, and Remi never suggests such a role.[61] Archibald's own reasoning, "that reconciliation with her father represents the re-establishment of proper social order, and that this in turn is symbolized by the restoration of her hand", is more plausible;[62] yet it is still undermined by the fact that the restoration does not happen during the reunion itself, in the direct context of the events for which it would stand as symbol.[63] Instead, there is a pause, a separation, a narrative hiatus between the two events that allows Remi to present the restoration of Joïe's hand not as a symbol of familial reunion or patriarchal restoration, but for herself alone, underlined by the episode's focus on the reason for the mutilation, which is also the reason for its repair: Joïe's adherence to God's law (7501-20).

The miraculous restoration of Joïe's hand could be seen as articulating a medieval preference for bodily "normalization", but this would be to misread Remi's signals: the hand is but one of a series of restorations. The order of the restorations runs husband, father, hand, and this might at first suggest ascending importance, but examination of Joïe's responses to each does not support this interpretation. At the news that her husband had not ordered her death and has been seeking her, "De joie li cuers li sautele" (6478: her heart jumps for joy); at her father's public confession to the pope, "S'est ademise par la presse; / De joie et de pitié engresse" (7129-30: she pushes through the crowd; impelled by joy and compassion). When the hand is restored, however, the focus moves at once to the heavenly voice that explains the miracle, thence to the recovery of the sturgeon and the discovery of the reliquary. For Joïe, the return of her hand is not, as might be expected, the climax of happiness and restoration; rather, her reactions imply that the reunions are presented in descending order of importance, beginning with her pure joy at her nuclear family's restoration, moving on to joy mingled with pity at the recovery of her father, and finally, at the restoration of her hand—nothing. The fact of the miracle is more important than its form and to Joïe it appears inconsequential. What Remi seems to be underlining is that Joïe is the same person with or without her hand: its recovery cannot and does not accomplish any essential change in her, and is the least of her concerns.

The occurrence of the second miracle, the reliquary enclosed in the sturgeon's stomach, suggests at first that Remi is plotting a movement towards a religious conclusion, a withdrawal from the secular world, and for a while the narrative does pause to contemplate the meaning of the Eastertide rituals which form the backdrop to the *dénouement* and its aftermath (7693-778). Joïe, however, remains a completely secular figure and Remi is at pains to emphasise this in describing the sexual reunion of Joïe and her husband following the feast on Easter Sunday ('[le] jour de la Surrection', 7779):

> Cele nuit jurent, ce me samble,
> En un lit andui tout ensamble
> Li bons rois d'Escoce et Joïe,
> Qu'encor jéu n'i avoit mie,
> S'avoit .viij. jors qu'il l'ot trouvée:
> Pour Dieu en firent consirée.
> Or sachiés bien que cele nuit
> Orent assés joie et deduit,
> Comme cil qui tant s'entr'amoient
> Et qui tant s'entre-desiroient.
> Perdu s'entr'estoient .vij. ans,
> Dont tante paine, tans ahans
> Eurent éu; or sont au port
> Venu de joie et de confort;
> Tant de joie ont que ne poroie
> Dire la moitié de leur joie. (7829-44)

> [That night, it seems to me, they both lay together in one bed, the good King of Scotland and Joïe who had not yet lain there, and yet it was eight days ago he had found her; for love of God they had abstained from it. Now be assured that they had copious joy and pleasure that night, as befits those who loved and desired each other so much. For seven years they had lost each other, through which they had had much distress and suffering; now they have come to the harbour of delight and solace. They have so much delight that I cannot describe a fraction of their bliss.]

Joïe is not a saint, an 'invincible virgin',[64] but an actively sexual being; like many saints, she makes a great sacrifice to take control of her own sexuality and to choose a sexual partner for herself, but clearly she has no desire to commit herself to a life of chastity and divine contemplation. Her earthly nature is emphasized in the reiteration of sexual pleasure here, which deliberately echoes the earlier description of the couple's coital delight on their marriage; the restoration of Joïe's hand might 'normalize' her appearance, but Remi does not intend it to detract from his earlier emphasis on Joïe's ability to live a full life.

Outside of its role in problematicizing her social status, her impairment, far from being the object of distaste, disgust or embarrassment, is used to supply Joïe with an identity, when the King of Scotland, declaring that he must have some name to use for her, gives her the appellation "Manekine" (vv. 1336–41):

> … il li mist le seurnon,
> Que Manekine la clamoit
> Pour çou que une main n'avoit… (7248–50)
>
> [he gave her the name that described her as "Manekine" because she was missing one hand.]

G. Huet equates *manekine* with modern French *manchote*, that is "one-handed" or "handless".[65] Joïe's self-imposed physical impairment therefore supplies the basis for a new nominal identity: she is both defined by and named for her impairment. As Francomano observes, "by giving her this name the king is also giving her a new hand: the first syllable of *Manekine* clearly resembles *main*, thus the name encodes both a hand and a lack of a hand".[66] That the (unnamed) king himself names her singles her out; and it is his action that underlines the anonymous stranger's difference, her otherness, while at once explicitly and publicly expressing his acceptance of (and also perhaps his affection for) her, both despite and because of her mutilation. This appellation is one she has no apparent reluctance to accept, and indeed she continues to use it when she is forced to leave Scotland: she later tells the Roman senator that she has been known as Manekine (5200–2). When he declares that he has never heard such a name and that nothing similar exists in his own country (5203–6), Joïe explains that '"cist qui le me dona/ Vit en moi aucune occoison/ Par coi il me donna tel non"' (5206–8: "he who gave it to me saw in me some reason for which he gave me such a name").[67]

From her initial act of self-mutilation, Joïe's impairment forms the central symbol of the text, both acting as identification and allowing the poet to explore in detail the social effect and repercussions of the amputation. Remi further emphasizes Joïe's handlessness throughout the text by making frequent reference to hands, both literally and metaphorically. Social routine and practice are seen in regular preprandial washing[68] and in physical guidance: the provost leads Joïe into the Scottish court "par le main" (1250: by the hand), and the senator, too, "La Manequine par la main/ Emmaine lès …, main à main" (6495–6: leads Manekine by the hand, next to him, hand in hand). The wedding ceremony requires the joining of hands: "Li prestres … /… posa/ Maintenant leur .ij. mains ensamble" (2035–7: the priest now placed their two hands together).[69] As Francomano observes, "throughout the romance, manucaption—the taking of hands—signals desire. For example, the poet has the [Hungarian] king take Joïe by the hand and draw her close to him each time he announces his incestuous intentions".[70] Metaphorical references to hands occur at key points in the narrative; for example, when the King of Hungary's council agrees that the marriage should take place immediately and Joïe's consent is shown to be considered a formality: "Or quident bien tenir ou poing/ Tel cose dont il sont molt loing" (645–6: Now they believe they indeed hold in their hand the very thing that they are so far from).[71] Again, when Joïe is found in Rome by the fishermen, she realizes "Qu'ele est en main de povre gent/ Qui li voelent estre preudomme" (4918–19: that she is in the hands of poor people, who wish to be courteous towards her). Even after Joïe's hand has been restored, references to hands continue to appear; for example, when the king and queen leave Hungary to travel round their estates, "En tel main laissierent la tere/ Que nus n'i conquist riens par guerre" (8129–30: they left the land in such hands that no-one would conquer it by warfare). The metaphorical use of hands thus serves to represent a locus of power, and simultaneously emphasizes the paradox that it is only by removing her hand, by taking on the role of Manekine, that Joïe can gain control of her destiny.

Ultimately, of course, *La Manekine* cannot be read as evidence of the treatment of the impaired in medieval society, and indeed Trevor Dean warns against drawing on literature for correspondences with history "as if historical and literary evidence were mutually reinforcing".[72] However, what Elizabeth Archibald calls "literary archaeology" can offer ways of understanding medieval thought and attitudes,[73] especially those outside the clerical community which are often attainable only through literary works. In *La Manekine*, the heroine's patient sufferings, and the culmination of the tale which reunites Joïe with both her hand and her family, provide a moral dimension overtly comparable with narratives intended to demonstrate inspirational saintly conduct. Yet the text's detailed exploration of Joïe's determined lack of self-pity and the uninflected behaviour of the majority of those who come across her seems intended to offer an object lesson in how to respond to impairment and the physically impaired in everyday life, advocating independence on the one side, a delicate sympathy and sensitivity without cosseting on the other.[74] The poem concludes with a meditation on its heroine who exemplifies that suffering should be borne patiently, for God will reward the faithful (8527-676), but Joïe's example clearly suggests that such rewards are not only to be sought in heaven, but can be earthly for those who refuse to be delimited by impairment. Joïe's dogged patience echoes that of tormented saints, but her physical behaviour also offers the impaired a model for living: even successful parenthood is not automatically precluded, and Joïe's passion for the Scottish king and enjoyment of their sexual life give her a human dimension far removed from hagiography and demonstrates that romantic love and sexual expression should not be beyond the reach of the impaired.[75]

Notes

---

[1] *Disability in Medieval Europe: Thinking about Physical Impairment during the High Middle Ages, c.1100–1400* (London and New York: Routledge, 2006). Metzler supplies a detailed discussion of the terminology used in the medieval and post-medieval periods in the introduction (1–9).

[2] Carl Ludwig von Bar and others, *A History of Continental Criminal Law*, trans. Thomas S. Bell and others (Association of American Law Schools: The Continental Legal History Series VI. Boston: Little, Brown & Co, 1916; repr. South Hackensack, NJ: Rothman Reprints, and New York: Augustus M. Kelley, 1968), 93, 108–9 *et passim*; see also Julia M. H. Smith, *Europe After Rome: A New Cultural History 500–1000* (Oxford: Oxford University Press, 2005, pp. 100, 108–9 *et passim*). The editors Barbara A. Hanawalt and David Wallace, in their introduction to *Medieval Crime and Social Control* (Minneapolis and London: University of Minnesota Press, 1999, ix–xvi), define vendetta as "violent self-help in solving disputes' and point out that many found this means of redress acceptable 'because it was a ready and often justifiable solution to perceived wrongs' that 'could be reconciled with both biblical and Germanic law" (ix); thus "[t]he law was viewed as a tool of vendetta and revenge, not necessarily as a final arbitrator" (x). Von Bar notes that, since law codes frequently allow for the payment of *compositio* as an alternative to physical penalties, the financial situation of the convicted criminal could affect the form of punishment actually imposed (71–2); indeed, in the late Carolingian period in Germany, "it is only a non-legal circumstance that a man who is not free and therefore possesses nothing, or at any rate is unable to pay the fine, is peremptorily subjected to a punishment of life or limb, which a free man possessed of property would avoid" (96).

[3] Von Bar, *Continental Criminal Law*, 92. R. W. Southern quotes Thomas Aquinas' unequivocal dictum that "[h]eresy is a sin which merits not only excommunication but also death" (*Western Society and the Church in the Middle Ages*. The Penguin History of the Church, vol. 2. Harmondsworth: Penguin, 1970, 17; see *Summa Theologiae* II:II, qu. xi, art. 3). See also Malcolm Lambert, *Medieval Heresy: Popular Movements from the Gregorian Reform to the Reformation*. 3rd edn. (Oxford: Blackwell, 2002).

[4] Von Bar, *Continental Criminal Law*, 93. Esther Cohen, describing the background to later medieval French law, concurs, observing that "[t]hough secular and ecclesiastical justice were theoretically two separate systems, they were in fact in constant touch" and "the boundaries of jurisdiction were extremely difficult to define. Thus the two parallel legal systems existed side by side,

formally independent of each other, but in reality constantly interpenetrating and influencing each other. The very vagueness of the dividing line provided a dynamic, developmental element" (*The Crossroads of Justice: Law and Culture in Late Medieval France* (Leiden, New York and Cologne, 1993, 17, 18)).

[5] *Suspended Animation: Pain, Pleasure and Punishment in Medieval Culture* (London: Reaktion Books, 2005), 116–17; Mills discusses a variety of visual sources. On textual sources, see Judith Perkins, *The Suffering Self: Pain and Narrative Representation in the Early Christian Era* (London: Routledge, 1995). Kathryn Gravdal discusses Old French saints' lives in "Plotting Rape in the Female Saints" Lives', Chapter 2 of *Ravishing Maidens: Writing Rape in Medieval French Literature and Law* (Philadelphia: University of Pennsylvania Press, 1991), 21–41; Amy V. Ogden focusses on Old French saints' lives and their modern reception in "The Centrality of Margins: Medieval French Genders and Genres Reconfigured" (*French Forum* 30, 2005, 1–23).

[6] "For the most serious crimes, the most serious penalties were reserved: the mutilation of ears, lips and tongue, the amputation of hands, feet and ears, the gouging out of eyes, or death by hanging, beheading or other means (dismemberment, burning, drowning, bur[ying] alive, the wheel)" (Trevor Dean, *Crime in Medieval Europe, 1200–1500*. Harlow: Longman, 2001, p. 24). Piers D. Mitchell notes that, in "[t]he Frankish courts of the Latin East", such crimes "ranged from armed assault and rape to medical malpractice" (*Medicine in the Crusades: Warfare, Wounds and the Medieval Surgeon*. Cambridge: Cambridge University Press, 2004, 134). Mitchell further comments on the extent of such penalties: 'Mutilation was a widely used punishment in the early years of the Frankish slates. There are many examples of this form of punishment, both within the framework of the law and by vigilantes. More common forms of mutilation included cutting off the nose, ears or genitals, amputation of a hand or foot or blinding with a hot iron. If such tortures and punishments really were handed out on a regular basis by those in power at the time, then it might be expected that a significant proportion of the population would have suffered disability or disfigurement of some kind' (*Medicine*, 136). Von Bar notes that some penalties imposed under the German *Sachsenspiegel* legislation were so cruel that '[e]ven the executioners complained' (*Continental Criminal Law*, 110; see also 110, n. 17).

[7] Yehudi Cohen, "Ends and Means in Political Control: State Organization and the Punishment of Adultery, Incest, and Violation of Celibacy", *American Anthropologist*, New Series, 71 (1969), 658–87, 673.

[8] Mitchell, *Medicine*, 134.

[9] Von Bar, *Continental Criminal Law*, 71. Jean W. Sedlar observes that similar laws operated in medieval Byzantium, Poland, Serbia and the Ottoman Empire, and suggests that under Stephen Dušan of Serbia, 'mutilation by blinding or loss of limbs was considered a relatively humane punishment, since it often replaced the death penalty' (*East Central Europe in the Middle Ages, 1000–1500*. Washington: University of Washington Press, 1994, 324).

[10] Von Bar, *Continental Criminal Law*, 72, n. 15. Leslie Lockett notes that in Alfredian law, "anyone who stole from a church might lose the hand which performed the crime; [t]he first objective of laws prescribing localized mutilations of this nature was, of course, to prevent repeated offences by the same bodily member" ("The Role of Grendel's Arm in Feud, Law and the Narrative Strategy of *Beowulf*", in *Latin Learning and English Lore: Studies in Anglo-Saxon Literature for Michael Lapidge, Vol. 1*, ed. Katherine O'Brien O'Keeffe and Andy Orchard. Toronto Old English Series 14. Toronto: University of Toronto Press, 368–88 (375)). Some amputations were indeed very precisely related to the crime: David S. King notes that one custumal prescribes the loss of testicles for a first offence of sodomy and the amputation of the *membre* for a second ("The Meaning of Amputation in the *chansons de geste*", *Symposium: a quarterly journal in modern literatures*, 62 (2008), 35–51 (40), citing *Li Livres de Jostice et de Plet* ed. P. Rapetti. Paris: Firmin Didot Frères, 1850, art. 22; 279). However, "visible bodily mutilation in Anglo-Saxon law was not always limited to the guilty limb" (Lockett, "Grendel's Arm", p. 376), and some custumals record various penalties that seem to have less logical relation to the crime committed, such as the amputation of an ear for a first theft of a plough or from a church, and loss of a foot for a repeat offence (*Coutume de Touraine—Anjou* (*c.*1246), art. xxii; *Les Établissements de Saint-Louis accompagnés des textes primitifs et de textes dérivés, avec une introduction et des notes*. 4 vols. Paris: Renouard, 1881–86, 1:14, cited by King, "Amputation", 40).

[11] "Prison before the Prison: The Ancient and Medieval Worlds", *The Oxford History of the Prison: The Practice of Punishment in Western Society*, ed. Norval Morris and David J. Rothman. New York: Oxford University Press (1995), 3–43 (24). Peters notes, however, that "penitential confinement" was encoded in monastic constitutions as early as the sixth century and by the twelfth century "each monastery was expected to contain a prison of one sort or another" (28); Guy Geltner suggests that medieval castles also offered places in which 'feudal lords occasionally imprisoned their subjects and political enemies for the duration of a trial, as a penal measure, or simply in order to collect ransom' ('Medieval Prisons: Between Myth and Reality, Hell and Purgatory', *History Compass* 4 (2006), 1–14 (2)); and Jean Dunbabin examines the liminal blurring between custodial and punitive imprisonment ('Custodial and Punitive Captivity', Chapter 7 of *Captivity and Imprisonment in Medieval Europe, 1000–1300*. Basingstoke and New York: Palgrave Macmillan, 2002, 98–113, also *passim*). Peters states that a system of punitive imprisonment was adopted by both the clerical and the secular inquisitions ('Prison', 30) and Dean observes that 'the birth of the prison, in the sense of punitive incarceration, at least, and perhaps too in the sense of confinement for the purpose of reform, is … located in the later Middle Ages' (*Crime,* 120; see also Geltner, *The Medieval Prison: A Social History*. Princeton: Princeton University Press, 2008, 3 *et passim*).

[12] In reference to the infliction of such punishments in the ancient world, Steven S. Kan observes that "[a] subject without a tongue can plow a field; a subject without a writing hand can watch gates; but a dead subject can accomplish nothing for the

master" ("Corporal Punishments and Optimal Incapacitation", *Journal of Legal Studies* 25 (1996), 121–30 (123)), and this may also have been a consideration in the Middle Ages. George Ives suggests a different reading, noting that, in some Anglo-Saxon law-codes, penal mutilations seem to have been intended as mortal wounds (*History of Penal Methods*. London: Stanley Paul and Co, 1914; repr. by Kessinger Publishing, 8).

[13] Although not all Germanic law codes prioritised mutilation: for example, in Lombard law mutilations were fairly rare; manual amputation was prescribed only for counterfeiters and those who wrote false charters; thieves, conversely, were branded on the forehead (Katherine Fischer Drew, trans., *The Lombard Laws*. The Middle Ages. Philadelphia: University of Pennsylvania Press, 1973, 252, n. 9).

[14] Cohen offers a reminder that written legislation does not necessarily equate to actual practice; recorded codes might not have been intended for everyday use in courts, but as "literary traditions, a record for posterity and a mirror for any society's self-perception" (*Crossroads of Justice*, 40). The custumals were thus not prescriptive documents, but, written by experienced practitioners of law who "made no attempt to formulate legal principles or posit general tenets, [they] instead gave minute and careful descriptions of their specific area's customs" (*Crossroads of Justice*, 10).

[15] Von Bar, *Continental Criminal Law*, 189; see *Coutumes et institutions de l'Anjou et du Maine antérieures au XVIe siècle: textes et documents, avec notes et dissertations*, ed. C. J. Beautemps-Beaupré. 4 vols. in 8 (Paris: A. Durand et Pedone-Lauriel, 1877-97). Nicole Gonthier briefly considers branding, amputation and blinding, quoting from medieval witnesses and custumals, in *Le Châtiment du crime au Moyen Âge, XIIe–XIVe siècles* (Rennes: Presses Universitaires de Rennes, 1998), 140–6.

[16] Von Bar, *Continental Criminal Law*, 151.

[17] Esther Cohen suggests that there was little or no sense of public ritual in the performance of mutilation or marking, "[n]or were the mutilations embedded within any kind of symbolic ritual. There was no need, for the message was simple, explicit and carried lifelong by the culprit. The act of infliction was therefore simply and expeditiously performed, without ceremony" (*Crossroads of Justice*, 166–7).

[18] See Barbara N. Sargent-Baur's introduction to Philippe de Remi, *Le Roman de la Manekine*, ed. and trans. Sargent-Baur, with contributions by Alison Stones and Roger Middleton (Amsterdam: Rodopi, 1999), 70–1. This volume, which includes a history of the manuscript by Middleton (41–68) and reproduces the relevant manuscript miniatures accompanied by a discussion by Stones ("The Manuscript, Paris BNF Fr. 1588, and its Illustrations", 1–39 plus plates), is not widely available, so citations in the present work will refer to the edition by Francisque Michel, which is available online and follows identical line numbering (*Roman de la Manekine, par Philippe de Reimes, trouvère du treizième siècle*. Paris: Maulde et Renou for the Bannatyne Club, 1840; *The Internet Archive*, stable URL <http://www.archive.org/details/romandelmaneki6800philuoft>). Some reference will also be made to the edition by Hermann Suchier, *Oeuvres Poétiques de*

Philippe de Remi, Sire de Beaumanoir (2 vols, Paris: Librairie de Fermin Didot et Cie, 1884–5), vol. 1 (1884). Translations throughout are my own.

[19] Hanawalt and Wallace cite the two Philippes among examples supporting their assertion that "[s]ince the literate men who were formulating laws and administering justice were reading and hearing imaginative literature as well as studying legal cases, literature and law were subject to strong, reciprocal influences" (*Medieval Crime*, x).

[20] Sargent-Baur, "Introduction", 91.

[21] Type 706 in the Aarne Thompson (AT) classification scheme (see Antti Aarne, *The Types of the Folktale: A Classification and Bibliography, translated and enlarged by Stith Thompson*. 2nd rev. edn. Folklore Fellows Communications. Helsinki: Suomalainen Tiedeakatemia, 1961).

[22] Catherine Velay-Vellantin, *L'Histoire des contes* (Paris: Arthème Fayard, 1992), 97.

[23] Given Remi's choice of subject for his romance, it is notable that penal amputation was not apparently a customary penalty in Clermont, Beauvais, whose customs were set down by his son (Philippe de Beaumanoir, *Coutumes de Beauvaisis*, ed. A. Salmon. 2 vols. Paris: A. Picard et fils, 1899, 1900; trans. F. R. P. Akehurst, *The Coutumes de Beauvaisis of Philippe de Beaumanoir*. Philadelphia: University of Pennsylvania Press, 1992); as S. H. Cuttler suggests, it is also unfortunate that Beaumanoir does not address "the topic of treason against the king or the kingdom" (*The Law of Treason and Treason Trials in Later Medieval France*. Cambridge Studies in Medieval Life and Thought, third series, 16. Cambridge: Cambridge University Press, 2003, 4).

[24] The theme of the Calumniated Wife, AT 706.

[25] This is not, however, the end of the poem, which continues for a further hundred lines or so, describing Joïe and her family travelling around their estates on their way home, and concluding with a moral promoting the spiritual benefits of suffering.

[26] In the oral versions of the tale, mutilation is always inflicted by an antagonist (Velay-Vellantin, *L'Histoire des contes*, 99), although similar self-mutilations feature in several written analogues (Elizabeth Archibald, *Incest and the Medieval Imagination*, Oxford: Clarendon Press, 2001, 168). G. Huet ("Les Sources de la *Manekine* de Philippe de Beaumanoir", *Romania* 45 (1918–19), 95) posits that Remi had drawn from written and oral versions of the tale ("Beaumanoir a composé son roman d'après *deux* versions du récit, l'une écrite et l'autre orale") and notes that Suchier had shown in his edition that the earliest written versions came from the north of England ("Suchier a prouvé que les plus anciennes versions *écrites* de ce thème sont anglaises, plus exactement originaires du nord de l'Angleterre"; see Suchier's 'Introduction' to his edition, xxiv-xxv). Suchier identifies two distinct versions of the tale, distinguished largely by the number of sons the heroine bears and the methods of exile and reunion, which ultimately derived from a single source (p. xxiv). From the evidence available at the time, Suchier stated that Remi's text had been composed *c.*1270 and influenced by the *Vita Offae Primi* and *La Belle Hélène de Constantinople*, but the dates Suchier

ascribes to *La Manekine* and the analogues (pp. xxiii-xxxiii) have been revised by more recent research and reveal that both the *Vita* (mid-thirteenth-century) and *Belle Hélène* (mid-fourteenth century) antedate Remi's poem. In these analogues, furthermore, the mutilation occurs as part of a later episode, where it forms part of the calumniated wife theme, and is not carried out by the heroine herself; in fact the heroine avoids mutilation in the former and in the latter invites it as a means by which her death can be proved (see Sargent-Baur, "Introduction", 111–12).

[27] Cf. Archibald (*Incest*, 165). Perspectives are clearly an issue in the text: Rosalind Brown-Grant asserts that Joïe "sees her father's wish to marry her as being motivated only by political expediency rather than by incestuous desire" (*French Romance of the Later Middle Ages: Gender, Morality and Desire*. Oxford: Oxford University Press, 2008, p. 195), while Archibald suggests that, by a lengthy exploration of the king's 'inner battle' on the subject of the marriage, the poet emphasizes that the ultimate decision "is based on his own desire rather than pure political expediency" (162–3).

[28] *Tradition and Re-creation in the Thirteenth-century Romance: 'La Manekine' and 'Jehan et Blonde' by Philippe de Rémi* (Faux Titre 48. Amsterdam and Atlanta, GA: Rodopi, 1990), 24, n. 6.

[29] Archibald notes that "[i]n many versions the mutilation is explained as the daughter's method of deterring her father by getting rid of the hand with which he fell in love, or by destroying her exact resemblance to her mother, or by making herself unfit to be queen" (*Incest*, 169-70).

[30] *Incest*, p. 170.

[31] The premise of the unworthiness of the physically deformed to enter into royal marriage is repeated later when the King of Hungary relates the affair to the Pope: '"Si respondi et itant dist/ Que ele n'estoit mie disne/ D'avoir roi ne d'estre roïne;/ Car tous ses membres n'avo[i]t mie"' (7076–9: "She replied and said thus much, that she was not at all worthy to marry a king nor to be a queen because she did not possess all of her members").

[32] *East Central Europe*, 31. That Remi was aware of this law is impossible to prove. Shepherd argues that the Hungarian setting has been utilized to suggest a connection between Joïe and St Elizabeth of Hungary (1207–31), but the parallels offered—'a Hungarian princess marries a foreign lord, is exiled from court, and lives an exemplary life under the direction of a confessor figure, becoming reconciled to the loss of rank and applying herself to domestic duties'—seem less convincing than her suggestion that "[i]n the Middle Ages, the country [Hungary] was a bridge between two worlds, East and West, the distant and the familiar, and as such provided an apt background for a fictional court, whose practices, modelled on those of thirteenth-century France, could yet be manipulated to justify the scabrous conduct of the Hungarian monarch" (*Tradition*, 49). Sargent-Baur similarly considers the possibility of the influence of St Elizabeth on Remi's text, and also of Margaret, who married Malcolm III of Scotland and was later canonized, and who had been born in Hungary (108).

[33] Paul Magdaliano, *The Empire of Manuel I Komnenos, 1143–1180* (Cambridge: Cambridge University Press, 1993), 442, 457.

[34] *A History of Medicine, vol. IV: Byzantine and Islamic Medicine* (Omaha: Horatius Press, 2001), 28.
[35] "Humour and the Everyday in Byzantium", *Humour, History and Politics in Late Antiquity and the Early Middle Ages,* ed. Guy Halsall (Cambridge: Cambridge University Press, 2002), 48–74 (65).
[36] Trevor Dean reports a case from Wischegrad in 1330, where an attack on King Charles and his wife, Elizabeth, left the queen without fingers on her right hand, 'later earning her the name "Kiktawa" in Polish, or "cripple-hand"' (*Crime*, p. 118).
[37] Shepherd accurately sees the text at this point as "dramatiz[ing] the choice between marriage and chastity", but then goes on to read Joïe's self-mutilation as representing her "commitment to Christ as his spiritual bride" (*Tradition*, p. 23). However, given the alacrity with which Joïe marries the King of Scotland when the opportunity arises, this interpretation seems to over-read the text's hagiographical elements. While the narrative states, in describing Joïe's reaction to her father's proposal, that the heroine "en Dieu a mise s'entente" (545: devotes herself to God) and refers to his suggestion as 'contre Dieu' (555: against God), these references seem intended to demonstrate her understanding of the immorality of incest, rather than to suggest any inclination to take the veil or to remain celibate.
[38] King offers a useful parallel in observing that, in the *chanson de geste*, amputation 'marks the guilty' ("A Motif Transformed: The Meaning of Lost Limbs in Arthurian Romance", *Arthuriana* 18:2 (2008), 31), and is a punishment specifically "for crimes … against public order" ("Amputation" 39, 35; cf. p. 45).
[39] Shepherd notes that "[p]unishment by fire and setting adrift were traditionally reserved for women who had sinned against the integrity of family life" (*Tradition*, 24).
[40] In the *chansons de geste*, a "missing member imposes shame and suspicion on the amputee" (King, "Amputation", 39).
[41] Michel's apparent misreading, *fanée* (v. 1262), has been amended here to *sanee*, following Suchier and Sargent-Baur. The clean healing of the wound seems to express divine approbation of Joïe and her action, which is later consolidated in the miracle of the finding and reattaching of her hand. Robert Barlett's description of the medieval view of healing in trials by ordeal offers a useful analogy: 'A man accused of a crime, or a man seeking to claim or defend his rights, would, after a solemn three-day fast, pick up a hot iron, walk three paces, and put the iron down. His hand would be bandaged and sealed, then, after three days, inspected. If it was "clean"—that is, healthy without suppuration or discoloration—he was innocent or vindicated; if the wound was unclean, he was guilty' (*Trial by Fire and Water: The Medieval Judicial Ordeal*. Oxford: Clarendon Press, 1986, p. 1); "these wounds—like amputation—were interpreted as manifestations of God's pleasure or displeasure with the accused" (King, "Motif Transformed," 36).
[42] A fundamental doubt already exists in the fact of her being a stranger and a foreigner, since strangers are frequently regarded with suspicion in the Middle Ages (see, for example, Norbert Ohler, *The Medieval Traveller*, trans. Caroline Hillier. Woodbridge: The Boydell Press, 1989, 79). Indeed, some medieval

legislation was directed at those outside a recognised group, and a criminal outside a group was seen as "an enemy" against whom any act was allowed (Von Bar, *Continental Criminal Law*, 108).

[43] Just before depicting Joïe's amputation, the poet observes "Onques mais feme ce ne fist" (725: never had any woman done this before), which may imply that Remi has himself invented this instance of self-mutilation, perhaps in order to explore fully its effect and social repercussions. Remi's emphasis here seems to be on the nature of the mutilation rather than the gender of the self-mutilator. Medieval hagiography suggests that traditionally it was women who carried out such mutilations in order to avoid enforced marriage; for this reason, Saint Oda of Hainault (d. 1158) cut off her nose, as did Saint Margaret of Hungary (d. 1270), while nuns were also recorded perpetrating self-rhinectomy to avoid rape; similarly, in the fifth century, Saint Brigid's prayer for deformity had led to one of her eyes bursting, later restored as she took the veil (Jane Tibbetts Schulenburg, *Forgetful of Their Sex: Female Sanctity and Society, ca. 500–1100*. Chicago and London: University of Chicago Press, 1998, 145–8, 150), and the torture and perhaps blinding of the third-century saint Lucy was recast by the "later medieval legend that she cut out own eyes to avoid marriage" (Armando R. Favazza, *Bodies Under Siege: Self-mutilation and Body Modification in Culture and Psychiatry*, 2nd edn. Baltimore, MD: Johns Hopkins University Press, 1996, 99), although Katrien Heene has challenged this apparent gender-bias, demonstrating from her study of twelfth and thirteenth century saints' lives of the Low Countries that males also practise self-mutilation and that avoidance of marriage is only one of several reasons ("'Ad sanguinis effusionem': Automutilatie en gender in middeleeuwse heiligenlevens," *Queeste: Tijdschrift over middeleeuwse letterkunde in de Nederlanden*, 6, (1999), 1–22).

[44] Exile was a penalty for a range of serious crimes in Roman law (von Bar, *Continental Criminal Law*, 29–30, 33–4, and notably 46, where banishment is characterised as a penalty imposed on the upper classes) and remained a penalty for grave or capital crimes in medieval Europe, including France (von Bar, *Continental Criminal Law*, 162–3; see also Dean, *Crime*, 127–8 *et passim*).

[45] This would have been appreciated by Remi's audience, since amputation for serious offences was still known in medieval French legislation of the period; for example, in the *Anciennes Coutumes d'Anjou et du Maine*, "one who laid hands on his lord had his hand cut off" (von Bar, *Continental Criminal Law*, 190 and n. 18). In contradistinction to the episode in Hungary, where it was fundamental, the issue of impairment *per se* leading to unsuitability for marriage is scarcely considered in Scotland, although Joïe does refer to her reasons for self-mutilation as she dreams she might marry the Scottish king despite her missing hand: "'En ne me souvie[n]t-il et member / Que je colpai pour çou mon menbre/ Que roïne ne déusse estre?'" (1707–9: "Don't I remember and recall about it that I cut off my hand for that reason: so I should not be queen?").

[46] The term 'court' (1557) can refer to a royal court or a law court (see Algirdas Julien Greimas, *Dictionnaire de l'ancient français: Le Moyen Âge*. Paris: Larousse, 1979; new edn. 1994, *s.v. cort* I. 3, I. 4, I. 5), and Remi may have used it

for this reason, to suggest that supposedly objective law-courts might be as prone to error or partiality as monarchs. It is also notable that the king apparently believes that he would have heard about a noblewoman being punished by amputation for wrongdoing (1559–60). Later, the king again outlines the double issue of the missing hand and his wife's unknown identity when he discusses his marriage with the senator in Rome, and declares that "de vrai cuer l'amoit;/ Et se ne set qui ele estoit/ Ne comment eut la main perdue;/ Qui fille ert ne dont ert venue…" (6383–6: he loved her with a true heart, and yet he does not know who she was nor how she had lost her hand; whose daughter she was nor whence she came).

[47] Cf. Sargent-Baur, who notes that Joïe's "injury, suggesting as it does a punishment for a serious crime, is one cause of the dowager queen's animosity" ("Introduction," 113).

[48] R. Howard Bloch observes that "the question of marriage is, ultimately, indissociable from that of land, of inheritance, and, in particular, of cognatic succession" (*Etymologies and Genealogies: A Literary Anthropology of the French Middle Ages*. Chicago and London: University of Chicago Press, 1983, 194) and Shulamith Shahar notes that blood and kinship ties on the distaff side were considered important (*The Fourth Estate. A History of Women in the Middle Ages.* 1983; rpr. London: Routledge, 1991, 101, cf. 131). Another, related, issue of Joïe's concealed past is that her sexual history, and thus her sexual integrity, is unknown.

[49] Given that, in the earlier episode, it is the barons who suggest that the King of Hungary marry his daughter, perhaps Remi is also implying doubt in the ability of barons to offer sound advice. In Hungary, the marriage also has clerical support, leading Elizabeth Archibald to suggest that the episode represents '[a] cynical reference to the corruption of the clergy and the frequent flouting of the incest laws' ("Incest in Medieval Literature and Society," *Forum for Modern Language Studies* 25:1 (1989), 8).

[50] Although Shepherd observes that the Dowager's "chief characteristic is that of trickery or deceit" (*Tradition*, 28), she fails to comment on the clandestine behaviour of her son or of the heroine, who certainly share this trait in the matter of their wedding.

[51] See, for example, Georges Duby, *Love and Marriage in the Middle Ages*, trans. Jane Dunnett (Cambridge: Polity Press, 1994), 6–9. It is also notable, and perhaps strange, that no banns are announced, although it is difficult to conclude whether this is problematic. Certainly, banns were required by the time Remi was writing; at the Fourth Lateran Council in 1215, "the institution of banns was fixed by canonical law" (F. L. Critchlow, "On the Forms of Betrothal and Wedding Ceremonies in the Old-French 'Romans D'Aventure'", *Modern Philology* 2:4 (1905), 497; cf. James A. Brundage, *Law, Sex, and Christian Society in Medieval Europe*. Chicago and London: University of Chicago Press, 1987, 362). However, medieval authors display little concern about anachronism and often depict practices from their contemporary society regardless of the narrative's temporal or geographical settings; ignoring customs or legal practices later adopted, and which would pose problems to the plot, would be just as simple. While Remi's text, with

its reference to Pope Urban (6875), may offer a temporal setting in the fairly recent past, both medieval popes of that name who held office prior to the date of composition offered by Sargent-Baur predate this canonical edict (Urban II 1088–99, Urban III 1185–7). Shepherd, who supports a composition date in the late 1200s (*Tradition*, p. 13), examines E. Schwan's identification of Remi's pope as Urban IV (1261–4), but also observes that "Jean Wauquelin, who made a prose adaptation of the romance in the fifteenth century, understood the Pope to be Urban II" (*Tradition*, 11).

[52] Cf. Archibald, *Incest*, 160.

[53] *Etymologies and Genealogies*, 85.

[54] Jane Bliss observes that "[t]he theme by which a wicked mother-in-law pretends the heroine has given birth to a monster is present in several romances of the Calumniated Wife type, but in *La Manekine* the supposed monster is the child of a really maimed mother" (*Naming and Namelessness in Medieval Romance*, Cambridge: D. S. Brewer, 2008, 149–50).

[55] "The Hands of Phillipe [*sic*] de Remi's *Manekine*," *Mediterranean Studies* 15 (2006), 2. I am grateful to the author for supplying me with a copy of her article.

[56] See Metzler, 39–44 *et passim*, and 86–9. Yet, given that the handlessness is not the sole issue with Joïe, perhaps the queen mother here is relying on a broader tradition, that deformity suggests "that a lineage … is flawed" (Henri-Jacques Stiker, *A History of Disability*, trans. William Sayers. Ann Arbor: University of Michigan Press, 1999, 50). Francomano notes that "the supposed birth of the monster recalls the threat of incest that set Joïe's adventures in motion" (2).

[57] Stiker, 70.

[58] "Introduction", 113.

[59] When mass is over, the assembled party goes at once to the fountain; the fish is caught and the reliquary marvelled at, while the rest of the sturgeon becomes the centrepiece of a celebratory feast (7635-88).

[60] Archibald, *Incest*, pp. 173-4; Thelma Fenster, "Beaumanoir's *La Manekine*: Kin D(r)ead: Incest, Doubling & Death," *American Imago* 39:1 (1982), 55-6.

[61] The hand, of course, plays no part in the husband-wife recognition scene either: it is the absence of Joïe's left hand that becomes 'the identifying mark repeatedly mentioned by the King of Scotland in his seven-year quest' to find his wife (Sargent-Baur, "Introduction", 113).

[62] Archibald, *Incest*, 174; cf. Francomano who see the hands as "the focal points of scenes in the romance where issues of marriage and lineage come to the fore" (4). Sargent-Baur offers a more simple symbolic reading, suggesting that Joïe's "physical healing is a metaphor of a healed relationship" ("Introduction", 113).

[63] Archibald's subsequent suggestion that Joïe's son may be a key factor, since "a male heir assures return to normal (patriarchal) life" (175-6), seems to offer the son, rather than the hand, as the pertinent symbol of reconciliation through the restoration of a disrupted patriarchy.

[64] Remi may have been influenced by the martyrdom of Saint Dympna, the daughter of a seventh-century king who fled her incestuous father only to be caught and beheaded, if rumours of her fate were in circulation prior to the

composition of the *Life* written soon after the discovery of her bones in the 1230s (Sargent-Baur, 111-12). "Invincible Virgins" is the title of Chapter 4 (106-44) of Mills's *Suspended Animation.*

[65] "Les Sources de la *Manekine*", 97.

[66] Francomano, 10.

[67] It is unclear how oblique this response may be. If the senator is saying that he does not understand the name, then Joïe does not in fact supply him with a plain definition, any more than Remi provides one for his audience. Huet suggests that the soubriquet, like Cinderella's, had simply travelled with the story in the oral tradition and that Remi, having learned the name when he first heard the tale, perhaps in childhood, thought it needed no glossing on its first use, but later changed his mind ('on comprend également pourquoi Beaumanoir a néligé d'expliquer le nom la première fois qu'il employait: ayant appris ce nom en même temps que le conte, peut-être dans son enfance, il n'aura d'abord pas cru qu'il avait besoin d'explication et se sera ravisé après coup', 'Les Sources de la *Manekine*', p. 98), although the gloss when it arrives makes no attempt at a precise definition. Alternatively, the senator may be commenting on the strangeness and uniqueness of the name, rather than seeking an interpretation. Sargent-Baur notes that Remi ignores matters of language in his geographically varied text, and suggests that such issues may not be problematic since "French was the *lingua franca* ... of much of the cultivated West" ("Introduction", 107). Although the King of Hungary's messengers, sent to seek a lady worthy of the widowed king's hand, are said to be well-educated (242) and know "pluseurs langages" (243: several languages), the text largely reflects William MacBain's remark that '[m]edieval literature depicts a "monolingual universe"' ("The Outsider at Court, or What is so Strange about the Stranger?", *The Court and Cultural Diversity, Selected Papers from the Eighth Triennial Congress of the International Courtly Literature Society*, ed. Evelyn Mullally and John Thompson. Cambridge: D. S. Brewer, 1997, 357–65, p. 361).

[68] It is notable that the term 'main' is not used in this context until after Joïe and her hand have been reunited. Earlier references tend to refer only to washing in general terms—"Quant mengié eurent, si laverent" (2289: When they had eaten, they washed)—or through metonymy: "Li trompéur l'iawe cornerent" (2276: The trumpeters announced the [arrival of] water). Conversely, later instances make explicit references to hands, for example, "Quant .../ ... il ourent lor mains lavées" (7693–4: when they had washed their hands).

[69] 'Usually at the same time as the question of assent to marry is being asked by the priest, he takes the right hand of the groom and that of the bride in such a manner that the pair hold[s] each other's right hand, and the celebrant then places his own hands over those he has brought together into a clasped position' (Critchlow, "Forms of Betrothal", 517).

[70] Francomano, 5.

[71] The matter of consent to marriage is one the text highlights three times: when the Hungarian king plans to marry Joïe without her consent, despite his initial proposal apparently considering the matter of Joïe's consent: '"Mais que il à vous

voeille plaire"' (542: 'supposing that it may please you'); when the King of Scotland deliberates on the need for Joïe's consent to marriage (1639–42); and when Joïe responds to the Roman senator's offer to house her by clearly outlining her refusal to participate in any sexual or marital relationship (5161–70), a situation the senator accepts.

[72] *Crime*, 145.

[73] *Incest*, 2.

[74] Such a response in the text is not limited to the aristocracy, for the fishermen who find Joïe in Rome treat her with a rough sensitivity and courtesy: they plan to take her in, lodge her with their womenfolk and sell her boat to acquire the means to pay for her board (4900–60).

[75] Thanks are due to Robert Mills for his interest in the project, and for offering valuable comments and bibliographical suggestions on the historical section of this essay.

'It Was No Sekenes': Discerning Disabilities in the Book of Margery Kempe

Marian E. Lupo

When one of the "most famows frerys in Inglond" comes to Lynn to preach, he refuses to permit Margery to attend his sermons unless she would either leave "hir sobbyng and hir crying" or admit to the community "it was cardiakyl er sum other sekeness." Margery refuses, knowing "wel be revelacyon and be experiens of werkyng it was no sekenes."[1] This conflict between the famous friar and Margery has been replayed in Kempe criticism, which alternatively pathologizes or valorizes Margery, either ascribing an undermining illness or a prodigious political agency to the character. Both interpretive modes rely on teratical approaches, which interpret deviations from able-bodied norms as either monstrous or exceptional. By taking seriously the historical specificity of this text, this essay claims that *The Book of Margery Kempe* is a key text contributing a new model of disability to Disability Studies: a jurisdictional model, which turns upon who has the authority to say whether a disability exists and how that disability is defined.

This essay shows how Kempe's text, as perhaps only a medieval narrative can, tests the limits of contemporary understandings of disability as well as the field of Disability Studies itself: it represents a body formed differently by its participation in the power/discourse structures of its time. Because it is hardly accepted by scholars that Kempe's text pivots on disability, this essay shows how Margery's deviations from able-bodied norms, such as her weeping/bellowing/falling down, are represented as either stigmatizing or in need of a cure, that is, represented as disabilities. Further, "disability," in its contemporary usage, often refers to a lack of control over the body and signifies a failure of agency, particularly when the body is thought of as a pliable instrument of the will. A recurring, if not central, issue raised by Kempe's text is the assumed causal relationship between control and agency. To focus on how Kempe questions a normative reading of agency, and our understanding of disability, I analyze how this text draws upon doctrinal and devotional discourses as sources of authority for Margery. Read against the Lollard controversy over lay theologizing, which was heightened by the secular writ to burn heretics (*De Hæretico Comburendo*, 1401) and codified by Archbishop Arundel's detailed proscriptions on lay preaching and teaching (*Constitutions*, 1409), the jurisdictional contours of Margery's authority emerge.

Central to the license Margery claims to publicly preach, teach, and engage in spiritual self-healing is a discursive authority contingent on her disabilities embedded within what I term the medieval vision industry. Margery employs two discourses, the *spirituum discretio*, or discernment of spirits, and the *imitatio Magdalenae*, or imitation of Mary Magdalene, in response to and within the constraints posed by the ecclesiopolitical power structure. Both discourses hinge on a lack of control over the body. Such a lack of control, paradoxically for contemporary audiences, authorizes Margery's interventions into her sociopolitical circumstances. Her disabilities are, quite literally, sources of discernment that permit Margery to say both whether they exist and what they mean. This jurisdictional model of disability produces juridical effects as it warrants Margery's lay theologizing in contravention of legal proscriptions.

Disability Studies

Kempe positions sickness as central to the narrative. The first proem lays out one of the several relationships between sickness and holiness that the narrative will pursue, spiritual healing: "Then this creature, of whom this treatise through the mercy of Jesus shall show in part the life, was touched by the hand of our Lord with great bodily sickness, where she lost reason and her wits for a long time until our Lord by grace restored her again, as it shall more openly be showed afterward" (Staley I.P1.3). It is also here that a relationship between bodily and spiritual illness is established: Margery went out of her mind because of her "great" (in Middle English, "grete") bodily illness. Finally, the beginning of the book also evokes Mary Magdalene, the woman who was healed of seven demons by Christ and who, by the late middle ages, was venerated as the "apostles of the apostles" and a female preacher: the book was begun, according to the second proem, "in the year of our Lord 1436, on the day next after Mary Magdalene" (Staley I.P2.6). Sickness is at the heart of chapter one of book one as Kempe recounts the sickness Margery suffered before, during, and after the birth of her first child and also begins the thread of clerical critique that runs throughout the book. It is because the confessor she sends for after childbirth, when she is in fear for her life, "was a little too hasty and began sharply to reprove her" that Margery "for the dread she had of damnation on the one side and his sharp reproving on that other side, . . . went out of her mind and was wonderfully vexed and labored with spirits for half a year, eight weeks and some odd days" (Staley I.1.7). Margery is healed by Jesus, who appears in a vision to her, asking her, "Daughter, why have you forsaken me, and I forsook never you?" (Staley I.1.8). Kempe thus establishes another relationship between holiness and sickness that runs throughout the book: the spiritual authority that arises from spiritual healing. As with the visionary Julian of Norwich, Margery's healing is established at that point in time from which she begins her privileged relationship with God: "And when this creature was thus graciously come again to her mind, she thought she was bound to God and that she would be his servant" (Staley I.2.8).

Sickness, particularly bodily sickness, appear again as central narrative elements when Margery returns from her first pilgrimage (Staley I.56.101-102), when Margery heals the woman who suffers as she did after childbirth (Staley I.75.130-31), and when Margery tends to her sick husband, an action for which she will receive "as much meed" (here meaning "reward") as if she was "in church to make [her] prayers" (I.76.132). We are told that Margery is called upon to pray for the dying (Staley I.72.126) and that Margery receives revelations as to whether a sickness will turn to death (Staley I.83.148). The pain of sickness is also central to the narrative: pain is both penance and a path for identification with Christ's Passion. When Margery returns from her one of pilgrimages in England, "God punished her with many great and divers sicknesses" (Staley I.56.101). The details of pain are amplified: she neither eats nor drinks during one of her illnesses, "but ever groaning till it was gone" (Staley I.56.101). Physical pain is also amplified when she recovers and is "houseled" (receives communion) following this bout of illness: "she cried whatever time she should be houseled as if her soul and body should have parted asunder, so that two men held her in their arms till her crying was ceased" (Staley I.56.102). Margery's sustained and often ambiguous relationship with physical pain is demonstrated in her prayer to Christ when she is sick: she asks him why he suffered so much pain for men's sins when she cannot suffer even this little pain, which she asks him to take away (Staley I.56.102). Kempe does not neglect mentioning even the smallest pain: on Margery's pilgrimage to Germany, we learn of the pain of lice, for example (Staley II.6.173). Sickness and pain represent well-established devotional paths to holiness as well as occasions for demonstrating holiness. Kempe's text challenges contemporary readers by presenting no easy resolution of the multiple relationships among sickness and holiness.

Rather, these multiple and often conflicting relationships among sickness and holiness surface as critical reading strategies in understanding Margery's weeping/roaring/falling down. The narrative gives the reader several options for determining the cause of Margery's weeping: "And therefore many people slandered her, not believing it was the work of God but that some evil spirit vexed her in her body or else that she had some bodily sickness" (Staley I.17.30). Again, "as soon as she perceived that she should cry, she would keep it in as much as she might, so that the people should not have heard it, for it annoyed them. For some said it was a wicked spirit vexed her; some said it was a sickness; some said she had drunk too much wine" (Staley I.28.51). When she is in Rome, "she wept bitterly, she sobbed violently and cried full loudly and horribly so that the people were oftentimes afraid and greatly astonished, believing she had been vexed with some evil spirit, not believing it was the work of God but rather some evil spirit, or a sudden sickness, or else simulation and hypocrisy falsely feigned by her own self" (Staley I.33.61). When she returns to King's Lynn, "[M]any said there was never a saint in heaven who cried so as she did, wherefore they would conclude that she had a devil within her which caused that crying. . . . Some said that she had the falling evil, for she with the crying twisted her body, turning from the one side into the other, and waxed all blue and gray, like the color of lead" (Staley I.44.77). Thus, the reader is given many possible readings of Margery's weeping: an evil spirit, drunkenness, sickness, hypocrisy, or the work of God. The good reader, like the priestly scribe who is converted to believing in Margery, and like the red ink annotator who later prepared the work with images, emphasis, commentary, summary, and emendations calculated to inspire a devotional reading, believes that Margery is inspired by God: this is the ostensible authority and purpose of this "short treatise and a comfortable for sinful wretches" (Staley I.P1.1).[2] By so believing in Margery's weeping as a gift from God, the reader may actually accrue spiritual grace: "And specially to those who doubt not or mistrust not in their asking, her crying greatly profited to the increase of merit and of virtue. To those who little trusted and little believed, perhaps there was a little increase of virtue and merit. But whether the people believed in her crying or not, her grace was never the less but ever increased" (Staley I.83.147). According to Kempe, everyone benefits from Margery's weeping, but especially those who believe, those "who doubt not or mistrust not in their asking."

Kempe's book thus foregrounds four issues raised by Disability Studies today: the sociohistorical construction of disability, the presence of pain, the contingencies of embodiment, and the knowledge that the disability perspective can contribute to understanding the human body/psyche. Lennard Davis explains that in the social model of disability, "disability is presented as a social and political problem that turns an impairment into an oppression either by erecting barriers or refusing to create barrier-free environments (where barrier is used in a very general and metaphoric sense)".[3] Pain, as an experience of the limitation of the body/mind, is perhaps the only universal experience, but it has become marginalized within the ideologies "of culture, democracy, capitalism, sexism, and racism," which are the ideologies of "the perfection of the human body and its activities".[4] In the shift from the "ideology of normalcy, from the rule and hegemony of normates, to a vision of the body as changeable, unperfectable, unruly, and untidy," Disability Studies also provides a way to enhance understanding of the mind/body by permitting the disabled to be heard.[5]

However, Kempe's book exceeds these issues just as it emphasizes how historically constructed disability is. For example, in Disability Studies, "impairment" is a "physical fact," which is hard to square with Kempe's fluid representations of illness or with equally fluid medieval medical theory. Considering Margery's impairment to be her weeping/bellowing/falling down underscores the social constructedness of disability and its dependence upon discourse. In addition, in embracing and describing pain, Kempe uses the well-established medieval discourse of the imitatio Christi, a discourse not without its speakers today, but that is superseded in popularity, if nothing else, by its mutation into the "no pain, no gain" physical fitness discourse, which sees pain as a path to physical perfection, not spiritual perfection. Finally, Kempe has almost always been understood as presenting an alternate understanding of the human psyche in her book, but this psyche has been understood as the mystical psyche, a psyche that in its otherworldliness obscures the social construction of her impairment.

Contemporary criticism, once it rejects the reading of Margery's weeping that is at the heart of the book's polemic, once it falls outside the group "who doubt not or mistrust not in their asking," replays the conflict between the famous friar and Margery. Some critics and readers continue to be annoyed by Margery's weeping. Nancy P. Stork argues that "we must explain why she annoyed her contemporaries and continues to annoy us today" by relying on an interpretation of Margery's weeping and cries as evidencing Tourette's syndrome.[6] Stork provides a chart at the end of the article demonstrating that Margery bellowed and wept more than the 'normal' mystic. She takes exception with Lynn Staley's *Margery Kempe's Dissenting Fictions*, and criticizes the author for writing "an entire book with barely a mention of Margery's weeping and bellowing".[7] Mary Hardiman Farley also challenges Staley by stating that "recent thinkers . . . are likely to see Margery as a cogent social critic, rhetorical saboteur, and even 'worthy heir to Chaucer,' romanticizing behavior her contemporaries consider intrusive or frightening".[8] Farley, in contrast, offers an interpretation based on modern diagnostic criteria, and she argues that Margery had a personality disorder. Richard Lawes claims that biologically-based psychopathology affords insight into the medieval mind; on this account, Margery suffered from postpartum psychosis and then temporal lobe epilepsy, illnesses that incited her to the autobiographical impulse.[9] Although avoiding the clinical language, Gail McMurray Gibbons repeats the clinical impulse in interpreting the text; she reads the central miracle of the book as Margery's "magical healing of a woman mad from childbirth," in which Margery "by triumphing over the perils of childbirth has both enacted her qualifying miracle of sainthood and fully asserted her own spiritual health".[10]

Each of these readings pathologizes Margery by secluding her within a drama of her own making and then using her illness as a "narrative prosthesis," that is, a narrative issue used "to resolve or correct . . . a deviance marked as abnormal or improper within the social context".[11] In these works, using narrative prosthesis to read Kempe's book is justified by modern diagnostic criteria, which are accepted as a grand narrative encompassing all ages because the criteria are "biologically based." The range of pathologies ascribed to Margery by contemporary diagnostic criticism also demonstrates how, even now, there is no one category into which to place her impairment of weeping/bellowing/falling down. Rather, the attempts to categorize Margery demonstrate the weakness of approaches based on "physical fact", on an impairment-based approach, since it reveals a taken-for-grantedness of the material, physical body/mind as prior to, rather than a result of and a continuing participation in, the formative effects of power/discourse, as Judith Butler maintains.[12] Thus, Kempe's book demonstrates not only the constructedness of disability but also reveals in Margery a body/mind differently formed by power/discourse.

In addition to lacking a historical context, at the core of the pathological approach, reductionist and condescending, is a denial of agency to Kempe. The author Kempe and the character Margery are collapsed, and Kempe is denied the agency, much less the authority, of authorship. The effect of this criticism is to return Kempe scholarship to a pre-Staley status. For example, Farley writes, "I find insufficient support for Lynn Staley's claim that it is a subtly crafted work of fiction," it is, rather, the "earnest report of . . . successful personality integration".[13] David Aers addresses this clinical approach to Kempe, noting that it uncritically deploys charged language with the political motivation of marginalizing *The Book of Margery Kempe*.[14] Farley articulates the assumption underlying the pathological line of criticism by stating that the issue of agency revolves around intellectual control.[15] Staley addresses this tendency early in her book when she asks, "How often do we ascribe the melodies of *Go Down Moses* to bourbon?"[16] Both David Aers and Lynn Staley have also challenged the gender bias inherent in pathologizing Kempe. Such criticism of Kempe's book replays the scorn that Margery welcomed as penance, without questioning whether or not this annoyance is deliberate and central to the text or whether their annoyance is the contemporary equivalent of the misogyny and proto-ableism that seeks to silence her weeping in the narrative.

At the same time, to ignore the sicknesses central to this narrative, especially Margery's weeping, is to undercut the narrative's achievement in creating a character that can be read as both sick and powerful, a character that can find authority and agency in sickness, a character that may even suggest a power immanent in sickness. Ruth Shklar not only contextualizes Kempe historically against the political and legal Lollard controversies of her time, but also draws the theoretical connections between Kempe's theological and political position, a necessary reading for a fifteenth-century author: "Kempe's unusual brand of political mysticism derives its rhetorical force and its interpretive difficulty from its proximity to unorthodox concerns".[17] The doctrinal confusion of her text, its juxtaposition of orthodoxy and heterodoxy, is at the heart of its "ecclesiopolitical polemic".[18] Moreover, by focusing on the accusations and examinations, Kempe "not so much proves her legitimacy as questions the processes of legitimation themselves" in a subversive mode of public writing in which she accords to herself and her scribe "the power reserved by the church of documenting legal process in official registers".[19] Shklar analyzes the exchanges between Margery and the church authorities to show, among other things, "her understanding of reading and writing as political acts monitored by various authorities".[20] Yet Shklar, like Staley, omits Margery's weeping/bellowing/falling down as if this sickness might render unachievable such astute strategies of critique.

If Kempe, as Staley and Shklar argue, does position Margery in relation to the politics of language, then one aspect of that politics implicated by her weeping/bellowing/falling down is the role of intellectual control in the use of language. Thus, even when readers distinguish between Kempe the author and Margery the character, the social construction of Margery's disability, then and now, precludes a serious interrogation of the claimed necessary relationship between agency and intellectual control. In other words, it seems impossible for contemporary readers to read Margery as both out of control, which is what either a holiness/sickness reading would imply, and a figure of agency, which is the very effect that she has in the narrative. Rather, the conflict in approaches follows the binaries established in the confrontation between the famous friar and Margery: she either holy or sick, either out of control or hypocritical, either saintly or demonic, either disabled or exceptional.

A Body/Mind Formed Differently

The Book of Margery Kempe resists these binaries, and the very placement of the conflict with the good friar two-thirds of the way through book one, in chapters 61 to 64, indicates that Kempe was careful in her negotiation of these binaries: the conflict is rhetorically placed at the same spot where one would include an opposing argument, where one would include material in an argument that might be too damaging elsewhere. A friar's diagnosis could have significant probative value as friars traditionally did care for the sick.[21] Margery's conflict with the friar also precipitates the difficulty she encounters in having her book written. When the famous friar preaches against her in St. James chapel yard, he is so vehement, to the extent of "smiting his hand on the pulpit," that even Margery's priestly scribe "dared not well speak of her". In fact, the priestly scribe's turning away from Margery dates from this sermon, and he "was in purpose never to have believed her feelings afterward" (Staley I.62.112). Thus, the proem that begins the book is Kempe's recursive revenge on the famous friar, both made necessary by the conflict and also transforming the conflict, Margery-style, into not only an occasion for her miracles, but also possibly the occasion for the book itself.

Margery's conflict with the famous friar, who is identified as the Franciscan friar Robert Melton in the margins of the manuscript,[22] involves the entire community against her. It is political from its inception and also one of Margery's darkest moments. Although the parish priest warned the famous friar of Margery's weeping, when Margery does begin to weep at his sermon, the friar orders her out because she "annoys the people" (Staley I.61.110). As to be expected, Margery tries to negotiate her exclusion. Two priests, including one who had read much scripture to her, go to the friar and try to persuade him to allow Margery to attend his sermons. He refuses, telling them that if she should make "any noise as she was wont to do", he would not only speak against it, but would not allow her to cry (Staley I.61.110). The friar maintains his position even though he approached yet again by a doctor of divinity and a bachelor of law, who send "for wine to cheer" the friar (Staley I.61.111). Later, "a worshipful burgess, who a few years after was mayor of Lynn," also approaches and is rebuffed by the friar (Staley I.61.111). These friends of Margery believe that if the friar knows more about Margery, specifically her revelations, the friar will not understand her as only sick. However, the friar, "trusting much in the favor of the people," popular opinion, refuses to acknowledge her weeping as a gift of God. Kempe demonstrates that the non-negotiability of his position is based as much on its political appeal as it is on some type of diagnostic certainty: the famous friar wins popular support through exclusion of the annoying Holy Woman.

And this is where Kempe most closely rehearses the politics of our contemporary medical model of disability: in the medical model, a physical attribute, an 'impairment', is constructed as a social fact, a disability that must be cured. Grounded in physicality, sustained through political appeal, the medical model permits the friar to adopt and maintain his non-negotiable position.[23] When the doctor of divinity and bachelor of law try to wine and dine the famous friar into accepting Margery, he replies, "if she might not withstand it when it came, he believed it was a heart disease ("cardiakly") or some other sickness, and, if she would be so known, . . . he would have compassion on her and steer the people to pray for her, and under this condition he would have patience with her and suffer her to cry enough, if she would say it was a natural sickness" (Staley I.61.111). Like the pathologically-focused critics, the friar is willing to tolerate Margery and suffer her weeping if she would admit that it was only a biologically based illness. Of all the pathologies attributed to Margery, the famous friar's is perhaps the harshest because it is the most mundane: the "cardiakly" is the common heart spasm.[24] Far from a gift from God, her weeping is simply the result of an errantly twitching heart or some other sickness that, by association, would be like a heart spasm. Medical works from the late fourteenth century prescribe homespun recipes to cure this simple ailment; the common use of ginger in these recipes as a remedy suggests that the "cardiakly" was nothing more than what we would call "heartburn."[25] Thus, the famous friar mocks Margery and her friends by calling her holy gift of weeping a type of indigestion. Kempe's emphasis on the credentials of Margery's friends is not only an indication of her political astuteness, but also a rhetorical strategy that emphasizes the vulgarity and rudeness of the famous friar.

The emphasis on her friends' credentials is also part of Kempe's consistent authorization of Margery within the medieval paradigm of the vision industry. When Margery refuses the friar's offer to submit to a medical model of her disability in order to attend his sermons by responding that she knew well "by revelation and by experience of it working that it was no sickness, and therefore she would not for all this world say otherwise than she felt" (Staley I.61.111), she also claims the authority of revelation and "experience of its working," or the good fruits of her revelations, elements of the medieval discourse *discretio spirituum*. Augustine crystallized transcendental experience into two types of experiences: first, the intellectual and cerebral direct communication with the ineffable, "mysticism," which does not lend itself to misapprehension; and second, the spiritual or imaginary vision, "seeing or hearing things with an inward or spiritual eye or ear", which could be deceptive. [26] The mystical experience was privileged over the concrete, material, and specific visionary experience, which could also be the tool "of the devil, and visionaries his minions".[27] The visionary experience was also the type of transcendental experience most often ascribed to the carnal and sensual nature of women. Because "both women and visions are perceived as potentially deceptive and deceiving, subject to the senses," women's visionary experiences were viewed as "flawed and a suspect expression of a flawed and suspect spirituality".[28] Nevertheless, women's visionary writing flowered from the twelfth to the fifteenth century, and their experiences were "eagerly read by their contemporaries".[29] To control the heresy and anarchy possible in this always potentially disruptive practice, the Catholic Church produced a discourse to control the vision industry, the *discretio spirituum*, the discernment of spirits, which derived from ecclesiastical doctrine.

The discourse of *discretio spirituum* established prescriptions for the acceptable forms of visions and the acceptable behavior of visionaries. It has seven basic elements: the first, and the most definite sign was "whether the person lives a virtuous life under the rule of a spiritual director"; second, as a result of the vision, "the soul feels inflamed by God's love" and the visionary's "obedience to Holy Mother Church" is strengthened; third, the visionary feels "a deep inward knowledge of the truth of the revelation"; fourth, the visions "are always and only of true things"; fifth, the visionary bears the appropriate fruit; sixth, "the day and hour" of their death is revealed to the visionaries; and seventh, "posthumous miracles . . . establish the status of the visionary beyond all question".[30] The *discretio spirituum*, embodied in scriptural sources and transmitted as a doctrine through scholastic and patristic writing, formed a "cultural substratum" by the late Middle Ages.[31] John Capgrave, for example, a contemporary of Kempe, used elements of the *discretio spirituum* to authorize his *Life of Saint Katherine*, a narrative that circumvents Arundel's proscriptions on vernacular theologizing and that begins with St. Katherine's vision of her marriage to Christ and the revelation to her, by the Virgin Mary, of her means of death.[32]

Although the *discretio spirituum* was an established discourse, and although Margery cites it appropriately to authorize her presence at the famous friar's sermons, the friar only continues to misread her by preaching against her publicly. Kempe emphasizes this misreading by placing, in Chapter 62, specific references to books that describe not only affective piety, but authorized women visionaries. The scribe recounts how he eventually came to be reconciled with Margery after reading the life of Marie d'Oignies, a visionary life written by Jacques de Vitry, Bonventure's "Prykke of Lofe", the *Stimulus Amoris*, Richard Rolle's *Incendio Amoris*, and the treatise of Elizabeth of Hungary, also an account of a visionary life (Staley I.62.112-113). Both Marie d'Oignes and Elizabeth of Hungary wept in devotion. In this self-reflexive passage, the scribe admits how he misread Margery, a misreading that heightens the importance of reading and writing to Kempe's self-authorization. In this passage Kempe also addresses, obliquely, possible charges of drunkenness and madness as the priestly scribe quotes the *Stimulus Amoris*: "'A Lord, of what shall I more noise or cry? You tarry and you come not, and I, weary and overcome through desire, begin to madden, for love governs me and not reason . . . . those who see me are irked and pity me, not knowing me drunk with your love. Lord, they say, 'Lo, yon mad man cries in the streets," but how great is the desire of my heart they perceive not'" (Staley I.62.113). Here Margery's altered state of consciousness is specifically justified in reference to holy drunkenness and madness. Kempe also emphasizes Margery's self-awareness: like those who see the author of *Stimulus Amoris*, those who see Margery "are irked and pity" her.

Kempe deliberately subverts and exceeds the *spirituum discretio*, a discourse whose purpose is to make the female visionary disappear behind the screen of her revelations. Margery never disappears from this text by adopting the acceptable behavior of visionaries, a fact that still continues to irk some readers. Rosalynn Voaden analyzes Margery's fashioning as a holy woman as paradoxical from its inception; her visionary authority undermined as "the intimate and instrument of the divine as well as rejected and despised by men".[33] Although Margery the character may be undermined, Kempe's narrative accomplishes a subversion of the hegemonic authority represented by the friar and the "favor of the people" that support him, the same people who slander Margery. Kempe inserts Margery into the most radical tradition of Christianity in her position as a female visionary who is rejected and despised. This radical tradition contains a critique of earthly authority; within this critique of the hegemony is a specific critique of ecclesiopolitical authority and the relationship it claims between intellectual control and agency. To accomplish this sustained critique, Kempe appropriates the raw material of the marketplace, the vision industry, and uses it to construct her own, improvisational meanings.[34] For example, Margery's persistent attempts to receive authorization from the clergy should be read as bricolage. She takes the one spiritual director/author of the vision industry, the indispensable element who legitimizes the female visionary as mediator of revelations, and multiples that authority, thus critiquing the vision industry through parody and also multiplying her authority while resisting the authority of any one director/authority.

To read *The Book of Margery Kempe* this way is not to exclude any other possible motivations behind the character Margery's pursuit of clerical authorization. She may seek to avert potential threats through multiple clerical authorization.[35] She may also, as Voaden notes, be "motivated by a fear of deception, by a desire for attention, and by an apparently insatiable thirst for clerical conversation".[36] The character may have all these motivations and more. However, to read Margery's pursuit of clerical approval as bricolage is to take seriously Staley's suggestion that we ask of the book all the questions we would ask of a "great" work of literature. The question, then, is what is Kempe the author doing within this narrative by reporting all these clerical authorizations? If she is using bricolage as I have suggested, an aesthetic associated with subversive subcultures and with parody, then the appropriated discourses reassembled in Kempe's narrative reflect aspects of a subcultural group life: bricolage uses objects/discourses in which the subculture's members can "see their central values held and reflected".[37] Kempe's *Book* has indeed been read by some scholars as originating from and addressed to a subcultural audience, one composed of interested religious and secular figures.

Kempe's portrayal of various authorizations could then also be read as not only a parody of the vision industry, but also as Margery's political gesture to create a community, a subculture, that would support her as well as understand her use of bricolage. John Goodman argues that Kempe's work is deeply polemical, arguing for a particular interpretation of Margery that justifies "the regulars and seculars at Lynn and Norwich who supported her against the strictures and qualms of their colleagues and against popular canards".[38] This subcultural community could be extended to include those regulars and seculars that she encounters on her pilgrimages, those who support her and know of her: not only "those no less than nineteen clerics or holy men who validate her way of life and visions" but also the "several clusters of holy men and women" who approve of her.[39] Janet Wilson finds that Kempe's disruptive influence upon fifteenth-century King's Lynn is evidence that the town was a "deeply disturbed social and religious milieu, one in which incipient dissatisfaction with the church and with contemporary forms of worship may have encouraged anti-clericalism".[40] In addition, "the religious milieu in East Anglia", an area second only to London in prosperity and arguably even more cosmopolitan in its contact with the continent through location and shipping, was "richly diverse and tolerated such individuality in devotional practices".[41] As with any religious work authored after Arundel's proscriptions against vernacular theology written or spoken, Kempe's book must carefully navigate the border of orthodoxy. It does this through a bricolage that reflects her subculture's concerns, primarily a concern with ecclesiopolitical authority and control manifested in the social construction of Margery as disabled.

Kempe's fashioning of the episode with the famous friar accomplishes her specific critique of and resistance to the claimed necessary relationship between intellectual control and agency, to the ideology that privileges the cerebral over the emotional, the third-person diagnosis over the first-person experience. After appropriating the discourse of the vision industry and affective piety to authorize Margery, Kempe notes that famous friar continues to speak against Margery in every sermon, whether Margery is there or not, and some people begin to say that "she had a devil within her, and some said to her own mouth that the friar should have driven two devils out of her" (Staley I.62.113). Here, where the hegemony condemns her, Kempe specifically mentions in her narrative that Margery has no control over the weeping: "[S]he wept, sobbed, and cried full sorely against her will; she might not choose, for she had rather wept softly and secretly than openly if it had been in her power" (Staley I.62.113-14). Margery's lack of control enables her to exercise agency. Because she cannot control the gift, she is still loud and visible, and most importantly, completely public. The famous friar reads her lack of control as disobedience and builds popular opinion against her to such an extent that Margery is almost banished from King's Lynn. Her friends come to her and advise her to leave town since so many people are against her. In a Kempian nod to the discourse of *discretio spirituum* in its reference to the authority of the spiritual director, Margery's confessor says to her, "Margery, what shall you now do? There is no more against you but the moon and seven stars. Hardly is there any man who holds with you but I alone" (Staley I.63.114). Christ also speaks to Margery about the matter, telling her, "Daughter, if he be a priest who despises you, knowing well wherefore you weep and cry, he is accursed" (Staley I.63.114). Christ's words to her, placed after her dialogue with her friends and confessor, establishes Christ as a friend of Margery, demonstrating Margery's deep inward knowledge of the truth of her revelation, an appropriated element of the *discretio spirituum* that Kempe uses to curse the friar.

Not only is the *discretio spirituum* used to explain Margery's lack of control, but also it justifies the transitory, contingent nature of her weeping. Christ finally intervenes in a revelation to resolve the crisis: "Daughter, I bid you go again into church, for I shall take away from you your crying so that you shall no more cry so loud, nor in that manner of way as you have done before, though you would" (Staley I.63.114). The element of *discretio spirituum* that the visions "are always and only of true things" is appropriated by Kempe to justify a contradictory position. This contradictory position critiques the claimed relationship between intellectual control and agency in enabling Margery to exercise agency: she is now able to attend the friar's sermons with her community. Still, the friar seems to succeed where all others failed in silencing Margery; as the narrative recounts it, "many people believed that she dared no longer cry because the good friar preached so against her .... Then they held him a holy man and her a false feigned hypocrite" (Staley I.63.114). The famous friar's political success reveals that the other side of the pathological focus is the construction of Margery as hypocrite; diagnosis draws credibility from the subject's disaccreditation.

The friar's focus on sickness/control rather than holiness allows Kempe to insert a protracted critique of the clergy within the narrative. Thus, following this episode, Margery is comforted by the Lord in an extensive monologue in which Christ dismisses the clergy: "there is no clerk in the world" who can teach Margery better that God (Staley I.64.116). In addition, the devil has no charity, and the famous friar and the people who support him are, by implication, associated with the devil. Christ becomes even more forthright than that: "there is no clerk who can speak against the life which I teach you, and, if he does, he is not God's clerk; he is the devil's clerk" (Staley I.64.116). "Under the habit of holiness is covered much wickedness," Christ tells her (Staley I.64.116). The friar's disbelief thus evokes the punishment Margery received for her own disbelief, her vision that lasted twelve days and in which she sees "divers men of religion, priests and many others, both heathen and Christian, coming before her sight so that she might not avoid them or put them out of her sight, showing their bare members unto her" (Staley I.59.107). The ungodly disbelief hidden by the habit of holiness is associated with naked male clerical authority in a vision with astounding congruence with Lacanian psychoanalytic theory: Margery sees that her entrance into the symbolic order is literally barred by the phallus. This vision, like her revelation from Christ about the famous friar, takes elements from the *spirituum discretio* and subverts them through bricolage: Margery feels a "deep inward knowledge of the truth of the revelation" at the same time as she questions 'obedience to Holy Mother Church' in the form of the naked male clerics or the famous friar. Kempe takes advantage of the requirement that visions "are always and only of true things" to authorize revelations that subvert clerical authority while granting Margery authority in excess of the clergy.

A Jurisdictional Model of Disability

As authored by Kempe, Margery not only claims religious authority through her visions and revelations, but also consistently exceeds the limitations of the discourse of *spirituum discretio* that authorizes her, demonstrating a failure to conform that exceeds the "profound conflict about their relation to authority" that mystic texts encode.[42] What is often understood as the character's failure to conform should rather be understood as the character's major success. Not only does Kempe specifically subvert ecclesiopolitical authority by recording and recounting heretical examinations in which Margery wins, as Shklar argues, but she does so by consistently using clerical authority's own discourse to resist it. Margery's visions and revelations can be understood are particularly threatening to secular and religious authority if they are understood not just as representations, which is how a contemporary audience might be tempted to read them, but as simulations that generate reality, which is how a medieval audience probably would have read them.

Medieval visionary experience, encompassing smell and sound as well as sight, proceeds from a theory of outwardness. The received impressions, rather than originating from inside the visionary, originate from outside models, and the spirit of the visionary generates rather than reproduces or copies the real. Similar to the third order of simulacra Baudrillard poses in his Symbolic Exchange and Death, medieval visions collapse the real with the imaginary, the true with the false. Simulations neither produce equivalents for the real nor reproduce the real – rather, a vision reduplicates and generates the real. Thus, the hyperreal exists – the more real than real, the generation of the real by its model. In this scenario, signs produce culture rather than culture producing signs. For example, Avicenna, one of the medical authorities mentioned by Chaucer's doctor of physic, theorized that the eye can see because the object of sight throws off a likeness of itself, a simulacrum; the simulacrum is received by the spirit that operates the *sensus communis*, which can see, hear, touch, taste, and smell, and the act of vision is completed.[43] Avicenna's model is just one of several medieval models of the senses and the imagination. Paul Strohm notes that "the sensory basis of images or phantasms might be differently described or illustrated from system to system, but remains fundamental to every medieval conception". Because "thought relies upon sense-derived images or phantasm," it is, "in a very important sense, more tangible and real to the medieval understanding than to our own".[44] By extension, visions and revelations would be more real that thought: they would be hyperreal.

Thus, it was possible for a medieval visionary to claim she had seen something that was really there in a way that would not be possible for a contemporary medical subject, who would be considered laboring under unbalanced chemicals in her brain. The contrast between the two approaches to visions also demonstrates the political nature of attempts to pathologize Margery as attempts to render her harmless. Because visions as simulations generate reality, have their own hyperreal ontology, their authorization poses a threat to established order and authority, secular or religious, medieval or modern. The visions authored by Kempe are dangerous simulacra that, through her use of bricolage, generate a remixed hyperreality that potentially vitiates the reality sanctioned by ecclesiopolitical authority.

Kempe uses this technique throughout the book in moments of affective piety that are disaffective or disobedient when read closely. In chapter 73, for example, Margery beholds Mary at her death. All the apostles kneel and ask Mary for grace. When Margery cries and weeps at this vision, the apostles command her to cease, and she replies, "Would you I should see the Mother of God die and I should not weep? It may not be, for I am so full of sorrow that I may not withstand it. I must needs cry and weep" (Staley I.73.128). Margery is both assertive and appropriately inflamed by love in her visions; her prerogative to weep and chide the apostles supported by Kempe's bricolage of the discourses of affective piety and discretio spirituum. She is later in Rome and forsaken by her fellowship because of the "priest who was one of her fellows and one of her countrymen" (Staley I.31.59). He slanders her so that "through his evil language" she is put out of the hospice of Saint Thomas of Canterbury where she was "houseled every Sunday with great weeping, violent sobbing, and loud crying" (Staley I.31.59). In response to this clerical rejection, Margery not only receives permission from a priest who could not understand English to say confession to him and receive communion, but she has a vision, she sees and hears in her "ghostly understanding," in which the Lord sends Saint John the Evangelist to hear her confession and grant her penance (Staley I.32.59). The effect of receiving a sacrament through a vision is not only to obviate any need for the clergy at all, but also to claim through revelation access to a higher authority than the clergy. Although both the bishop of Lincoln and the archbishop of Canterbury fail to give Margery permission to wear white clothes (Staley I.15-16.27-29), and although the German priest, "through the stirring of the English priest who was her enemy", asks her to obey him by wearing black clothes, Margery eventually asserts the authority of her revelations again when she obeys the commandment of "our Lord Jesus Christ" and bids her "ghostly father, Wenslawe by name" to "give her leave to wear again her white clothes. And, when she told him the will of our Lord, he dared not once say no. And she wore white clothes ever after" (Staley I.34-37.62-67). Margery repeatedly circumvents the clergy through Kempe's unorthodox juxtaposition of Margery's ghostly understanding – the *discretio spirituum* – and the ghostly hierarchy of sainthood that authorizes Margery.

But there is also and at the same time within Kempe's visionary bricolage the parody that Baudrillard ascribes to hyperreality by the "anticipation and immanence of the code" in her visions.[45] After she chides the apostles, Margery prays that she may die soon because it is so painful for her to attend both Christ's death and Mary's death. In answering her, Mary confirms that Margery has received plenary remission for her sins. The parody is in this reward given to Margery, a reward which is anticipated and immanent in the code of her vision, but which is given to a visionary neither meek nor humble, a visionary who effaces the apostles. The vision of Saint John the Evangelist hearing her confession parodies clerical authority in its excessiveness: she appeals to an über-clergy in the form of an apostle to go over the head of her enemy, in a critique of the latter's assertion of authority. In the revelations that authorize her wearing of white clothes, a wardrobe considered confrontational, there is the parody of male clerics so intent and yet impotent to control even the most superficial aspects of female behavior, female dress. Specifically, since Wenslawe speaks no English, Kempe parodies the effectiveness of earthly ecclesiopolitical speech.

The visionary reality Kempe generates through Margery also exceeds the medieval visionary paradigm by employing a discourse that Paul Strohm calls the "oppositional imagination," a discourse often identified with the Lollards. As described by Strohm, the oppositional imagination functions as a "political unconscious", and it "produces an unending stream of representations alternative to every established and agreed-upon signification".[46] As Shklar notes, Kempe skillfully deploys "what was by 1436, when the first part of the *Book* was written in its final form, a long history of Lollard controversy" and responds to the "complex gendering of Lollardy" as a central aspect of Margery's self-presentation as "a female mystic and reformer".[47] Both female preaching and criticism of the clergy were elements of the oppositional imagination by 1436 in this book written after the "initially savage repression and a longer-term process of intimidation" against secular and religious heterodoxy initiated by the Oldcastle Rebellion of 1410.[48] The first four prohibitions of Arundel's *Constitutions* of 1409 specifically target and outlaw unlicensed lay preaching. William Sawtry, the first victim of the conflation of ecclesiastical and secular authority under Henry V reflected in the *De Haeretico comburendo* of 1401, was for a time before 1399 Kempe's parish priest.[49] In addition, the manuscripts of the Norwich heresy trials, 1428-31, "gives the impression that Lollardy was well established in at least parts of East Anglia immediately before the trials".[50] And of course, and more significantly, Kempe tells us that she is familiar with the language of the oppositional imagination through Margery's encounters with clerical authorities who accuse her of Lollardy and heresy and with secular authorities who identify her as Cobham's (Oldcastle's) daughter, that is, the metaphorical offspring of a rebel (95-100).

In Kempe's fashioning of Margery's revelation following her confrontation with the famous friar, she demonstrates that the oppositional imagination has not only not been quelled, but also now is generated as hyperreality in Margery's visions and revelations. After telling Margery that any clerk who preaches against her life is the "devil's clerk", Christ says to her that he will chastise those who "grudge and have great pain to suffer the grace that I show to you" (Staley I.64.117). Margery responds by saying that since Christ says that all men will be saved, that she "must also will the same" (Staley I.64.117). Christ answers her by saying that those who are damned are "well worthy" to be damned, the implication being that he has damned the devil's clerk, the famous friar, to hell himself (Staley I.65.117). In this revelation, Kempe employs elements of the oppositional imagination that appear in legal documents surviving from Margery Baxter's heresy trial at Norwich. According to the deposition of

Joan Clyford, Baxter said that "Thomas of Canterbury that people call Saint Thomas of Canterbury was a false traitor and is damned in hell because he . . . promoted and encouraged many heresies in the Church which deceive the simple people." Likewise, "the cursed pope, cardinals, archbishops, bishops, and particularly the bishop of Norwich, and others who uphold and sustain heresies and idolatries, ruling generally over the people, shall have within a short time the same or worse punishment."[51] Clyford's deposition would have been structured in response to the tenets of heterodoxy as identified by clerical authority in the questionnaire used during depositions, not necessarily by what would have been considered heterodox by the witnesses.[52] The damnation of the clergy occupies paragraphs four and five of Clyford's deposition, indicating its place as a heretical belief subordinate only to refusing to take oaths, veneration of images, and disbelief in transubstantiation.[53] Anti-clericalism in the form of criticism of the clergy was considered an aspect of anti-sacerdotalism and, thus, heretical.[54] For example, in the deposition of Hawisia Moone, condemnation of the clergy occupies the sixth and seventh paragraph of the deposition, following several paragraphs that establish as heretical disbelief in the sacraments as mediated by the clergy.[55] Within the utopian elements of the oppositional imagination was an unmediated relationship with God. Kempe uses this utopian element of the oppositional imagination to curse a clerical member who seeks to interrupt that relationship, who offers her, in exchange for the holiness of her weeping as granted by God, his praying for her sickness.

In this extended dialogue with Christ, Kempe also demonstrates that the medical model of Margery's sickness is a political model that seeks to silence female weeping as a form of female preaching. The damnation of the cleric is linked to prohibitions on female preaching in the words of Christ that follows, in which Christ says to Margery, "Daughter, I sent once Saint Paul unto you to strengthen you and comfort you so that you should boldly speak in my name from that day forward. And Saint Paul said unto you that you had suffered much tribulation because of his writing, and he promised you that you should have as much grace in return for his love as ever you had shame or reproof for his love" (Staley I.65.118). Margery's loud crying and roaring have been silenced as a form of female preaching of the love of God because they are only evidence of a disease. Margery's noise making, her speaking and weeping, are linked throughout the book. In chapter 27, when her pilgrimage fellowship complains to the legate, the latter says "As for her weeping, it is not in my power to restrain it, for it is the gift of the Holy Ghost. As for her speaking, I will ask her to cease until she comes where men will hear her with a better will than you do" (Staley I.27.47). In chapter 40, they are again associated when the German priest miraculously understands her story of Holy Writ told in English: "So blessed may God be that made an alien to understand her when her own countrymen had forsaken her and would not hear her confession unless she would have left her weeping and speaking of holiness" (Staley I.40.71). In this revelation, thus, not only does Margery accrue grace through the tribulations she suffers because of Saint Paul's writings, but Kempe also inserts into the narrative further authorization for Margery to speak and weep boldly just at those times when she has been silenced most profoundly.

Kempe also, in this passage, through explicit reference to Saint Paul, refers the audience back to Margery's conflict with other clerics, the archbishop of York and his clerks, an episode in which Kempe again skillfully uses the discourse of the oppositional imagination through bricolage. When the archbishop requires her to swear that 'you shall neither teach nor challenge the people in my diocese', Margery refuses to comply by citing a gospel story and by drawing a distinction between preaching and speaking of God (Staley I.52.93). "'A, sir,' said the clerks, 'here we know well that she has a devil within her, for she speaks of the gospel.'" Immediately a great clerk brought forth a book and laid Saint Paul for his part against her that no woman should preach' (Staley I.52.93). Margery then responds by drawing a distinction between preaching in a pulpit, which she does not do, and simply 'communication and good words,' which she asserts she will continue to do (Staley I.52.93). The problem with her speaking seems to be not only that she speaks of the gospel, though, but that she also speaks poorly of priests. One of the clerics, a doctor of divinity, says to the archbishop, "'Sir, she told me the worst tales of priests that ever I heard'" (Staley I.52.93). The archbishop, of course, wants to hear the tale, and Kempe thereby inserts in the episode a tale that disparages priests in the form of Margery merely complying with the request of the archbishop. In Margery's story, a "wayward" priest who, resting one night in a fair garden with a pear tree in bloom, beholds a bear, "great and violent, ugly to behold, shaking the pear tree and knocking down the flowers". The beast "greedily devours" the flowers and, after he eats them, "turning his tail end in the priest's presence, void[s] them out again at the shameful part" (Staley I.52.93). Although the archbishop says he is satisfied by Margery's subsequent exegesis of the tale, which includes her identification of the priest with the pear tree and the bear, the exegesis evokes not only the damnation of clerics in the heresy trials, but also Clyford's specific accusation that Baxter blasphemed communion by stating, "if every sacrament is God and the true body of Christ, there are numerous gods, because a thousand and more priests made a thousand such gods and afterwards eat these gods and, having eaten them, discharge them through their posteriors into foul smelling privies, where you can find plenty of such gods if you want to look".[56]

Kempe appropriates and improvises upon the oppositional imagery of many white things (tree blossoms, hosts) being eaten by a priest/bear and discharged through the posterior. By placing this story in the mouth of Margery, a woman whose "incorporation into the body of Christ", in communion and otherwise, "is the very height of spiritual attainment",[57] Kempe locates the clergy's attempt to silence Margery in the realm of the profane. In addition, by claiming archbishopric approval of Margery's tale, Kempe seeks to convince the audience that the archbishop would not have understood this parody (the story of the bear) of a parody (oppositional imagery of communion). Thus, the authorities are portrayed as dimwitted, a critique of ecclesiopolitical authority that underlies both this episode and the narrative evocation of this incident in Margery's protracted dialogue with Christ. In this dialogue Kempe also emphasizes the intellectual grace Christ gives to Margery following her conversion, the "grace enough to answer every clerk in the love of God" (Staley 14), an intellectual grace that confounds the intellectual control/agency binary forced upon her by the famous friar.

By confounding this binary, Kempe insists that Margery be read as a mediator for supernatural forces. The friar eventually agrees with this interpretation of Margery, but then insists that she is a mediator for an evil supernatural force. After Margery begins to redeem herself within her community by the weather miracle she performs when the parish church is burning, her place within the community secure for the moment, 'a good friend of the said creature met with the friar who had preached so sorely against her and asked how he thought of her. The friar, answering sharply against her, said, "She has a devil within her," nothing moved from his opinion, but rather defending his error" (Staley I.67.121). By "defending his error," Kempe now casts the friar in the position of a heretic. Rather than turn his condemnation to another bodily illness, such as the 'the falling evil,' [epilepsy] or turning to the medieval counterparts to psychiatric illness, "the elf take" and "woodnesse" [madness],[58] the friar resorts to a variation of the "evil spirit" explanation. Significantly, although contemporary teratical criticism frequently ascribes various psychiatric/mental disorders to Margery, Margery's contemporaries never place her in such a category. Rather, the friar and the people who accuse Margery of vexation by an evil spirit are diagnosing Margery with an illness that partakes of medical/physical and religious/spiritual elements, using a medieval discourse of illness more fluid than contemporary biological determinism.

In medieval discourse, the bodily spirit partook of the physical constitution of the body through the humoural theory and provided the link by which the mind communicated with the bodily organs; "disordered reason" was treated as though it were a purely physical function for doctors while philosophers insisted that reason, ordered or disordered, was outside medical control.[59] The narrative's repeated references to Margery's weeping as being the result of vexation by an evil spirit carries both medical and philosophical/religious connotations because the spirit/mind was not necessarily identified with the brain. The occasional identification of Margery's weeping with the falling evil supports this interpretation. In the falling evil, or epilepsy, the person may see or hear things not there, a disturbance due to a failure of the spirit to properly mediate between the body and soul.[60] In one sense, all visions are spiritual, the result of mediation by the spirit between body and soul. In another sense, visions are spiritual in that the spirit of the visionary person is seized by either a good spirit or bad spirit to produce the visions. As Augustine writes, "But when a good spirit seizes or ravishes the spirit of a man to direct it to an extraordinary vision, there can be no doubt that the images are signs of other things which are useful to know, for this is a gift of God".[61] Thus, when the friar accuses Margery of having a devil within her, he moves to the far end of the medieval body/mind spectrum, from indigestion to possession.

The friar uses his position of authority to recast the terms of the debate, which Kempe responds to with the discourse of the imitatio Magdalenae, a discourse with demoniacs as a central concern. Her most elaborate use of this discourse follows her final conflict with the famous friar. Margery, in spite of her weather miracle, and in spite of ceasing her weeping while present at the famous friar's sermons, continues to assert her holiness because, as Kempe notes, "there was never a clerk who preached openly against her crying but the Gray Friar" (Staley I.69.123). After recounting, in chapter 68, numerous incidents involving clergy who did not exclude Margery when she wept, the narrative turns to two specific clergy who, in accordance Christ's promise to Margery that "he should ever provide for her", take up Margery's part against the famous friar:

> So our Lord … made them mighty and bold to speak for his part in excusing the said creature, both in pulpit and, in addition, wherever they heard anything moved against her, strengthening their arguments by Holy Scripture sufficiently, of which clerks one was a White Friar, a doctor of

> divinity. The other clerk was a bachelor of canon law, a well-labored man in scripture. (Staley I.69.123)

In this continuing war of authority with the famous friar, bolstered on Margery's part by the learning of her champions, Margery loses yet again: "And then some envious persons complained to the Provincial of the White Friars that the said doctor was too conversant with the said creature, forasmuch as he supported her in her weeping and in her crying and also informed her in questions of Scripture when she would ask him any" (Staley I.69.123). The provincial forbids the White Friar to speak to Margery again. The connection between the famous friar and the "envious persons" is clear: in supporting Margery, the two clergy members openly oppose the famous friar. The hegemony responds by separating Margery from her most authoritative supporter, the doctor of divinity. The other clerk also charges her not to "ask him questions as she had done before" (Staley I.69.123). Margery is thus isolated from open clerical authorization as a Holy Woman. Although Kempe ultimately asserts Margery's authority in eventually eating with the White Friar again, which is also a fulfillment of her prophecy, the narrative returns with a rebuttal to the famous friar most powerfully in Margery's vision of Mary Magdalene.

With this vision, Kempe provides an alternative reading to the famous friar's pathologization of Margery by skillfully employing the discourse of *imitatio Magdalenae*. In the Making of the Magdalene: Preaching and Popular Devotion in the Late Middle Ages, Katherine Ludwig Jansen describes the rise in the late middle ages of a form of affective piety more humble than the *imitatio Christi*, the *imitatio Magdalenae*, a rise she attributes to the increase in popular penitential devotion following the Fourth Lateran Council of 1215.[62] As she notes, "affective piety was above all emotional piety, and of that there was no greater example than Mary Magdalene".[63] In the *imitatio Magdalenae*, the "devotee, rather than take on the wounds of Christ himself, instead, through deep compassion, partook of the Magdalene's grief, sorrow, and emotional suffering at the foot of the cross".[64] In medieval England, Mary Magdalene "became a popular saint for the dedications of hospitals" because she was "linked to healing through the episodes of anointing [and] her special place at the resurrection".[65] Sixth-three hospitals were dedicated to Mary Magdalene in England, including one foundation established in the twelfth century at Lynn.[66] As Jansen explains, in the sixth century, Pope Gregory the Great preached a homily in which he converged three Marys from the New Testament into one saint: the female sinner who washes Jesus's feet with her hair; Mary, sister of Martha, "at whose beckoning Jesus raised Lazarus from the dead"; and the demonically possessed Mary Magdalene whom

Jesus healed of seven demons and who then became his devoted disciple.[67] Mary Magdalene became the "exemplar of hope and repentance", the "apostle of the apostles" who, following the Pentecost, received a mission to preach.[68]

As represented in *The Digby Mary Magdalene*, a non-cycle play composed in East Anglia "probably late in the fifteenth century,"[69] Mary is of an affluent family, becomes corrupted through exposure to tavern life, is healed by Christ's exorcism of her seven demons, persuades Christ to bring her brother Lazarus back to life, is present at the crucifixion and the resurrection, converts the pagan "land of Marcyll" through preaching, performs a miracle, goes out into the wilderness, and then dies after receiving confession and communion from a hermit. The formerly affluent, weeping penitent is linked to female preaching and the spiritual grace of speaking in tongues:

> Of alle maner tonggys he yaf us knowing
> For to understond every langwage
> Now have the dysypyllys take ther passage
> To dyvers contryes her[e] and yondyr
> To prech and teche of hys hye damage [the Passion].[70]

Following this assertion of preaching and teaching, the play turns to Jesus, who shows himself in heaven and who, in the course of vesting Mary Magdalene with the mission of converting the pagans, praises his mother Mary who is "the muske ayens the heryts of vyolens / the jentyll jelopher ayns the cardyakyllys wrech".[71] As the medicine against heart spasms and pain, Mary Magdalene is positioned in a complex discursive relationship with Margery as her healed weeping rival, the woman who according to the gospels saw the risen Christ before even his own mother.

Kempe employs this discourse in a series of visions she inserts within the narrative following Margery's confrontation with the friar that authorize Margery within the *imitatio Magdalenae*. In the last of these visions, she again uses bricolage to generate a remixed hyperreality that potentially vitiates the reality sanctioned by ecclesiopolitical authority. In this vision, the risen Christ appears to his mother and asks her leave to appear to Mary Magdalene. She consents because Mary Magdalene, like Margery, "has full much sorrow for your absence" (Staley I.81.144). Witnessing "these ghostly sights" causes Margery to "weep, to sob, and to cry full loudly" without measure (Staley I.81.144). She then hears and sees Mary Magdalene weeping at Christ's grave and her encounter with Christ upon his resurrection. In generating this *noli me tangere* scene, though, Margery resists responding obediently as Mary Magdalene does. After

Christ tells Mary Magdalene not to touch him, Margery sees Mary Magdalene complying and going forth "great joy" to announce his resurrection to the apostles. Kempe discontinues Margery's identification with Mary Magdalene at this point:

> "[T]hat was a great marvel to her that Mary rejoiced, for, if our Lord has said to her as he did to Mary, she thought she could never have been merry. That was when she would have kissed his feet, and he said, 'Touch me not.' The creature had such great sorrow and heaviness in that word that ever when she heard it in any sermon, as she did many times, she wept, sorrowed, and cried as if she would have died of the love and desire that she had to be with our Lord" (Staley I.81.144).

In this passage, Margery identifies herself as loving Christ even more than Mary Magdalene, and also being capable of more sorrow than her, but she does so by resisting the place of Mary Magdalene as a woman identified with carnal, deceiving, sensual nature. Further, Kempe employs the discourse of affective piety so that Margery can both resist the authority of his prohibition and use her resistance to produce more sorrow.

Although Mary Magdalene is one of several female saints that Kempe refers to more than once in her book, she is the only saint, aside from Mary, the mother of Jesus herself, who occupies such an extensive narrative position in the visions. The book itself, begun on the day after Mary Magdalene's feast day, signals not only that Margery should be read as a holy woman who is following the *imitatio Magdalenae*, but also that the figure of the Magdalene resonates throughout the narrative. When Christ gives Margery the grace to answer any clerk, he is giving her as a grace the analogue of Mary Magdalene's gift of tongues, both arguably intellectual graces. Both gifts authorize a life of preaching and teaching. Margery's gift of weeping is similarly authorized through identification with the *imitatio Magdalenae*. Within the other many similarities between Margery and Mary Magdalene, such as formerly affluent status and the ability to reclaim the purity of virginity, it is Mary Magdalene's status as an ex-demoniac turned preacher/saint that directs the reader to understand Margery as possessed by the spirit of Christ, not by a devil. This identification seems complete when Kempe has Christ say to Mary Magdalene, following his resurrection, "Yes, Mary, . . . I shall never forsake you, but I shall ever be with you without end" (Staley I.81.144), words that echo the healing language of Christ to Margery when he appears to her during her childbed sickness, "Daughter, why have you forsaken me, and I forsook you never" (Staley I.1.8). As Mary Magdalene was healed of seven demons, indicating a very severe possession, so

Margery was healed of the spirits that disturbed her after her childbirth. Thus, the *imitatio Magdalenae* functions as a source of discursive authority, creatively employed, to self-authorize Margery in her confrontation with the friar's medical model of disability and his social construction of her as possessed.

Conclusion

The friar's social construction of Margery's weeping/crying/falling down, first as a physical disability, "cardiakyl er sum other sekeness", and then as a physical/spiritual disability, possession, foregrounds a central conflict in the sociohistorical setting that Margery resisted and exceeded. This central conflict is one of ecclesiopolitical authority over vernacular lay theologizing (preaching/teaching/weeping) and, arguably, lay spiritual self-healing.[72] Self-healing, for the purposes of Kempe's text, can be understood, in part, as resisting the social construction of an impairment as a disability. It is tempting to make further claims based upon the parallels between demoniacs and female saints in the thirteenth century, including the experience of an "unusual degree of illness".[73] The female demoniacs preaching in the thirteenth century "launched a potentially dangerous and subversive brand of authority in the world", an authority based on illness; the clerisy initially thought they could control the demoniacs. [74] But any such claims would need to consider the origins, nuances, and replication of the moral model of disability, in which an impairment is constructed as a punishment (or grace). Likewise, it is for future scholarship to explore how canonist Jean Gerson, the putative formulator of the *spirituum discretio*, may have produced/outlawed/legitimized an ontology now considered to be disabled.

For the purposes of the claims made in this article, it is enough to show how Kempe skillfully employs the medieval discourse of *discretio spirituum*, the oppositional imagination, and the *imitatio Magdalenae* to counter and to exceed the friar's medical model of Margery as disabled, both reflecting the social tensions of her time (Christ, for example, ordains Margery "to be a mirror" among the people (Staley 136)) and providing an alternative reality to these tensions through her use of visionary bricolage. Kempe uses the lack of control central to the social construction of Margery as impaired as opportunities for agency, which enables Margery to directly protest ecclesiopolitical oppression in the narrative, a narrative that may be occasioned by the oppression she suffers from the famous friar. Finally, Margery resists attempts to control and marginalize her through the alternative reality her visions generate. If the medium is the message, then Margery, as a visionary woman who publicly preaches, teaches, and weeps/cries/falls down, not only contravenes Arundel's first four constitutions and oppressive ecclesiopolitical power, but demonstrates the power of the oppressed to self-authorize their own generation of reality. Such a power, contingent upon historically specific discourses and formations of power, contributes a new model of disability to Disability Studies: a self-authorizing or jurisdictional model, in which inherent in the social construction of disability is the power of the disabled to determine whether a disability exists and how that disability is defined: in Kempe's words, to assert "it was no sekenes" and then explicate a profoundly multi-dimensional ontology. Although today we may lack the richness of discourse to render disability as inherently self-discerning, *The Book of Margery Kempe* helps us begin to recognize people constructed as disabled, even those deemed to possess the least agency, as potentially self-authorizing.

Notes

[1] Lynn Staley (ed), *The Book of Margery Kempe* (Kalamazoo, MI: Medieval Institute, 1996), 146-7. This essay follows Staley's scholarship in drawing a distinction between Margery Kempe as author ("Kempe") and Margery Kempe as character ("Margery"). Subsequent references to Kempe will be in parentheses and, except when otherwise noted, refer to Staley's 2001 translation.

[2] Kelly Parsons, "The Red Ink Annotator of The Book of Margery Kempe and His Lay Audience," in *The Medieval Professional Reader at Work: Evidence from the Manuscripts of Chaucer, Langland, Kempe, and Gower*, eds Kathryn-Kerby-Fulton and Maidie Hilmo (Victoria, BC: University of Victoria, 2001), 29

[3] Lennard J. Davis, *Bending Over Backwards: Disability, Dismodernism & Other Difficult Positions* (New York, New York University Press, 2001), 23.

[4] Davis, 32.

[5] Davis, 39.

[6] Nancy P. Stork, "Did Margery Kempe Suffer from Tourette's Syndrome," *Mediæval Studies* 59 (1997), 264.

[7] Stork, 263.

[8] Mary Hardiman Farley, "Her Own Creature: Religion, Feminist Criticism, and the Functional Eccentricity of Margery Kempe," *Exemplaria* 11, no. 1 (1999), 1.

[9] Richard Lawes, "Psychological Disorder and the Autobiographical Impulse in Julian of Norwich, Margery Kempe, and Thomas Hoccleve," in *Writing Religious Women: Female Spiritual and Textual Practices in Late Medieval England*, eds. Denis Renevey and Christiana Whitehead (Toronto: University of Toronto Press, 2000), 279-80.

[10] Gail McMurray Gibson, *The Theatre of Devotion: East Anglian Drama and Society in the Late Middle Ages* (Chicago: University of Chicago Press, 1989), 64-5.
[11] David T. Mitchell and Sharon L. Snyder, "Representation and Its Discontents: The Uneasy Home of Disability in Literature and Film, in *Handbook of Disability Studies*, eds. Gary L. Albrecht, Katherine D. Seelman, and Michael Bury (Thousand Oaks, CA: Sage, 2001), 198; Davis, 180 n. 33.
[12] Judith Butler, *Bodies That Matter: On The Discursive Limits of "Sex"* (New York: Routledge, 1993), 1-16.
[13] Farley, 2.
[14] David Aers, *Community, Gender, and Individual Identity: English Writing, 1360-1430* (London: Routledge, 1988), 52.
[15] Farley, 4.
[16] Lynn Staley, *Margery Kempe's Dissenting Fictions* (University Park, PA: Pennsylvania State University Press, 1994), 3.
[17] Ruth Shklar, "Cobham's Daughter: The Book of Margery Kempe and the Power of Heterodox Thinking," *Modern Language Quarterly* 56, no. 3 (1995), 278.
[18] Shklar, 278.
[19] Shklar, 279.
[20] Shklar, 284.
[21] Darrel W. Amundsen, "Medieval Canon Law on Medical and Surgical Practice by the Clergy," *Bulletin of the History of Medicine* 52 (1978), 23.
[22] Janet Wilson, "Communities of Dissent: The Secular and Ecclesiastical Communities of Margery Kempe's Book," in *Medieval Women in their Communities*, ed. Diane Watt (Toronto: Toronto University Press, 1997), 161 n.30.
[23] Michael Oliver, *The Politics of Disablement* (Basingstoke, UK: Palgrave Macmillan, 1990), 1-11.
[24] George Henslow, *Medical Works of the Fourteenth Century* (London: Chapman and Hall, 1899; New York: Burton Franklin, 1972), 67.
[25] Henslow, 67, 134.
[26] Rosalynn Voaden, *God's Words, Women's Voices: The Discernment of Spirits in the Writing of Late-Medieval Women Visionaries* (Woodbridge, UK: York Medieval Press, 1999), 15-6.
[27] Voaden, 19.
[28] Voaden, 19.
[29] Voaden, 17.
[30] Voaden, 49-50.
[31] Voaden, 48-9.
[32] Karen A. Winstead, "Introduction", in *The Life of Saint Katherine by John Capgrave*, ed. Karen A. Winstead (Kalamazoo, MI: Medieval Institute Publications, 1999), 1-5.
[33] Voaden, 117.
[34] Dick Hebdige, "Subculture: The Meaning of Style," in *Literary Theory: An Anthology*, eds. Julie Rivkin and Michael Ryan (Oxford, UK: Blackwell, 1998), 1070.

[35] Sarah Beckwith, *Christ's Body: Identity, Culture and Society in Late Medieval Writings* (London: Routledge, 1993), 97.
[36] Voaden, 123 n. 45.
[37] Hebdige, 1071.
[38] Anthony Goodman, "The Piety of John Brunham's Daughter, of Lynn," in *Medieval Women*, ed. Derek Baker (Oxford, UK: Basil Blackwell, 1978), 349.
[39] Voaden, 123 n. 45.
[40] Wilson, 156.
[41] Wilson, 154.
[42] Beckwith, 20.
[43] Ruth E. Harvey, *The Inward Wits: Psychological Theory in the Middle Ages and the Renaissance* (London: Warburg Institute, University of London, 1975), 43.
[44] Paul Strohm, *England's Empty Throne: Usurpation and the Language of Legitimation, 1399-1422* (New Haven, CT: Yale University Press, 1998), 27.
[45] Jean Baudrillard, "Symbolic Exchange and Death," in *Literary Theory: An Anthology*, ed. Julie Rivkin and Michael Ryan (Oxford, UK: Blackwell, 1998), 500.
[46] Strohm, 32.
[47] Shklar, 280.
[48] Strohm, 67; Shklar, 290-91.
[49] Strohm, 43; Shklar, 280 n. 9.
[50] Norman P. Tanner, "Introduction," in *Heresy Trials in the Diocese of Norwich, 1428-31*, ed. Norman P. Tanner (London: Offices of the Royal Historical Society, 1977), 29.
[51] Tanner, *Heresy Trials*, 292.
[52] Tanner, "Introduction," 20; Strohm, 48-9.
[53] Tanner, *Heresy Trials*, 291-2.
[54] Tanner, "Introduction," 21.
[55] Tanner, *Heresy Trials*, 140-41.
[56] Tanner, *Heresy Trials*, 292.
[57] Beckwith, 25.
[58] Henslow, 89.
[59] Harvey, 8.
[60] Harvey, 43
[61] Qtd. In Voaden, 46.
[62] Katherine Ludwig Jansen, *The Making of the Magdalen: Preaching and Popular Devotion in the Later Middle Ages* (Princeton, NJ: Princeton University Press, 2000), 15.
[63] Jansen, 92.
[64] Jansen, 92.
[65] Jansen, 111.
[66] Jansen, 111, n. 37.
[67] Jansen, 33.
[68] Jansen, 35, 81.

[69] John C. Coldewey, "Introduction to *The Digby Mary Magdalene*," in *Early English Drama: An Anthology*, ed. John C. Coldewey (New York: Garland, 1993), 186.

[70] *Digby Magdalene*, 1343-47 (Coldewey, ed.)

[71] *Digby Magdalene*, 1352-63

[72] Nicholas Watson, "Censorship and Cultural Change in Late-Medieval England: Vernacular Theology, the Oxford Translation Debate, and Arundel's Constitutions of 1409," in *Speculum* 70, no. 4 (Oct. 1995), 824-25.

[73] Barbara Newman, "Possessed by the Spirit: Devout Women, Demoniacs, and the Apostolic Life in the Thirteenth Century," in *Speculum* 73, no. 3 (July 1998), 750.

[74] Newman, 769.

ILLNESS AND AUTHORITY: THE CASE OF FRANCIS OF ASSISI

DONNA TREMBINSKI

While many scholars of Francis of Assisi would acknowledge that his early hagiographers emphasized the saint's suffering, and that such suffering on the part of the saint helped to introduce the practice of affective experiential piety to medieval Europe, few have fully explored the role that Francis' infirmities played in his position as the founder of a new mendicant order and the leader of a reform movement within the Catholic Church. Francis' authority in his capacity of a reformer, when discussed at all, is most often discussed in terms of informal authority based upon his suffering as *imitatio Christi* and his mystical visions of God's will. Indeed, as Caroline Walker Bynum has suggested, the suffering Francis experienced as a result of his asceticism and his disabilities demonstrated his nearness to Christ and Christ's corporeal experience and created a foundation from which Francis exerted a mystically-driven, informal authority. She further argued that Francis' model of using illness and disability to access authority was employed much more often, and effectively, by women who challenged a Catholic hierarchy that denied them formal authority.[1] Francis, however, was not a woman and he was not automatically excluded from traditional avenues of authority within the church (though his own writings and that of his hagiographers suggest that he did often eschew them).[2] He was the founder of a mendicant order whose membership within his own lifetime numbered in the thousands. Until his resignation, which occurred some time before 1221, he was the leader of that order,[3] though tradition (and much historiography) suggests that he did not always feel confident in his ability to lead. In this context, the focus on Francis' disabilities and suffering as a way of accessing informal authority seems out of place. Yet, as the earliest witnesses to Francis' extraordinary life attest, a great tension existed between a debilitated, suffering Francis and the saint's role as an official authority figure within the order. Indeed, as an exploration of early hagiography of St. Francis will demonstrate, the very source of Francis' informal mystical authority, his suffering and illnesses, was problematic for his expression of formal authority and perhaps ultimately resulted in Francis' withdrawal from such a position.

It is, of course, well known that Francis resigned his leadership position in Franciscan order sometime before 1221, turning that duty over first to Peter Catani and upon Peter's death, to Elias of Cortona. It has long been argued that Francis' decision to resign was prompted both by his desire to lead a humble life and by his own recognition that he was not able to lead an order the size of the Franciscan order, even as early as 1217.[4] This conjecture may in part be based upon the reality that Bonaventure's official lives of Saint Francis, the *Legenda maior* and the *Legenda minor,* both written circa 1263 and officially adopted as the official *vitae* of Francis at the order's general chapter in 1266[5] contain no reference to the saint's growing disabilities interfering with his ability and even his legal right to lead his order. Yet, as an examination of earlier *vitae* of Francis and contemporary canon law collections demonstrates, while Francis and his early biographers clearly believed that his disabilities greatly aided his personal spiritual growth, they also obliquely attest that his infirmities undermined his ability to lead his order effectively. Moreover, early Franciscan hagiography of the saint reveals a clear tension between the wishes of Francis not to have his infirmities treated in any way, and those of his superiors within the order and of the ecclesiastical hierarchy to ensure that Francis sought out medical attention.

The dating and relative reliability of early hagiographies of St. Francis have been debated since Paul Sabatier published his *Life of Saint Francis of Assisi* more than a century ago.[6] The so-called 'Franciscan question' still has no definitive resolution, but there is current scholarly consensus concerning the relative dating and authority of the various texts.[7] The earliest known *vita* of Saint Francis was written by an acquaintance of the saint, Thomas of Celano. It was completed soon after the death of Francis, circa 1228, probably with the express purpose of promoting the status of Francis' cult.[8] Thomas wrote a different *vita* nearly 20 years later, completing what is now referred to as the *Vita secunda* before the summer of 1247.[9] By this time, a number of other *vitae* had been written. Henry d'Avranches' *Legenda versificata* was written perhaps as early as 1230[10] and Julian of Speyer's *life,* based on the *Vita prima* of Thomas of Celano was composed circa 1235.[11] The manuscript tradition of sources then becomes more complicated. The *Umbrian Choir legend,* most recently attributed to Thomas of Celano as well, was written between 1237 and 1244, just before the then minister-general of the order, Cresentius of Iesi, requested that still-living members of the order who had personal remembrances of Francis record them for posterity.[12] This resulted in two texts that have survived to the present day. The *Legend of Three Companions,* said to have been written by three of Francis' earliest companions, Leo, Angelo and Rufino was largely completed between 1241 and 1247[13] and was based, in part, on the earlier *Umbrian Choir Legend.*[14] A second collection of personal reminiscences about the saint was likely collected between 1244 and 1260. It is quite clear that this collection, now called the *Assisi Compilation,* includes very personal and very intimate recollections of the saint.[15] Perhaps in an effort to control the various legends and stories that were circulating about saint Francis, a request was made at the Franciscan General Chapter of 1260 for the creation of an official life of Francis.[16] The new minister-general of the order, Bonaventure of Bagnoregio wrote two lives in response to this request, the *Legenda maior* and the *Legenda minor,* which were completed in time for the general chapter of 1263.[17] In 1266, the order decided to adopt Bonaventure's *legendae* as the official versions of Francis' life and ordered all other *vitae* removed from their houses and, if possible, the houses of other orders.[18] While Thomas of Celano's *vitae* of Francis are early and Bonaventure's are those the order chose to adopt, most historians recognize that amongst the most important witnesses to the historical Francis are the recollections found in the *Anonymous of Perugia*[19] *Legend of the Three Companions*[20] and the older portions of the *Assisi Compilation.*[21]

Based upon these early *lives* of Francis, it is possible to glean a somewhat coherent account of Francis' medical history.[22] Born circa 1182,[23] Francis was the son of a relatively wealthy fabric merchant. He lived a comfortable life until his conversion to devout Christianity, a conversion that culminated in his famous rejection of his father's patrimony before the bishop of Assisi.[24] Even in his youth, Francis seemed to experience periods of ill health,[25] however, during the last ten years of his life, Francis' developed seriously debilitating disabilities.For much of his life the saint suffered several fevers and other unnamed illnesses.[26] By 1220, Francis' eyes had begun to cause him constant pain and he was experiencing a decline in his visual acuity, a problem for which he would eventually be ordered to seek medical help on perhaps as many as three occasions.[27] In 1224, the saint, in meditation and prayer on Mount Alverna, saw a vision of a crucified seraph and received the stigmata, the wounds of Christ. According to early hagiographies, Francis kept these wounds a secret from all but his closest friends, but they caused him a great deal of pain.[28] By the time of his death in 1226, Francis was almost totally blind, unable to walk due to his various infirmities and suffering mightily from illness and the effects of carrying the stigmata.[29]

There has been some debate about what, precisely, caused the deterioration of Francis' health so that by his mid-forties he was so debilitated that he was almost blind and at times was so weak that he could not walk. No doubt the saint's extremely ascetic lifestyle contributed to his developing infirmities, but many other, more medically oriented suggestions have been put forward to explain them. For instance, Francis' eye pain and blindness have been variously attributed to glaucoma, iritus, trachoma and corneal ulcers.[30] The recurring fevers and weakness Francis experienced as symptoms have been diagnosed variously as malaria, dropsy, and tuberculoid leprosy.[31] Whatever the proper diagnosis for Francis' various ailments and infirmities, the reality appears to have been that by the 1220s at the latest, it is likely that Francis was in no condition to govern an order whose members, even then, numbered in the thousands. Though it is most often presented in Franciscan hagiography as Francis' personal decision to step down from his position of leadership in the order, in fact, canon law of the early thirteenth century dictated that this should occur, given the severity of his infirmities. In spite of canon law that required all ill and disabled prelates to step down from their positions of authority, the Francis of early hagiography was reluctant to seek out secular cures for his ailments unless explicitly ordered to do so.

Francis' seeming ambivalence about secular medical treatment reflects the uneasy relationship between the practice of medicine and ecclesiastical doctrine and law in the Middle Ages. As Judith Perkins has argued, since the beginning of Christianity, Christian identity has been fundamentally linked with the suffering self.[32] Naturally, this led to some difficulties in assessing whether or not a Christian should seek medical intervention for illnesses and disabilities. On the one hand, God was the author of all things, including any infirmities experienced. Moreover, suffering was regarded as redemptive, so seeking out medical therapies to diminish suffering from infirmities could be regarded as counterproductive to salvation. On the other hand, from the second century forward, some Christian thinkers have presented Christ as a healer, and medicine, like the ailments themselves, could be considered a gift from God.[33] Thus, from the patristic period to the High Middle Ages, ecclesiastical opinion was divided on the suitability of Christians consulting physicians. Vincent of Beauvais' massive encyclopedia, the *Speculum maius* demonstrates the lack of consensus perfectly. His question entitled "how the counsel of doctors is to be used" in the *Speculum naturale* cites four authorities for consulting physicians, four against and one opinion that is ambivalent.[34] In canon law, it was not until the Fourth Lateran Council of 1215 that the question of how a Christian should seek medical advice was addressed, and it comes in the form of an admonition to physicians who should ensure that a patient see a "physician of the soul", that is a priest, before applying a secular medical cure as "corporeal infirmity is sometimes caused by sin".[35] It should be noted that this canon seems to expect that individuals will seek out medical attention when in need, though this is not particularly advocated. Rather, the goal of that canon is to ensure spiritual health is the first priority for both patient and physician.

Codified collections of canon law also suggested uncertainly about how Christians, especially ill or infirm religious, should treat their illnesses. Perhaps the most well known of these codifications is Gratian's *Decretum*, completed circa 1145 and used as a textbook in the law school developing at Bologna almost since its completion.[36] Gratian's work does not discuss the whether Christians should or should not seek medical advice, nor does it directly question the suitability of an ill individual as a leader for a religious order. Rather, the question he posed was whether ill or infirm[37] bishops should be replaced. Based upon a letter written by Pope Gregory I,[38] Gratian states that while a bishop can never be replaced while he is still alive, regardless of how sick or unable to perform his duties he might be, a steward can be appointed to do his duties in his stead.[39] Gratian expands upon the necessity of such stewards in chapter three of the same question, suggesting that while sick or infirm clerics ought not to lose their benefices and thus their sources of income, a steward should be appointed to ensure that their duties to the community and the church are fulfilled.[40] Although the ecclesiastical law laid out in Gratian's work does not refer specifically to a situation such as Francis', one could expect that rather than step down, he would have been asked to choose a suitable stand-in as a leader for the order.

Gratian's *Decretum* was never officially adopted by the church as a definitive statement of its laws, however it did become a useful tool in the training of lawyers of canon law. Used as a teaching tool, masters of law produced commentaries on the text as they lectured about it. One of the earliest of these commentaries was *Summa parisiensis*, written circa 1160 by an unknown Italian master teaching in or near Paris.[41] The *Summa parisiensis* largely echoes the position of Gratian on the issue of how ill clerics should be replaced by a steward and should not lose their income. However, he cites one exception to this rule: a bishop who is ill with leprosy should not retain his episcopacy. This, he explains, is a parallel application of canon law that prohibits those diagnosed with leprosy from living with their spouses.[42] In some communities, lepers were regarded by those around them as 'dead to this world', a position with which the anonymous author of the *Summa parisiensis* would seem to agree.[43] Had thirteenth-century physicians diagnosed Francis' various ailments the way some modern scholars do, as tubercular leprosy, the commentary provided by the *Summa parisiensis* would have been critically important. While not a bishop, as the head of the newly-founded order, Francis would have been in a similar position of authority and may have been forced to resign. Yet, none of the testimonial and hagiographic literature at our disposal indicated that Francis was ever diagnosed with leprosy. Rather his various ailments and disabilities were treated as though they had unrelated causes. The reluctance of Francis' physicians to diagnose the saint with leprosy, should he indeed, as Schatzlein and Sulmasy argued, have had leprosy, is unsurprising. During the High Middle Ages, it would have been unthinkable to imagine Francis, the *alter Christus* who lived a life of apostolic poverty, suffering from a disease that had long been associated with sin. More surprising, however, has been the reaction of modern scholars to the possibility that Francis could have been suffering from leprosy. Very few scholars have referenced the work of Schatzlein and Sulmasy, published in 1987, and fewer still have incorporated the possibility that Francis suffered from Hanson's disease in their work.[44]

In spite of his physicians' reluctance to provide a single cause for Francis' growing number of ailments, the symptoms the saint was experiencing, particularly after 1220, would have been enough of an issue for canonists of his own time. While Gratian's *Decretum* was never officially adopted by the Catholic Church, Pope Gregory IX's commissioned another collection of canons, this one written by his chaplain and confessor Raymond of Peñafort, which would overshadow Gratian's work and be accepted and promulgated as law by the church. Gregory's decretals are important both for their content concerning ill clerics, which differ substantially from Gratian's work and because of the close personal connection between Gregory and Francis. Gregory IX began his life as Ugolino of Segni, a member of a wealthy family from northern Italy (Compagnia) and the nephew of Innocent III. After Innocent's election, he was appointed to the position of papal chaplain. As his experience and knowledge grew, he was rewarded with successive posts, the last of which was cardinal-bishop of Ostia in 1206. He also worked as a legate for Innocent's successor, Honorius III. In 1227, when he was perhaps already eighty years old, Ugolino was chosen to be pope. He was, in fact, the pope who oversaw Francis' canonization, yet even before his ascension Ugolino had been a friend to the fledgling Franciscan order.

Ugolino met Francis and some of his followers in Florence around 1217.[45] Moorman suggests that Ugolino, in a position of power and having the pope's ear, was in a good situation to foster the Franciscans, whom he believed would inject new life and devotion into the Catholic Church.[46] By 1218, Ugolino was taking greater control over many aspects of Franciscan organization.[47] When Francis left to preach Christianity to the Muslims, heading for Syria in 1219, Ugolino took charge of the affairs of the order in Europe. In that year, he asked Honorius to ensure that the friars would be welcomed where ever they preached.[48] Against Francis' wishes of absolute poverty not just for the friars but for the order itself, Ugolino also began the process of providing convents for the friars, a step that angered Francis upon his return.[49] When Francis abdicated his position of leadership of his order sometime between 1217 and 1220, both Peter Catani and Elias of Cortona managed the order under the watchful eye of the order's protector. And, most significantly for the purposes of this argument, it was Ugolino who first ensured that Francis received treatment for his worsening vision, a dictate that was seconded by both Peter and Elias.[50]

Given the close connection between Ugolino, the future Pope Gregory IX, and St. Francis, and the interest the former took in both Francis' order and the saint's health, the differences on the subject of ill clerics between Gratian's *Decretum* and the concordance of canons commissioned by Gregory IX are intriguing. Like Gratian's work, Gregory's decretals insist that ailing clerics and bishops should keep their living, even if a steward must take over their duties. It was the church's duty to care for the sick.[51] However, the criteria given for when and why a person should be removed from his ecclesiastical duties are more clearly stated. Quoting another letter of Gregory the Great, the decretal states that churches ought not to be afraid of finding stewards to replace officials, since "if others were to be discouraged by the example of an individual's illness, it would perhaps not be possible to find [those] who are able to fight for the church".[52] Had this law been applied directly to Francis, the saint would have been forced to resign his position at the head of the order, particularly as his blindness and physical weakness sometimes must have made it impossible to do even the simplest of tasks. On the surface of the evidence for Francis' life, however, there is no indication that it was his infirmities that encouraged Francis to resign his leadership role in the latter half of the 1210s. Bonaventure's official *life* of Francis, the *Legenda maior,* suggests that Francis resigned his position and asked for a guardian to ensure his humility.[53] However, a more comprehensive exploration of the early tradition of Franciscan hagiography suggests that his infirmities, and the official ecclesiastical reaction to them, may have played a more important part in Francis' resignation than is generally believed.

Bonaventure's two official *vitae* of St. Francis were in some ways sanitized and fictionalized accounts of Francis' life. Francis was presented as more moderate and more conventional than he had been portrayed in earlier *vitae.*[54] This is certainly clear with respect to Francis' illnesses and disabilities for unlike earlier texts, they are never the focal point of a chapter or story. Nor do his disabilities stop Francis from living a life of profound asceticism according to Bonaventure's *vitae.*[55] When Francis discovered his eye disease, caused in Bonaventure's understanding by his continual weeping, Francis immediately consulted with doctors. Though the doctors tell him he must stop weeping to preserve what his left of his eyesight, Francis turns this advice on its head, suggesting that he would prefer to become blind rather than restrain his tears in prayer.[56] Francis is again urged to seek treatment by his fellow friars (not his superiors), only agreeing to receive treatment in the form of a cauterization on his eyes, because it would allow him to suffer through the very painful treatment and had the added benefit of being good for his health.[57] Generally speaking, discussions of Francis' infirmities are used by Bonaventure as tropes to illustrate the saint's patience, humility and piety. God was, in Bonaventure's words preparing Francis' "soul to join with the anointing of the holy spirit."[58] Even in his final days, when the saint could no longer walk, Bonaventure describes Francis as "fixed on the cross with Christ,"[59] for his disability has been caused not by his increasingly weakened condition as it had been in earlier texts— for Bonaventure it was the result of his stigmata, shaped like nails, growing out of his feet.[60] Thus, unlike earlier versions of Francis' *vitae,* illness and disability take on a lesser priority in Bonaventure's *Legenda maior* and *minor,* most often serving to teach the saint or to demonstrate his complete devotion and obedience to God.

The Franciscan position towards the necessity of secular medical intervention was not always so clear as Bonaventure suggests in his official hagiographies of Saint Francis. Indeed, Francis' earliest rule, the one that did not receive papal approval, includes a passage that urges brothers not to seek medical attention too readily, for that desire to care for the body before the soul, Francis wrote, "comes from evil".[61] Giulia Barone has argued that some *lives* of Saint Francis, perhaps representing an earlier tradition, provide evidence that the earliest Franciscans did not seek medical attention,[62] a possibility that may explain why early candidates for admission to the Franciscan order were questioned extensively about the state of their health, and why some unhealthy friars were refused entry.[63] Yet, this position on seeking medical treatment conflicted with some thirteenth century ecclesiastical opinions and with the opinion of later leaders of the Franciscan Order, in particular, St. Bonaventure.[64] The tension between what appears to be Francis' own view about the intervention of physicians and those of the higher ecclesiastical authorities to which the order and even Francis himself were obedient becomes clearer in the examination of Francis' earliest *vitae* written before Bonaventure's official *lives* were promulgated.

The earliest *vitae* of Francis, written by Thomas of Celano and Julian Speyer just after Francis' death in 1226, describes the disease of his eyes as the first severe ailment Francis experienced. Moreover, they both suggest that the ailment was made worse by the harsh asceticism Francis practiced for most of his life.[65] Though his fellow Franciscans often urged him to seek medical aid for all his infirmities, but especially his eyes, both Thomas and Julian write that Francis thoroughly refused to seek such treatment.[66] Francis finally had to be ordered to seek treatment by Brother Elias, who was by then the leader of the Franciscan Order.[67] This order was reinforced by Ugolino, the protector of the order, who warned Francis not to refuse treatment for his infirmities.[68] Though Thomas and Julian both make reference to the fact that Francis had asked Ugolino to become the protector of the Franciscan order, neither discuss how or why Elias would have been in a position to order Francis to do anything, for the discussion of how Francis abdicated his position of leadership within the order is surprisingly absent from both accounts.

Henri d'Avranches' versified *life* of Saint Francis, again written within a few years of Francis' death, describes Francis' eye disease in more detail than had Julian or Thomas. In his account, it is the saint's optic nerve that pains him and it was the resulting inflammation of his eyelids that caused Francis' vision to deteriorate. According to Henri, the saint scratched and rubbed his eyes causing a secondary infection to occur. In spite of the pain, the loss of vision and the infection, Francis still refused to call on doctors, lest "he seem not to want to suffer these divine lashes".[69] This sounds very much like the saint who wrote in his first rule that friars should not be eager to accept medical help for disabilities and ailments. Yet, as in Thomas of Celano's *Vita prima* and Julian of Speyer's *life* of Francis, Brother Elias was able to encourage the saint to receive medical treatment in the versified *life*.[70] The treatments did not help. Indeed, according to Henri, the saint saw doctor after doctor, none of whom could cure his illness or relieve his pain.[71] In spite of the greater emphasis on Francis' disabilities, and his suffering, there is still no link made between these issues and his changing position within the Franciscan order. Like Thomas and Julian, Henri avoids commenting on Francis' withdrawal from leadership.

It is not until the second generation of material about Saint Francis, written between 1235 and 1247 but considered as, or even more, reliable than the earlier *vitae* because of their reliance on sources who were close to Francis during his life, that the first discussions of Francis' resignation begin to occur. In the *Umbrian Choir Legend,* no direct reference is made to Francis' resignation, but near the end of his life, Francis blesses Elias, saying "you took my burdens on your shoulders and courageously met the needs of your brothers".[72] This surely implies that Francis had left the administration of the order in the hands of Elias.

In the *Legend of the Three Companions,* a new legend about Francis is told, one which was explicitly intended to explain the saint's reasons for his resignation from leadership within his order. Francis saw a vision of a black hen with a dove's feet with so many chicks she was unable to keep them under her wings. Francis interpreted this vision to mean that he would have so many followers that he would not "be able to protect them with his own strength".[73] The legend links this vision with Francis' decision to entrust the order to the church and to Ugolino, cardinal-bishop of Ostia.[74]

While the *Legend of the Three Companions* suggests, albeit in the vaguest of terms, that Francis believed he would be incapable of providing guidance and protection for a large order, the *Assisi Compilation* initially negates that entirely, suggesting that it was, in fact, Francis' humility that allowed him to remove himself from his leadership role. He promised always to obey the minister-general, the provincial generals and any guardian appointed to oversee him.[75] Yet other, perhaps older parts of the *Assisi Compilation*[76] hint at a different possibility. Once when he was asked why he gave up his position as the leader of the order, Francis replied that he wished the brothers would follow his footsteps more, as he believed that some prelates of the order were leading the friars astray. Later, during a bout of illness, the saint woke up and reportedly said, "who are those people who took my religion and my brothers from my hands. If I go to the general chapter, I will show them what I will."[77] This passage has most often been interpreted as showing the concern of some of the original companions of St. Francis that the order was already by the 1240s moving in a direction that was inimical to Francis' vision for his brothers, but should some version of the reported incident have actually occurred, it might also possibly suggest that Francis, at times, felt that his order had been removed from his control, perhaps against his will. In another chapter of the *Assisi Compilation*, a young brother asks Francis why he tolerates brothers who do not follow the saint's example of living in poverty, humility and simplicity. The saint's answer is that in spite of his illness, which he had had since his conversion, when he had the order, he had taught them well by example and through his preaching. When he resigned, Francis said to his brothers that his increasingly severe infirmities meant that he would not be able to care for the brothers any longer as a minister, though he suggests to the friar that had the brothers not already begun to fall away from his example and ideals, he would have felt well enough to lead the order in spite of his failing body.[78] The older portions of the *Assisi Compilation* do discuss Francis' resignation and, in fact, reiterate the link between his stepping down and his infirmities.[79]

As a compilation of the texts and remembrances of St. Francis that had been written and recorded as a result of the minister-general's request in 1243, Thomas of Celano's *Vita secunda* reflects many of the same themes found in the *Legend of the Three Companions* and the *Assisi Compilation.* Francis' vision of himself as a black hen unable to protect all of her chicks under her wings is retold in much the same way it was in the *Legend of the Three Companions,* though Francis states in this version of the tale that his concern is for defending his chicks/friars from those of his own flock who were not fully devoted to Franciscan ideals.[80] The story of Francis' resignation is retold, making reference to both the saint's humility and his infirmities, neither of which allowed him to stay on as minister-general of the order.[81] In comparison to the earlier texts upon which Celano's *Vita secunda* is based, though Thomas decentres Francis' illness again, as it is the focus of the text only for two chapters near the end of the second book. Moreover, Francis' obedience in seeing doctors is not mentioned. Instead, the lesson Thomas teaches in relation to Francis' infirmities is that it is the saint's duty to ensure that he cares for his disabled, infirm body, act as a friend to its needs as it had done in the past by being a friend to his soul's desire for asceticism.[82]

The tensions that play out in the earliest hagiographies of Francis, those written between 1228 and 1263, of course reflect tensions within Franciscan membership about Francis' wishes for the order and about what could be expected of the order as it grew in size and popularity. These conflicts ultimately resulted in a split between the Spirituals and Conventuals. However, with respect to illness and disability, the early hagiographies seem to reflect a different sort of tension, that which existed between Francis' wishes with respect to his position within the order and with respect to how he ought to treat his infirmities, and the wishes of the ecclesiastic administration that supported the Franciscans on the same matters.

Francis' reasons for his resignation as the leader of the Order of Friars Minor ultimately remain unknown. While a surplus of early hagiographies of St. Francis exists, there are very few records of early Franciscan chapters-general or chapters-provincial. No record exists of the chapter at which Francis made his abrupt announcement of resignation. In fact, it is not known for certain in which year the saint resigned[83] and indeed, some early chronicles of Franciscan leadership (though, it should be noted, not the earliest chronicles) suggest that Francis remained minister-general until his death.[84] Moreover the earliest *lives* of Francis did not discuss his resignation at all and those later texts that did describe it cite both Francis' desire to remain humble and his infirmities as a reason for his stepping down. Peter Catani and Elias of Cortona, the first individuals to take Francis' place at the head of the order, are referred to variously as vicars and minister-generals in their own right.[85] Naturally these gaps and differences in the textual record have led to uncertainty about how and why Francis resigned his position. However, the role of Ugolino, later Pope Gregory IX who promulgated Raymond of Peñafort's decretal collection, as protector of the order suggests a possible way to rationalize the evidence. Ugolino became the order's protector at Francis' request circa 1217.[86] From that time, he began to exert greater and greater control over the order. It is not inconceivable that the same man, a canon lawyer himself who, when he became pope, promulgated a collection of law that included new discussions of how ill clerics and prelates should place stewards in their place encouraged Francis to do precisely this. While the evidence is certainly circumstantial, as demonstrated above, Francis is reported to have cited his growing disabilities as one of the reasons for his resignation. Moreover, the role of Peter Catani and Elias of Cortona in the order during Francis' lifetime seems less like that of a minister-general and more like that of a steward. Neither was elected by the order, the common practice for choosing leaders within the order after Francis' death; rather both were chosen by Francis himself, [87] and though Francis called both ministers-general of the order, the papacy, in particular, referred to both as vicars or stewards.[88] This suggests that although Francis may have regarded his removal from leadership as an act of humility that was permanent, others within the ecclesiastical hierarchy and even within the order understood it to be an administrative necessity that created a situation of stewardship, which was, in fact, how Elias and especially Peter treated their positions.

With respect to whether friars should seek medical attention for their ailments and infirmities, the hagiography outlined above depicts a clear conflict between Francis' wishes and those of others, particularly the wishes of Ugolino and Elias. Francis' earliest preference, made clear in the *Regula non bullata*, was to avoid seeking medical care for disabilities and illnesses as much as possible. Equally clear, however, was the desire on the part of Ugolino and Elias that Francis submit to treatment, something he did out of obedience to those more 'superior' in the order. This is perhaps why, when Francis finally agreed to have his eyes treated through cauterization, he wished to wait for the presence of Brother Elias to begin treatment, for here would be proof positive that he was ordered to accept treatment. As noted above, by the time of Bonaventure this tension over Francis (and by extension Franciscans) receiving medical treatment seems to have been resolved, at least according to the content of the hagiographical literature concerning the medical treatment of St. Francis. Bonaventure, unlike earlier hagiographers, presented the saint as agreeing to the treatment not because he had been ordered to do so, but because, upon the encouragement of doctors and the friars, he recognized that the treatment would aid his infirmity and also be a sort of ascetic act.[89]

The history of disability has, in many respects, been a history of marginalization: the marginalization of differently-abled individuals within various cultures and societies and the marginalization (until quite recently) of the study of disability. Of course, no one could argue that the study of Francis of Assisi has been a marginal endeavor for medievalists of all disciplines; and yet, serious study of Francis' disabilities and the potential impact of those disabilities, has been marginalized. There are reasons for this— Francis' decision to embrace a life of apostolic poverty and to understand his suffering as a way of sharing Christ's incarnate experience did impact medieval European modes of belief. The saint did establish a remarkably successful order, once which continues to flourish today. Moreover, today, as in the thirteenth century, there are serious ramifications to seeing Francis's suffering as other than an opportunity for *imitatio Christi*— a saint who demonstrates his humility and love of God by kissing lepers and then contracting leprosy, as Schatzlein and Sulmasy have suggested he did, presents a rather daunting theological problem. Nonetheless, Francis did experience serious infirmities throughout his life and recentring Francis' disabilities is essential to understanding the whole of his life. If his earliest hagiographies are to be believed, Francis had a tendency towards illness even in his twenties, and by his mid-forties, through a combination of underlying illnesses, harsh living and perhaps receiving the stigmata, Francis was experiencing terrible eye pain and was so disabled that at times he was not even able to walk. Perhaps Saint Francis welcomed his suffering, but Francis was also a man functioning in a position of authority within the hierarchy of the medieval Catholic Church. As the canon law of the period demonstrated, in this context, Francis' illnesses and infirmities were a distinct liability, a liability that may have resulted in his premature resignation as the leader of the Franciscan Order.

Notes

[1] Caroline Walker Bynum, *Holy Feast, Holy Fast: The Religious Significance of Food to Medieval Women* (Berkeley: University of California Press, 1987), 255. Caroline Walker Bynum, "...And Woman his Humanity: Female Imagery in the Religious Writing in the Religious Writing of the Mater Middle Ages" in *Fragmentation and Redemption: Essays on Gender and the Human Body in Medieval Religion* (New York: Zone Books, 1992), 151-179. Working from Bynum's position, Jacques Dalarun has recently suggested that Francis helped to create greater religious opportunities for women in religious life by creating "a bridge between masculine religion and a new religion, feminized as the languishing body of Christ is feminized". Jacques Dalarun, *Francis and the Feminine,* trans. Paula Pierce and Mary Sutphin (St. Bonaventure, NY: Franciscan Institute Press, 2006), 279.

[2] Indeed, Jacques Dalarun has suggested that the repeated use of feminine imagery (of mothers and of hens, for example) in reference to Francis as the leader of his order may have come about as a way of allowing the hagiographers to write clearly about Francis' governance appeared to be guidance without force or dominance. See Jacques Dalarun, *Francis and the Feminine,* 268.

[3] Traditional scholarship has suggested that Francis was the first minister-general of his order. See, for instance, Rosalind Brooke's discussion in her *Early Franciscan Government: Elias to Bonaventure* (Cambridge: Cambridge University Press, 1959). Recently, however Jean François Godet-Calogeras has argued that Francis never resigned from his position as Minister-General of the Franciscan Order as he never possessed that title to begin with. See Jean François Godet-Calogeras, "Francis of Assisi's Resignation: An Historical and Philological Probe" in *Charisma und religiöse Gemeinschaften in Mittelalter,* ed. G. Andenna, M. Breitensten and G. Melville, 281-300 (Berlin, Hamburg and Münster: LIT Verlag, 2005).

[4] On this reasoning, see for instance, John Moorman, *A History of the Franciscan Order from its Origins to the Year 1517* (Chicago: Franciscan Herald Press, 1968), 50-52 and Rosalind Brooke, *Early Franciscan Government: Elias to Bonaventure (*Cambridge: Cambridge University Press, 1959), 76-83. Jacques Dalarun has recently lamented the tendency of many scholars to unquestioningly believe the truthfulness of Francis' humility described in early Franciscan sources. See Jacques Dalarun, *Francis and the Question of Power (*St. Bonaventure, NY: Franciscan Institute, 2007), 194.

[5] So important did the order think the establishment of a single official document outlining Francis' life was, that it ordered all other lives and testaments about Francis burned. See J. A. Wayne Hellemann, "Francis of Assisi: Saint, Founder, Prophet" in *Francis of Assisi: History, Hagiography and Hermeneutics in the*

Early Documents, ed. J. A. Hammond, 15-38 (New York: New City Press, 2004), 29.

[6] Paul Sabatier, *Life of Saint Francis of Assisi,* trans. Louise Seymour Houghton (New York: Charles Scribner's Sons, 1894, 1930). On Sabatier as the originator of the Franciscan question see Michael Cusato, "Towards a Resolution of the Franciscan Question: Introduction to the Roundtable" in *Franciscan Studies* 66 (2008), 479-481; Jacques Dalarun, *The Misadventure of Francis of Assisi: Towards a Historical Use of the Franciscan Legends,* trans. Edward Hagman, 30-41 (St. Bonaventure, NY: Franciscan Institute Publications, 2002); Luigi Pelligrini, "A Century of Reading the Sources for the Life of St. Francis of Assisi," *Greyfriars Review* 7:3 (1993): 323-346.

[7] Of course scholarly consensus has been turned over many times, most recently by Jacques Dalarun's *Vers une résolution de la question franciscaine: La légende ombrienne de Thomas de Celano (*Paris: Fayard, 2007) which argues that the previously unknown author of the *Umbrian Choir Legend* was likely Thomas of Celano.

[8] Thomas of Celano, *Vita prima sancti Francisci,* in *Fontes Franciscani,* ed. E. Menesto and S. Brufani, 273-424 (Assisi: Edizioni Porziuncola, 1995). On dating see St. *Francis of Assisi: Early Documents*, ed. Regis Armstrong, J. A. Wayne Hellmann and William Short. 3 vols. (New York, London, Santa Mesa: New City Press, 1999-2001), 1.171.

[9] Thomas of Celano, *Vita secunda sancti Francisci,* in *Fontes Franciscani,* 441-639. For dating see *Francis of Assisi: Early Documents,* 2.233.

[10] Henry d'Avranches, *Legenda sancti Francisci versificata,* in *Fontes Franciscani,* 1131-1242. For dating, *Francis of Assisi: Early Documents,* 1.423.

[11] Julian of Speyer, *Vita sancti Francisci,* in *Fontes Franciscani,* 1025-1095. On dating, *Francis of Assisi: Early Documents,* 1.363.

[12] *Francis of Assisi: Early Documents,* 2.63.

[13] *Legenda trium sociorum,* in *Fontes Franciscani,* 1373-1445. The first sixteen chapters of this text have been definitively dated as composed between 1241 and 1247. The date for the remainder of the text is more uncertain, but it almost certainly was composed before 1260. *Francis of Assisi: Early Documents*, 2.63.

[14] Dalarun, *Résolution,* 136-142.

[15] *Compilatio assisiensis* in *Fontes Franciscani,* 1471-1690. On dating see *Francis of Assisi: Early Documents,* 2.115-116.

[16] On the possibility that the order wanted to some extent control the "official" version of Francis' *life,* see Aviad Kleinberg, *Flesh Made Word: Saints' Stories and the Western Imagination* (Cambridge, Mass: Belknap Press, 2008), 218-219. See also *Francis of Assisi: Early Documents,* 2.495.

[17] *Francis of Assisi: Early Documents,* 2.503.

[18] Ibid.

[19] See Jacques Dalarun's brief discussion of this early source, dated to approximately 1241 in *Misadventures,* 176-179.

[20] See Jacques Dalarun's brief literature review about this source in *Misadventures,* 189-190.

[21] The history and textual tradition of the so-called *Assisi Compilation* is quite complicated. Dalarun posits that the oldest manuscript dates from 1311, but parts of the manuscript, especially paragraphs 50-100 and 107-120 can be dated to as early as the 1240s, perhaps even before Crescentius' call for remembrances of Francis. Much of the rest can be dated to between 1247 and 1260. See Dalarun, *Misadventures,* 204-206. Without an earlier manuscript example, however, it is impossible to date all parts of the *Assisi Compilation* to before Bonaventure's official *lives.* As Enrico Manestò has argued, it is impossible to definitively state whether the *Assisi Compilation* was written before or after Bonaventure's texts. See E. Manestò, "Introduzione," in *Fontes Franiscani,* 1449-1471, 1462. On the difficulty of dating the different parts of the *Assisi Compilation* more generally, see, the introduction to the English translation of the *Assisi Compilation* found in *Francis of Assisi: Early Documents,* ed. R. J. Armstrong, J. A. W. Hellmann, and W. J. Short, 113-116 (New York: New City Press, 2002), 113-114; Ferdinand Delorme, "La 'legenda antiqua s. Francisci' du MS 1046 de la Bibliothèque communale de Pérouse," in *Archivum franciscanum historicum* 15 (1922): 23-70.

[22] Of course, using hagiographical sources to establish Francis' illness may be problematic. As Jacques Le Goff has succinctly summarized, the splinters in the Franciscan order over the meaning of Francis' Rule and the question of poverty within the order resulted in hagiographies that were written to persuade members of the order about the "truth" of Francis' position on this issue. See Jacques Le Goff, *Saint Francis of Assisi,* trans. Christine Rhone (London and New York: Routledge, 1999), 17-22. Le Goff suggests his own way forward, using the myriad of early hagiographies of Francis, along with the saint's own writings to establish cultural norms for different words and concepts. Certainly, like all texts, the hagiographies of St. Francis may obscure more about Francis than they reveal. However, by comparing the content of the hagiographies for similar language in discussions concerning Francis' disabilities, it is possible to glean a semblance of an understanding about Francis' various ailments and various peoples' responses to them.

[23] The exact year of Francis' birth has not been resolved. On this subject see Moorman, 4.

[24] This famous episode is recounted in most of Francis' early *lives,* including *The Legend of the Three Companions* (LTS), 3:19-20 and Thomas of Celano's *Vita prima* (VP) 1:15.

[25] This period is attested in most early versions of Francis' *vitae.* VP 1.2, Julian of Speyer's *Life of Saint Francis* (JS) 1, Henri d'Avraches' *Versified Life of St. Francis,* (HdA) 1, Bonaventure's *Legenda maior* (LM) 1.1.2 and his *Legenda minor* (Lm) 1.1.2.

[26] Occasional mentions of illness are found in VP 1.21; JS 6, 12; HdA 12; the *Assisi Compilation* (AS) 80, 100, 119; LM 1.6.2, 1.7.11, 1.8.10.

[27] VP 2.4-2.5, 2.7; JS 12; HdA 12-13; AS 68, 83, 86; VS 89, 93,125; LM 1.5.8-9.

[28] VP 2.3-2.4; JS 10; HdA 12; LTS 17; VS 135-138; LM 1.13.3-7, 1.15.2; Lm 1.6.3-4, 1.7.1.

[29]For a summary of Francis' medical history see Joanne Schatzlein and Daniel P. Sulmasy, "The Diagnosis of St. Francis: Evidence for Leprosy," in *Franciscan Studies* 47 (1987): 181-217, esp. 183-184.
[30] For a summary of the possible diagnoses of Francis' eye disease, see Rosario Zeppa, "San Francesco's Blindness," in *The Journal of Paleopathology* 3:3 (1991), 133-135.
[31] See Joanne Schatzlein and Daniel O Sulmasy, "The Diagnosis of St. Francis".
[32] Judith Perkins, *The Suffering Self: Pain and Narrative Representation in the Early Christian Era* (London and New York: Routledge, 1995).
[33] On the complexities of the position of medicine within medieval Christian faith see, for instance, Joseph Ziegler, *Medicine and Religion c. 1300: The Case of Arnau da Vilanova* (Oxford: Oxford Historical Monographs, 1998), 215-222 and Irina Metzler, *Disability in Medieval Europe: Thinking about physical impairment during the high Middle Ages, c. 1100-1400* (London and New York: Routledge, 2006), 38-47.
[34] Vincent of Beauvais, *Speculum naturale (*B. Belleri, 1624, repr., Graz: Akademischen Druck-u. Verlagsanstalt, 1967), xxxi, 99. See also Ziegler, 223.
[35] Lateran IV, Canon 22.Cum infirmitas corporalis non numquam ex peccato proueniat, dicente Domino, languido quem sanauerat: Uade et amplius noli peccare, ne deterius aliquid tibi contingat, decreto praesentistatuimus et districte praecipimus medicis corporum, ut cum eos ad infirmos uocari contigerit, ipsos ante omnia moneant et inducant, quod medicos aduocent animarum, ut postquam infirmis fuerit de spirituali salute prouisum, ad corporalis medicinae salubrium procedatur, cum causa cessante cesset effectus. Hoc quidem inter alia huic causam dedit edicto, quod quidam in aegritudinis lecto iacentes, cum eis a medicis suadetur, ut de animarum salute disponant, in desperationis articulum incidunt, unde facilius mortis periculum incurrunt. Si quis autem medicorum huius nostrae constitutionis postquam per praelatos locorum fuerit publicata, transgressor extiterit, tamdiu ab ingressu ecclesiae arceatur, donec pro transgressionehuiusmodi satisfecerit competenter. Ceterum cum anima sit multo pretiosior corpore, subinterminatione anathematis prohibemus, ne quis medicorum pro corporali salute aliquid aegrotosuadeat, quod in periculum animae conuertatur." See *Decrees of the Ecumenical Councils: Nicaea to Lateran V,* ed. N. Tanner. 2 vols. (Washington DC: Georgetown University Press, 1990), 245-246. The English translation of this canon can be found in H. J. Schroeder, *Disciplinary Decrees of the General Councils: Text, Translation and Commentary* (St. Louis: B. Herder, 1937), 236-296. Now in public domain and available at http://www.fordham.edu/halsall/basis/lateran4.html. Accessed July 15, 2009. See also Metzler, 46-47.
[36] On the history of Gratian and his *Decretum* see James Brundage, "The Teaching and Study of Canon Law in the Law Schools", in *The History of Medieval Canon Law in the Classical Period,* ed. Wilfried Hartmann and Kenneth Pennington, 98-120 (Washington: Catholic University of America Press, 2008); Peter Landau, "Gratian and the Decretum Gratiani" in *The History of Medieval Canon Law in the Classical Period: From Gratian to the Decretals of Pope Gregory IX,* 22-54; and

Anders Winroth, *The Making of Gratian's* Decretum (Cambridge: University of Cambridge Press, 2000), 5-8.

[37] As Irina Metzler has argued the Latin words *infirmus, aeger* and *egrotus* were used almost interchangeably to mean either a sick or impaired individual. See Metzler, 4-5.

[38] Letter 11.29. See the *Patrologia Latina,* ed. J. P . Migne (Paris: Garnier fratres, 1866-1882), 77:1141-1142. An English translation can be found in Gregory the Great, *The Letters of Gregory the Great,* trans. John R. C. Martyn (Toronto, PIMS, 2004), 774-775.

[39] "Et quod nusquam canones precipiunt, ut pro egritudine episcopi episcopus succedat, et ideo iniustum est, ut, si molestia corporis irruit, honore suo priuetur ergrotus. Sed suggerendum est, ut si quid, in regime, egrotat, dispensator illi talis requiratur, qui possit eius curam omnem agere et locum illius in regimine ecclesiae (ipso non deposito) conseruare, ut neque Deus omnipotens offendatur, neque ciuitas neglecta esse inueniatur. Gratian, *Decretum,* ed. A. L. Richter (Graz: Verlagsanstalt, 1959), 2.7.1.1, column 566.

[40] This is the particular topic of 2.7.1.3, c. 567, a chapter which begins with the rubric "infirmitatis causa loco suo quis priuare non debet".

[41] For an overview of what is known about the author of the *Summa parisiensis,* see Terence McLaughlin's introduction to the critical edition. Terence P. McLaughlin, "Introduction", introduction to *The* Summa parisiensis *on the Decretum gratiani* (Toronto, PIMS, 1952), XVII-XX and XXXI-XXXIII.

[42] "Sed solum si fuerit leprosus, tunc non debet retinere cathedram, sicut in corpore canonun est, ubi similiter inuenitur quod propter lepram aliquis separatur a cohabitatione uxoris." *Summa parisiensis,* ed. Terrance McLaughlin, VII.2, 134.

[43] The extent to which communities considered the lepers in their midst officially dead and had rituals to affirm that status has been debated in recent years. Carole Rawcliffe has argued that there is no evidence that leper masses or other rituals that allowed lepers to become "dead to the world" ever existed in England. She further argues that such rituals, if they did exist, need not mean that the leper was marginalized or persecuted, a conclusion this commentary on Gratian's *Decretum* would seem to refute. On the historiography of the so-called 'leper mass', see Carole Rawcliffe, *Leprosy in Medieval England* (Woodbridge: Boydell, 2006), 21-28.

[44] In fact, other than Francis' suffering as *imitatio Christi,* the impact of Francis' disabilities in his life have been little discussed, even amongst those who study the history of disability. The most striking example of this can be found in Henri-Jacques Stiker's work *A History of Disability,* in which he argues that Francis succeeded in having the previously marginalized value of poverty "accepted as a positive value". Yet in noting this, Stiker fails to comment on Francis' obvious and myriad other infirmities, going so far as to imply he had none by saying "It may be remarked that in the course of the inquiry into St. Francis, I seem to have lost sight of the truly disabled." See Henri-Jacques Stiker, *A History of Disability,* trans. William Sayers (Ann Arbor, MI: University of Michigan Press, 2002), 83.

[45] Brooke, 63-65; Moorman, 46; Dalarun, *Power,* 94.

[46] Moorman, 47.
[47] Brooke, 64; Moorman, 48.
[48] Bull. Franc. I, 2; Moorman, 50.
[49] VS 28.58. See also Brooke, 64 and Moorman, 51.
[50] VP 2.5. Ugolino's order to Francis is also found in later sources for the saints' life, such as the *Legend of Perugia,* 42 and the *Mirror of Perfection*, 91. See also, Giulia Barone, "S. Francesco, S. Bonaventura e la malattia," in *San Bonaventura Francescano* (Todi: Centro di studi sulla spiritualità medievale, 1974), 271-278, 272.
[51] "fraternitas tua diuini contemplatione iudicii praebeat aegrotanti". Raymond of Peñafort, *Decretalium gregorii,* in *Decretalium collectiones,* ed. A. L. Richter (Graz: U. Verlagsanstalt, 1959), cc.1-928, 3.6.1, c. 481.
[52] "…quia, si alii eius essent exemplo deterriti, forte non posset qui militaret ecclesiae inueniri". Ibid. The decretal is nearly word for word repeated from the register of Gregory's letters. "quia diuersis in Ecclesia militantibus, uaria, sicut nosti, saepe contingit infirmitas. Et si hoc fuerunt exemplo deterriti, nullus de caetero qui Ecclesiae militet poterit inueniri…" . See the *Patrologia Latina,* 77:544-545. No recent translation of this letter into English exists.
[53] LM 6.4.
[54] See Kleinberg, 218-219. A number of scholars have noted Bonaventure's return to conventionality in the *Legenda maior and Legenda minor.* See for instance, Thomas Renna's discussion of a more conventional discussion of Francis's gift of prophecy in Bonaventure compared with Thomas of Celano's works in Thomas Renna, "St. Francis as Prophet in Celano and Bonaventure" in *Michigan Academician* 33.4 (2000), 321-332. General OneFile Web. (Accessed Mar 1 2010). See also Michael Cusato, "Talking About Ourselves: The Shift in Franciscan Writing from Hagiography to History (1235-1247)," in *Franciscan Studies* 58 (2000): 37-75, in which he concludes by suggesting that Bonaventure's two *legendae* of Francis represented a return to more traditional modes of hagiography than had been seen in the *Anonymous of Perugia* and the *Vita secunda* of Thomas Celano, which tended to advocate for a return to the apostolic poverty many of the Spirituals believed Francis had embraced.
[55] To give but one example, Bonaventure writes that once, when Francis decided to use a feather pillow because his head and eyes were sore, a demon got into the pillow and did not allow him to pray or meditate at all. Thus he ordered the pillow removed. "Unde cum nocte quadam propter infirmitatem capitis et oculorum, praeter solitum morem ceruical de pluma positum haberet ad caput, daemon in illud ingressus, ipsum usque ad horam matutinalem inquietatum multimode a sanctae orationis studio perturbauuit, donec, uocato socio, puluinar cum daemonio fecit extra cellulam longius exportari." LM 5.2, FF. 815.
[56] "Cum enim ex continuo fletu infirmitatem oculorum incurisset grauissimam, suadente sibi medico, quod abstineret a lacrimis, si corporei uisus caecitatem uellet effugere, uir sanctus respondit: 'Non est, frater medice, ob amorem luminis, quod habemus commune cum muscis, uisitatio lucis aeternae repellenda uel modicum, quia non spiritus propter carnem, sed caro propter spiritum beneficium lucis

accepit.' Malebat siquidem corporalis uisus lumen ammitere quam lacrimas, quibus oculus mundatur interior, ut Deum uidere ualeat, repressa deuotione spiritus impedire." LM 5.8, FF. 819. "Quodam namque tempore, cum consilium daretur a medicis et instanter suaderetur a fratribus, ut contra infirmitatem oculorum pateretur sibi per cocturae subueniri remedium, humiliter uir Dei assensit, pro eo quod id non solum medela contra aegritudinem corporis, uerum etiam materia foret exercendae uirtutis." Lm 5.1, FF. 994.

[57] "Cum autem semel daretur consilium a medicis, et instanter suaderetur a fratribus, ut pateretur sibi per remedium subueniri cocturae, humiliter uir Dei assensit, quia salutiferum hoc simul et asperum esse cernebat." LM 5.9, FF. 819. "Quodam namque tempore, cum consilium daretur a medicis et instanter suaderetur a fratribus, ut contra infirmitatem oculorum pateretur sibi per cocturae subueniri remedium, humiliter uir Dei assensit, pro eo quod id non solum medela contra aegritudinem corporis, uerum etiam materia foret exercendae uirtutis." Lm 5.1, FF. 994.

[58] "Et quia spirtuali auditui dat intellectum inflicta uexatio, facta est super eum manus Domini et immutatio dexterae Excelsi, diutinis laguoribus ipsius corpus affligens, ut coaptaret animam ad sancti spiritus unctionem." LM 1.2, FF. 782.

[59] "Christo igitur iam cruci confixus Franciscus...:, LM 14.1, FF. 898. "[Franciscus] *Christo* igitur iam *cruci* uir Dei *confixus*". Lm 7.1, FF. 1006.

[60] "...;quonium propter excrescentes in pedibus clauos ambulare non poterat..." LM 14.1, FF. 899. "Et quia propter excrescentes in pedibus clauos ambulare non poterat," Lm 7.1, FF. 1006.

[61] "uel si forte sollicite postulauerit medicinas nimis desiderans liberare carnem cito morituram, quae est animae inimica, a malo sibi euenit et *carnalis est,* et non uidetur esse de fratribus, quia plus diligit corpus quam animam". Francis of Assisi, *Regula non bullata* 10, FF. 195.

[62] Barone, 273

[63] On this subject, see Angela Montford, *Health, Sickness, Medicine and the Friars in the Thirteenth and Fourteenth Centuries* (Aldershot: Ashgate, 2004), 30-31.

[64] Barone, esp. 278-279.

[65] VP 2.4, FF. 373. JS 12.

[66] "[Franciscus] hoc facere penitus recusabat", VP 2.4, FF. 374, JS 12, FF. 1082.

[67] VP,2.4, FF. 375, JS 12, FF. 1083.

[68] VP 2.5, FF. 378, JS 12, FF. 1084.

[69] "Frontis et insignes gemmas animaeque fenestras/ Obturant nubes, perturbant nubila, neruum/ Scilicet opticum dolor intollerabilis angit;/ Cacochymis pupilla rubet densataque uisum/ Palpebra deformat, aciesque molestia torquet./ Inuitat dolor ipse manus, digitique medelam/ Dum praebent, adimunt; est namque uenenifer ille/ Tactus, et intendens etiam nocumenta iuuando./ Hoc etenim uirtus uisiua remittitur, ex quo/ Incipit esse frequens,/ palpebrarumque medulla/ Prurit, et inficitur tunicae septemplicis humor./ Ille dolens, ultra quam posset credere quisquis/ Non sentiret idem, patienter sustinet omnem/ Corporis accidiam: diuinaque ne uideatur/ Nolle flagella pati, medicos adhibere recusat." HdA 12, FF. 1199.

[70] HdA 12, FF. 1199-1200.
[71] HdA 13, FF. 1200-1201.
[72] See the *Umbrian Choir Legend,* in *Francis of Assisi: Early Documents,* 474.
[73] Uiderat namque gallinam quamdam paruam et nigram, habentem crura pennata cum pedibus in modum columbae domesticae, quae tot pullos habebat quod non poterat eos sub alis propriis congregare, sed ibant in circuitu gallinae exterius remanentes. Euigilans autem a somno coepit cogitare de huiusmodi uisione, statimque per Spiritum sanctum cognouit se per illam gallinam figuraliter designari et ait "Ego sum illa gallina, statura pusillus nigerque natura, qui debeo esse simplex ut columba et affectibus pennatis uirtutum uolare ad caelum. Mihi autem Dominus per misericordiam suam dedit et dabit filios multos quos protegere mea uirtute non potero, unde oportet ut eos sanctae Ecclesiae recommendem quae sub umbra alarum suarum eos protegat et gubernet". LTS 16, FF. 1436.
[74] LTS 15, FF. 1437.
[75] AC 11, FF. 1484-1485. See also AC 39, FF. 1512.
[76] cf. note 21.
[77] "Et paulo post cum infirmitate nimia grauaretur, in uehementia spiritus in lectulo se direxit. 'Qui sunt isti, ait, qui Religionem meam et fratrum de meis manibus rapuerunt? Si ad generale capitulum uenero, eis ostendam qualem habeam uoluntatem.'" AC 44, FF. 1517. This anecdote likely dates from circa 1247, as it appears to be drawn from the *Vita secunda* of Thomas of Celano. See VS 188, FF. 607.
[78] "Quoniam licet tempore quo renuntiaui et dimisi officium fratrum, coram fratribus me excusarem in capitulo generali, quod propter infirmitatem meam de ipsis curam et sollicitudinem habere non possem, tamen modo, si secundum uoluntatem meam fratres ambularent et ambulassent, propter ipsorum consolationem nollem, quod alium ministrum haberent preter me, usque in diem mortis mee." AC 106, FF. 1649. This anecdote comes from what is believed to be the oldest portion of the so-called *Assisi Compilation,* drawn from the remembrances of one's Francis' oldest companions, Brother Leo.
[79] "Et nunc, propter infirmitates quas tu nosti, dulcissime Domine, *curam eius habere* non ualens, ipsam recommendo ministris". AC 39, FF. 1512.
[80] VS 16, FF. 464.
[81] "Et nunc propter infirmitates quas tu nosti, dulcissime Domine, *curam eius habere* non ualens, ipsam recommendo ministris." VS 104, FF. 571.
[82] "Respondit filius diligenter ad patrem, a Domino sibi dari uerbum resporisionis agnoscens: 'Dic mihi, si dignaris, o pater, qua diligentia corpus tuum, dum potuit, tuis obtemperauit mandatis?'. Qui ait: 'Testimonium illi perhibeo, fili, quia per omnia obediens fuit, in nullo sibimetipsi pepercit, sed quasi praeceps ad cuncta ferebatur imperia. Nullum subterfugit laborem, nullum declinauit incommodum, tantummodo iussa posset perficere . In hoc perfecte conuenimus ego et ipsum, ut sine aliqua repugnantia Christo Domino seruiremus'. [5] Et ait frater: 'Ubi est ergo, pater, liberalitas tua, ubi pietas et summa discretio? Estne ista fidelium amicorum redhibitio digna, beneficium libenter accipere nec tempore necessario danti pro merito respondere? Quid seruitii Domino tuo Christo absque auxilio corporis

hactenus impendere potuisti? Nonne, ut ipse fateris, propter hoc se omni periculo dedit?' 'Fateor, fili', ait pater, 'hoc esse uerissimum'. Et filius: 'Estne hoc rationi conueniens, ut tam fideli amico in tanta necessitate desis, qui se et sua pro te usque ad mortem exposuit? Absit a te, pater, auxilium et baculus afflictorum, absit a te hoc peccatum in Domino!' 'Benedictus et tu', inquit, 'fili, qui sapienter meis disceptationibus tam salutaria remedia propinasti!' Et coepit hilariter loqui ad corpus: « Gaude, frater corpus, et parce mihi, quia, ecce iam tua placita libenter perficio, libenter tuis querulis affectibus subuenire festino!' VS 160, FF. 626-627.

[83] Moorman suggests 1220, p. 51 while Rosalind Brooke suggests as early as 1217, pp. 78-83.

[84] See "A List of the General Ministers" dating from the 1260s in *Francis of Assisi: The Early Documents,* 3.824. However, this list may be of non-Franciscan origin, which may account for the confusion. The first unquestionably Franciscan source about the early minister-generals of the order dates from just after the turn of the fourteenth century and does suggest, though does not explicitly state, that Elias of Cortona had taken over the role of minister-general during Francis' lifetime. See *Francis of Assisi: The Early Documents,* 3. 827-3.828. It is significant that neither text mentions Peter Catani. On this subject also see Brooke, 110.

[85] Brooke, 106-115; Dalarun, *Power,* 190.

[86] Moorman, 46; Brooke, 64.

[87] Brooke, 113; Dalarun, *Power,* 88.

[88] Brooke, 111.

[89] "Cum autem semel daretur consilium a medicis, et instanter suaderetur a fratribus, ut pateretur sibi per remedium subueniri cocturae, humiliter uir Dei assensit, quia salutiferum hoc simul et asperum esse cernebat." LM 1.5.9, FF. 819. "Quodam namque tempore, cum consilium daretur a medicis et instanter suaderetur a fratribus, ut contra infirmitatem oculorum pateretur sibi per cocturae subueniri remedium, humiliter uir Dei assensit, pro eo quod id non solum medela contra aegritudinem corporis, uerum etiam materia foret exercendae uirtutis." Lm 5.1, FF. 994.

DEFINING MENTAL AFFLICTIONS IN MEDIEVAL ENGLISH ADMINISTRATIVE RECORDS

WENDY J. TURNER

From at least the twelfth century, administrative records in medieval England made special note of any lack of mental capacity on the part of a convicted criminal[1] and, from the mid-thirteenth century, of any mentally disabled landholder unable to assume the responsibilities associated with holding land.[2] English authorities gave lesser or no punishment for crimes committed by those persons unable to discern.[3] Moreover, Henry III claimed for the crown the right of guardianship over all lands held by mentally disabled persons.[4] Until the end of the fifteenth century, English medieval administrations kept track of both mentally compromised criminals and mentally incapacitated persons holding lands. A comparison of the terminology used to define mentally ill criminals and mentally disabled landholders reveals that medieval English society employed a range of terms to describe mental conditions; furthermore, given the designations inherent in their use of these terms, they had an understanding of a continuum of mental disabilities, even if these were not discretely defind.

Most English medieval records were kept in Latin, and the clerks and officials keeping the records of mentally incapacitated persons used this Latin vocabulary with little change from antiquity. The Romans had divided their terminology for mental disabilities into two distinct groups: persons who were *furiosus*—raging, passionate, or unsettled persons—and persons who were *non compos mentis*—mentally lacking, slow, or unperceptive persons.[5] Other Latin terms in the category of the mentally unsettled include *fatuus*, a foolish and silly person, or imbecile; *stultus*, a fatuous or stupid individual; and *vecors*, a senseless or mad person. As with *furiosus*, these terms indicate an unsophisticated or unsettled mind with a low or limited capacity for reason; though, because they imply rage or no constraint, these terms also allude to an uncontrolled body in conjunction with the uncontrolled mind. Terminology describing passive mental disabilities—the *non compos mentis*, those persons without mental capacity—includes those persons who did not know right from wrong, who were born without full mental powers, or who had trauma to the brain. An individual who had become injured or ill might be portrayed with a related phrase, *non sane mentis*, without mental health. Another term for passive mental disability that became popular in later medieval England is *idiota,* which indicated an uneducated, ignorant, and base individual. In Rome, this term most often referred to a commoner, rather than a mentally incapacitated person. In subsequent years it took on the more dramatic meaning of dull-witted or inward-looking becoming identified in medieval England with someone born with low comprehensive ability.

The Romans added to these terms of no constraint and passivity descriptive qualifiers to indicate duration or severity such as *a nativitate*, from birth. Latin also included terms that span the gap between unconstrained and passive mental anguish. *Freneticus*, for example, is to be frantic, as when a person is affected with delirium caused by fever; this franticness could be passive or active in its presentation. Similarly *amens* or *demens* is to be insane and out of one's mind. Persons with *demencia* were literally *insanitas*, because they were unsound or unhealthy. Other mental conditions could affect the ill person such as *mania*, a Latin derivative of a Greek word meaning derangement often accompanied by agitation or hallucinations. The term *lunaticus*, a moon-sick individual, though quite popular in Early Modern English vocabulary, was not often used in Roman or medieval English administrative records. It describes a cyclical or periodic illness, perhaps worsening with the full moon.[6] Latin and Roman vocabulary and law had influenced English practice; the Romans even had a type of guardianship – inspired the later practice in England, after the transmission of the *Corpus* of Roman law to England in the twelfth century.[7]

Terms for Mental Incapacity in Medieval England

Terminology for Mentally Ill Criminals

Medieval English society characterized mentally incompetent criminals using specific descriptions and terms. For the records from 1200 to 1500, 139 terms were collected out of approximately the same number of records for mentally incapacitated criminals. The descriptions provide insight into how mentally ill criminals were treated and socially categorized by their communities and the royal authorities. For instance,

Ralph Russel and Maud Levying, pardoned later for their crimes, are described as "*infirmitate*," ill.[8] Mentally incapacitated criminals quite often are referred to as "knowing neither good nor bad (*sciens nec bonum nec malum*)."[9] This phrase was commonly used to describe the lack of intent on the part of both the mentally incompetent and the temporarily mentally ill who committed crimes. This is not just a few court clerks; others, such as ecclesiastical writers,[10] observed that unless an individual could distinguish between good and bad, they must be accounted as not acting feloniously, as when Drew (*Drogo*) de Henle killed two boys and was found to have acted out of "fury and not by felony," "*furiam et non pro feloniam*."[11] Drew still could have stood trial for his crime "if any will proceed against him"; though, the justices pardoned Drew and would only push for a further trial if someone knew of a reason to punish this person who had been in the pardonable state of *furiosus* at the time of the homicides.

Terms used to depict mentally incapacitated criminals portray the state of their mental or emotional health and unconstrained behavior (see *figure 1*). Most of the time a mentally incapacitated criminal is described as having the characteristics associated with being in a state of *frenesis* (madness, insanity, frenzy) or a state of *furor* (rage or fury).[12] As such, a person is often referred to as a *freneticus* (mad, insane, or frantic person) or *furiosus* (enraged or furious person). Someone described as being in the state of *furor* quite often implied a level of passion even if that was not stated outright—which to the medieval writer was not a romantic passion but rather a passion such as that of Christ's suffering. This passion accompanied his or her fury. For example, the mentally incapacitated Henry Bruneman of Tydington was charged with the murder of Hugh de Faucumbe in 1298 and was found not to have committed a felony since there had been no "malice aforethought (*malicia excogitata*)."[13] Henry was ill and murdered Hugh "while in a fit of madness (*dum in frenetica passione*)." Together these two terms—*freneticus* and *furiosus*—make up nearly forty-five percent of all of the descriptions of those persons who have some type of mental condition and who commit a crime. In every case, it is the individual's acting out, of his being out of control or in "a frenzy" or "a passionate rage" that causes him to misjudge the situation and commit murder or arson or some other crime.

The third most common term has already been mentioned; it is the phrase *sciens nec bonum nec malum,* knowing neither good nor evil. This description engages the issue of criminal mental health by going to the heart of the matter—that these mentally incapacitated persons cannot discern. Without an internal mechanism by which to judge a situation, these persons did not know right from wrong and as such were not held accountable for their actions. The courts often treated them as if they were children.[14] In one example, John Argent killed his two sons. A record of miscellaneous matters says John was without understanding "*de bono et malo*" while in "*frensie*;"[15] and the following year the writer of the letter patent for his pardon described him as having been a furious and frantic person.[16] In another example, William le Bachelor killed the wife of Warin le Soutere "while in state of fury and great agitation" ("*furore et magna furiositate*") but he was not found guilty because he was without a sense of right and wrong.[17] One official in a letter close (an official, private and sealed letter) wrote, "Madmen committing crimes in their madness ought not by law to undergo the extreme penalty nor to forfeit their goods or chattels."[18] This does not say they should not stand trial nor be punished; mentally incapable persons did stand trial for their crimes, were jailed, sometimes bound or chained, and, even if pardoned, could receive a punishment, though never as if they had committed a felony.

Other terms follow in frequency of usage for mentally ill criminals, including *demens*, *lunaticus*, and a variety of illnesses. The terms *demens* and *amens* are interchangeable (generally meaning out of one's mind, but also insane, senseless, or distracted); and upon occasion one or the other also might appear in association with fever or illness. The Coroners' rolls describe Edith Rogers, for example, as "*demens et insanis*," out of her mind and insane (or unhealthy); Edith "by reason of her own negligence and insanity" fell into a well and drowned.[19]

Lunaticus can describe someone with a cyclical condition, or someone thought to be affected by the moon, *a luna*, such as Richard Thurbern of Brent. Richard was suspected of larceny, which he, his neighbors, and jurors all said was untrue, except that they did suspect that he stole a fowl, "which he took in his madness at a time when he was lunatic."[20] The term *lunaticus* is rare, though *a lune* as part of the description—as in *furiosus a lune,* furious by (because of) the moon—is more common. Two interesting examples of the term *lunaticus* occur in conjunction with trespass. These two men each wandered away from his community. Thomas Corderye of Ropsled and Simon le Vineter of Drauton are each recorded as "*lunaticus*." They had both "gone wandering," which may or may not have influenced the choice of this term—it is difficult to tell with so little evidence. Whether or not the episodes were monthly also cannot be determined from extant records, nor should it matter. It is important that a king's official classified Thomas as having "become a lunatic" indicating an onset point in time to his condition and another official recorded the friends and family of Simon as having taken him "often" to Croyland for his recurring condition.[21]

Infimitas as a term has been included on the chart, and all illnesses that were described in the records are included under that term whether the records used the term *infimitas* directly or not. Many ill perpetrators of the law had a fever with their illness, which might account for the mental condition.[22] It was during a high fever that many people are described as raging or mad.[23] Maud Levying, wife of Walter, was so ill ("*infirmitate*") in 1284 that she could not tell "good from evil"; she became mentally furious and frantic ("*furiositate et frenesi ducta*") killing her children, John and Alice.[24] Ill persons might also be described as simply sick or feverish and thrashing. In 1248, Matilda, the wife of Ralph Carson, killed her two sons when she was mad ("*laborans frensy*").[25] In 1281, Amy (*Amya*) murdered her son, John, "the son of Stephen Brumman," while she was "mad for fifteen days (*rabie pro xv dies*)."[26] In 1325, Walter Makepays killed Adam de Grenhamerton while suffering from "a certain great illness, as well it is said he was mad in his madness (*quaedam magna infirmitate qua dicitur frenesis unde freneticus fuit*)."[27] These individuals and many others were ill at the time they committed a homicide, probably without knowing what they had done.

The terminology used to describe criminals and other aggressive persons in the records include terms of inappropriate activity, lack of discernment, not knowing right from wrong, and ignorance. These terms also include persons with an inability to remember, with cyclical ailments, or with difficulties at the time of the full moon. These persons are all out of control in one way or another, even those who are ill to the point of being insensible and unable to control their actions. If landholders with mental incapacities were not only passively dull-witted but also uncontrollable, they too might be described using these terms.

Terminology for Mentally Incompetent Landholders

Henry III began taking an interest in the lands of mentally incapacitated persons in the mid-thirteenth century. He claimed the prerogative right to be the guardian of all the lands of mental afflicted persons. During the thirteenth century, the phrase *non compos mentis* was preferred over other descriptive terms or phrases for mentally incapacitated landholders. By the fourteenth century, *fatuus* and *idiota* dominated in usage for these disabled landholders where they had been little used in the preceding century. The data in *figure 4* shows the total number of recorded terms used per year entered into the database for each of the terms indicated.[28] Clearly, the number of appearances in the upper graph on *figure 4* demonstrates the increase in usage of the terms *idiota* and *fatuus*. The lower graph depicts the somewhat steady use, with a slight decline after 1310, of *non compos mentis* and "other" terms.[29]

In *figures 5* through *8*, the yearly percentage of usage was calculated from the total number of terms entered per year for each term, demonstrating the relative importance instead of the absolute importance.[30] In other words, each term has been weighed against all the others for each year, giving each the importance per year it had in relation to all the other terms. The running average that is also plotted on these four graphs de-emphasizes the fluctuations in the data, providing an additional metric representing the overall long-term trend in the usage of each term; this curve appears superimposed over the percentages per year. The trend curves for each term were generated using a running "boxcar" average, of ten years prior and ten years post, of the percentages for each year. For example, the running average of the yearly percentage of usage for a particular term in 1358 would be the sum of the usages for that term for the years 1348 through 1368 (ten years on either side of 1358) divided by the sum of the usages of all terms during that twenty-one year span and converted to a percentage. Because of the technique for calculating a running average, the beginning of the trend curve is plotted ten years after the first individual observations, and it ends ten years before the last observation. Conclusions drawn from the curve showing the running average reflect only trends that may be prevalent over twenty years or more, which may indicate a shift in legal practice or belief. Use of a running average may also indicate an individual year during which a profound relative change in the frequency of usage for one or more terms occurred, such as when the collective "other" terms are declining from 1200 to 1275. Yet, because their usage is generally rare, both charts demonstrate that their use is constant, but infrequent (see *figure 6*). Use of the trend line in conjunction with the yearly occurrence plot, which emphasizes short-term usage, allows for a complete examination of both short-term and long-term patterns of term usage.

Over time, certain terms became more or less prominent, and the increase in records cannot account fully for the fluctuations in terminological use or for changes in terminology over time. Errors of about ten percent are possible; therefore, short-term fluctuations (i.e., from year to year) of less than ten percent can be considered insignificant.[31] For example, *idiota* took on more significance in a relative sense (see *figure 5*). A comparison of the major terms for landholders per year to the percentage of the total terms demonstrates that *idiota* came into regular use sometime in the 1270s, and it quickly became used by clerks over forty percent of the time in reference to mentally incompetent landholders. This usage leveled off at approximately fifty percent of the total usage throughout the fourteenth and fifteenth centuries.

The investigations into charges of incompetence were carried out by a variety of persons depending on several factors including the type of property, the origin of the complaint, and time of year. In some instances, several hearings might have been held to ascertain the level of competence of a person. The king wanted to be certain in questionable cases of mental disorder before stripping someone of his property rights. For example, Nicholas Glamorgan was examined at least twice and in both instances he was unable to handle the basic tasks necessary for managing property. Without the cognitive ability necessary, Nicholas could not manage his extensive properties (stretching over several counties) and he was discounted as a lord. "Nicholas, who by examination before the Council, has been found to be an idiot (*idiota*), and incapable of managing his lands ... [and] having upon examination before the king in the chancery, [has (again)] been found to be an idiot (*jdeota*)."[32]

The term *idiota* had a fairly even rise to prominent use, whereas the frequency of usage for the terms *fatuus/fatuitas* and *non compos mentis* mirror each other throughout the period from 1200-1500, although after 1300 *fatuus* is relatively and absolutely more important (see *figures 7* and *8*). It is interesting to see that from about 1320 to 1355 *fatuus* tends lower in usage (*figure 7*), while *non compos mentis* is higher (*figure 8*). In the period 1320 to 1355, legal and administrative record keeping was undergoing some changes and this change along with other factors affected the records of this period. Some of the important influences on this period were a disabled government, poor harvests that led to famine, "severe deflation,"[33] and the Black Death (1348-49). Edward II was deposed for poor administration of the government (1327) and Edward III during part of that period was a child (coming to the throne at fourteen years old). There are generally fewer records of the mentally incapacitated for these years, when the courts and various administrative arms of the crown were reshuffled several times, which may account in part for the altering use of terms from 1320 to 1355.

After this period of economic instability, *fatuus* regains dominance in usage, increasing in the records from 1355 to 1430. In 1427 for example, John Thymolby was heir to a manor held in chief of the king, but he was a "*fatuus naturalis*"[34] and, therefore, became a ward of the crown. A few years later, William Butteveleyn is also described as a "*fatuus naturalis,*" and he also became a ward of the king who provided for the care of

William and his properties in four counties.[35] About 1430 to 1470, *non compos mentis*, along with a small but significant percentage of the "other" terms,[36] is used with more frequency, while both *idiota* and *fatuus* decline somewhat in percentage as a result. Common for the usage of *non compos mentis*, in 1340 Joan Chyvene is described as "*non est compos mentis sue*, but she enjoys lucid intervals."[37] Periodic ailments having a lucid and non-lucid oscillation are often found in conjunction with *non compos mentis*, though not always and not exclusively. This change in term usage from *fatuus* to *non compos mentis* occurs during the so-called "Wars of the Roses," and also the end of the wars with France. During this period, there was a rapid succession of kings, councilors, protectors, and usurpers, and the fluctuation in terminology may represent an overall instability in administration, administrators, and record keeping.

The most frequently used term for landholders during this three-hundred-year period out of the nearly 1000 descriptions is *idiota* (see *figure 2*), which meant "idiot" commonly and more broadly "mentally incompetent." *Idiota* often occurs in conjunction with the term *fatuus*, which in English would most closely translate to "fool," "foolish," "senseless," or "fatuous," although all of these words have taken on connotations that may not be true to the intended meaning in medieval England. For example, in an inquisition post mortem Bartholomew Sakevill was said to have been "fatuous and an idiot . . . from the time of his birth (*fatuus et idiota . . . a tempore nativitatis sue* ").[38] The use of either *idiota* or *fatuus* accounts for almost half of all term usage when clerks were describing mentally incapacitated landholders in the administrative records. *Figure 2* includes all variations for each term, including plural forms and derivations for gender, tense, declension, and so on. *Idiota/idiocy* occurred 435 times, *fatuus/fatuitas* 427 times, while all other individual terms and their variations combined total only 230. After *idiota* and *fatuus*, the next most commonly observed term was the phrase *non compos mentis* that literally meant "not mentally controlled" or "no mental control" and like the other terms, the chart includes all forms and word orders, such as *non est compos sue mentis*.[39] In a few cases, such as that of Bartholomew, the royal officials had not always seen other documentation on a person's history and, therefore, might have no idea what had been said earlier about the individual. By way of illustration, in a letter patent written before the above description, Bartholomew was said to be "*non compos mentis sue.*"[40]

Often terms appear in combination in a document and, given their frequency of usage, it might be expected that the most frequent phrase was *fatuus et idiota,* as above with Bartholomew. The conditional form of this phrase is often used when the clerk was explaining the reason as to why the king had the right to take the individual's lands, writing, *racione fatuitatis et idiocie* ("by reason of his senselessness and idiocy"). For example, "*racione fatuitatis et idiocie Johanis Bertelot*" was taken into the custody of the king.[41] John Bertelot was described in other documents as "*fatuus et idiota*," fatuous and an idiot and "has existed as such since birth."[42] Other phrases were used to describe the mentally incompetent with far less regularity; they include *idiocie et non compos mentis*[43] and *non compos mentis et fatuus*. For instance, John Cofe was described: "Cofe is a natural fool and he is without mental ability" ("*Coof [Cofe] est fatuus natural et non compos mentis sue.*")[44] Other types of combinations were helpful to the official trying to decide legal status—"from birth," "natural," "by the moon"—with *a nativitate* (from birth), as in the example above of Bartholomew Sakevill, being the most common: it appears 87 times compared to 16 appearances of *naturalis*, and 3 *a lune* (by the moon), which was more frequent among criminal descriptions.[45]

Scribes used other terms upon occasion and their use, both because they are rare and for that reason could indicate specific conditions, is worth some scrutiny. One such term is *ignorant*, which meant generally "not to know" and more specifically in the context of the mentally incapacitated "incapable of knowing." For example, in a *post mortem* inquisition for 1401, Ralph (*Radalphus*) Punchard is described as a "foolish idiot without a healthy [sane] memory . . . *ignorant* (incapable of knowing)" his surroundings.[46] Ralph's ignorance was not of something specific, but a general state of not understanding.

Another lesser-used term for mentally incapacitated landholders is *lunaticus,* someone often described as being affected specifically by the moon or who seems to have cycles of mentally incapacity as the moon has cycles. Only a few landholders in the administrative records of England are referred to as *lunaticus*, most of the time this was a term used for uncontrolled persons guilty of a crime. Landholders described as "lunatics" were done so only by association with the moon rather than with the direct term of *lunaticus*. For example, in 1302, the escheator examined William Berchaude and found him to be "manifestly an idiot (*idiota & non compos mentis sue*), and [he] has been so from his birth (*tempore nativitatis*)." William did not "enjoy lucid intervals" but the escheator had "heard [that] at lunations (*Lunaconnes*) [William] is worse and raves with madness (*furose* [sic])."[47] What exactly this indicates is harder to explain. It may be that William has "phases" like the moon, perhaps something akin to a modern bipolar disorder. William's family had other mentally incapacitated members, who were not labeled as *lunatics*. William's maternal uncle, John Danethorp, was "an idiot from birth" and his lands had been under the king's protection as well.[48]

It is not impossible to find multiple members of one medieval family who all had some type of mental disorder. It is, however, impossible from the scant evidence given in each record to make any kind of judgment as to what precisely this phenomenon indicates genetically, socially, or culturally, especially when each person was labeled differently.

Comparison of terms of passive and uncontrolled mental disabilities

Generally the data in *figures 1* and *2* especially are helpful in understanding what terms were used in what instances—whether the individual was considered a threat to the community, ill, disabled (as in unable to work), or a simpleton. A comparison of all of the terms provides the overall continuum of terminology (see *figure 9*), from the most passive (*idiota*) to the most aggressive (*freneticus*), since officials used those terms at the right-hand end of the spectrum in *figure 9* for the most aggressive or out of control persons guilty of homicide. The officials did not alter their vocabulary just because a person was normally a respectable member of the community; they would have still described him as frantic, furious, or not knowing good from bad. For example, Margaret Talbot who, while ill, murdered her two girls, Agnes and Maud. The records say that she was "*furia*" and "did not know good from bad."[49] Emma Hereward was granted a pardon for her murder of a neighbor's child, Maud, while demented ("*demenciam*") "on condition that she make peace with the relatives."[50]

Examining the few instances in which "non-standard" terms (those from the opposite end of the spectrum) were used to describe an individual—such as a term of passivity for a criminal or a term of aggressiveness for a landholder—provides a clearer sense of what the justices or scribes might have meant by these terms. For example, in 1265 William Pilche of Sonky is described as *fatuus*; according to the above definitions, he was therefore a foolish person or imbecile.[51] Yet, he is in the records for homicide. William met Augustine le Fevere on the road at night, the latter disguised as "a terrible monster uttering groans and refusing to speak though adjured [presumably by William] in God's name." William, not knowing how to qualify a joke from reality, "rushed upon him as a monster and killed him."[52] The words used by the recorder of the events implies that William did not normally "rage" but was a passive individual, who even thought enough in the moment to invoke

God's name, but could not reason deeply enough to recognize a disguise in the dim light.

Two of the instances in which terms often used for criminals were applied to landholders are both complex social situations. In the first, Thomas Corderye inherited a messuage in Bristol, and claimed that he was too impoverished to come to court to claim the land. Then suddenly, it seems, he "became a lunatic and went wandering."[53] Because his land was held in chief from the king, the king chose to take the land into his own hands. Thomas was later found confined as a lunatic ("*lunaticus*"), and was released since his lands were now in ward to the king. Thomas apparently had a mental condition of some kind in which he had some periods that were better than others. In the second case, John Dychton was to become the guardian of his mentally incompetent relative but he got lost on the way to deliver the paperwork to court. The escheator investigating the relative seems to have lost patience with John and not only "dared not" turn the wardship over to John, but also said John was "*non compos mentis* ... and ... manifestly frantic and an idiot (*manifestus frenetic est et idiota*)."[54] What exactly the escheator meant here is difficult to tease out. John got lost, which does not seem a good reason to describe someone as a *freneticus,* but, without more information, the description of John gives the impression that he had some kind of outburst. Perhaps he acted frantic and foolish once he returned unsuccessful. In this case, more information would be necessary to decide precisely what the esheator meant here by "*Johann de Dychton ... frenetic est et idiota*."

Insanus is the complicated term near the middle of the chart (*figure 9*). It was used equally for both landholders and criminals, though again because of the scarcity of records for criminals compared to those of landholders, the proportion favors use for criminals. Still, *insanus* seems to be used as a general term for a person with an "unhealthy mind" who is possibly prone toward physical uncontrollability. John de Inteberwe, for example, held land and was married, and yet "had been kept in bonds for fifteen years because of his insanity and . . . he labours under the same insanity (*adhuc in eadem laborate insania*) so that he cannot rule himself or preserve his lands and possessions."[55] Squatters had encroached on John's lands, and the king was taking steps to have John's wife recover them. The terms *idiota*, *fatuus*, or *non compos mentis* would not work as descriptions for John's condition presumably because of the physical aggressiveness of John in his affliction. John is in "bonds"; he is not an ordinary simpleton, nor intellectually slow. John was active or dangerous to the point that he had to be restrained, and a term was used that more adequately described his condition, *insanus*.

Another landholder described as *insanus* is Geoffrey Luterel. Geoffrey is not only described as laboring with insanity, but also of laboring with infirmity and of being *non compos mentis*. The officials had difficulty pinning Geoffrey with a particular description, though they do not say Geoffrey was bound or incarcerated. Geoffrey was married with children and was so afflicted that "he is incompetent for the rule of himself (*infirmitate laboret quod nec adregimen sui*) and his lands."[56] At different times, the officials, describing Geoffrey as being *insanus*, *infimitas,* and *non compos mentis*, were most likely examining a man who was physically somewhat uncontrolled, ill, and perhaps fatigued with his affliction. They did not describe him as a *lunaticus*, perhaps because he does not have lucid times, or because he did not have them regularly; but because he is married with children, he seems to have either had a late onset or he had better times and worse times within a continual incapacity.

Some Conclusions

It is important for scholars to recognize that medieval scribes and administrative officials did not use their terminology randomly. The various terms for mental illnesses and incompetence had specific meanings for those authors and their audiences, and they chose the right term for each condition as they assessed it. The analysis here incorporates variations used by officials, such as the description of John Gerard in 1251 of being in "mental disorder [unable to comprehend] ... living in continual dementia (*mentis sue incompotem ... demencia continua exstitesse*)."[57] The terminology in the administrative records presents a continuum of discrete conditions and symptoms of mental difficulties from the physically passive to the highly aggressive. Officials using these terms often described landholders in the records as *idiota* or another word for slow thinking or lack of memory, while they used terms of franticness or fury to describe the conditions of those guilty of crimes. These descriptions reflect the ill person's having lashed out while in pain or with fever. Certainly there must have been healthy individuals with these types of physically aggressive conditions who were carefully monitored to keep them from committing a crime, and they, therefore, do not appear in the records. John de Inteberwe may be one such person, and he came into the records because of his lands. Some terms in the middle of the spectrum were more descriptive of specific symptoms—*lunaticus* invoked a cyclical condition, while *sine intellectum* stated clearly that a person lacked the ability to understand.

The statistical analysis of the terms used to portray the mentally incapacitated in England from the thirteenth to the fifteenth century, demonstrates a wide variety of nominally understood conditions. A fourteenth century scribe would not have written "mad" (*furiosus*) or "lunatic" (*lunaticus*) when he meant "simpleton" (*idiota*). He knew the difference between these conditions and would have used the appropriate term. Moreover, he had a spectrum of terms from which to choose and would have used them in combination if that better described the condition of the person he saw before him. Finally, the official describing the mentally afflicted person before him implied certain behavioral patterns with the words he chose to use, signaling to readers the reasons for a person's misbehavior or crime, or substantiating removal from responsibilities because of a lack of ability and social awareness.

Notes

[1] Basil Clarke, *Mental Disorder in Earlier Britain: Exploratory Studies*, (Cardiff: University of Wales Press, 1975), 58-61; and Sara M. Butler, *The Language of Abuse: Marital Violence in Later Medieval England,* Leiden and Boston: Brill, 2007, 114-116.

[2] Clarke, 58-9; Wendy J. Turner, "*'Afflicted with Insanity': The Care and Custody of the Feeble Minded in Late Medieval England*, dissertation at UCLA [2000], 232-235.

[3] Ralph V. Turner, *The English Judiciary in the Age of Glanvill and Bracton, c. 1176-1239*, (Cambridge: Cambridge University Press, 1985), esp. 234-7; and G. O. Sayles, introduction, *Fleta vol. IV*, Selden Society series v. 99, (London: Selden Society, 1984), xv.

[4] Aside from chapters 11 and 12 in the *Prerogativa Regis* in *The Statutes of the Realm*, vol. I. King George III, 1810, (London: Dawsons of Pall Mall, reprinted 1963), see also: W. Turner, "Mental Incapacity and Financing War in Medieval England," in *The Hundred Years War: A Wider Focus, vol. 2*, edited by L.J. Andrew Villalon and Donald Kagay, (Leiden and Boston: Brill, 2008); David Roffe and Christine Roffe, "Madness and care in the community: a medieval perspective," *BMJ* 311 (1995): 1708-1712, accessed on the Internet 6/18/2003 at BMJ.com; and Basil Clarke, *Mental Disorder in Earlier Britain: Exploratory Studies*, (Cardiff: University of Wales Press, 1975).

[5] Latin scholars have translated *furiosi* into English in a variety of ways. On the one hand, according to J. A. C. Thomas the editor of *The Institutes of Justinian: Text, Translation and Commmentary*, (Amsterdam and Oxford: North Holland Publishers, 1975), *furiosi* were those mentally ill persons "capable of lucid intervals" (Thomas, 57). He often uses the English word "lunatic" to translate *furiosi*. On the other hand, J. A. Crook, author of *Law and Life of Rome, 90 B.C.-A.D. 212*, (Ithaca: Cornell University Press, 1967, reprint 1987), writes that the

ancient Romans distinguished between two kinds of feeble-mindedness, "someone born insane," the *furiosi*, and "someone who had become mad," the *mente capti*. Latin-English dictionaries will give various interpretations of the word *furiosi* including, raging, raving, mad, furious, passionate—all words of action, movement. *Furiosi* probably began as a description of a feeble-minded person akin to someone exhibiting pure anger, someone completely out of control. The image of, and variety of actions associated with, a complete lack of mental and physical control, suffices to describe some mentally ill persons. *Non compos mentis*, the lack of mental capacity, is associated with the term *furiosi* in at least one Roman legal text—*Code* 5. 70. 1 (*furiosus*) and 3 (*si pater tuus mentis compos non est*). Roman law did not seem to care about the time frame of the loss of capacity, just the present mental state of the individual, meaning that they did not necessarily make an issue of being born mentally incompetent, though that was noted with an added *a naturalis* or *a nativitate* when clarification was needed. Still, medieval readers of Roman law saw the two terms as different and interpreted them separately much as Crook did: *furiosi* being those who raged and *non compos mentis* being those who were passively unable to reason, often emphasizing a *loss* of mental capacity rather than the alternate definition of *without* mental capacity. It is important to look at when and how these terms were used since the legal scholars of the Middle Ages drew their distinctions between the terms based on the laws and circumstances in which the terms were used. It seems, though, given the evidence I present in this paper, that the division was not only between at birth and later life, a time oriented division, but also saw a the stronger division between rage and passivity in both Rome and medieval England .

[6] The biblical "epileptic demoniac" of the Gospels was called a *lunaticus* in medieval versions of the Bible. See: Matt 17: 15-20 and Luke 9: 38-43. For more information on Church law regarding the mentally incapacitated, see: R. Colin Pickett, *Mental Affliction and Church Law: An Historical Synopsis of Roman and Ecclesiastical Law and a Canonical Commentary*, (Ottawa, Ontario: The University of Ottawa Press, 1952), 2, 12. For Roman distinctions of periodic mental disorder, see: *Code* 5. 70. 6, *Cum aliis quidem hominibus continuum furoris infortunium accidit, alios autem morbus non sine laxamento ingreditur, sed in quibusdam temporibus quaedam eis intermissio pervenit, et in hoc ipso multa est differentia, ut quibusdam breves indutiae, aliis maiores ab huiusmodi* ... "It sometimes happens that the affliction of insane men remains continuous, and with others the attacks of disease are suspended, and lucid intervals occur, and in this latter instance a great difference exists, for some of the lucid intervals are short, and others are of long duration." R.W. Lee, *The Elements of Roman Law with a translation of the Institutes of Justinian*, 4th edition, (London: Sweet & Maxwell, 1956, 1986).

[7] This guardian was called a *curator,* who was to be the nearest *agnate* (male relative, or relatives, from the father's side). *Institutes* 1. 23. 3, 4. If no *agnate* existed, then an appropriate magistrate would appoint a *curator*. During the Roman Republic, the use of *agnates* as *curators* fell into disuse and the *praetor* replaced this practice by claiming a more general jurisdiction over the custody of all the

mentally incapacitated persons, much as the crown did in England in the thirteenth century. See also: Vacarius's *Liber Pauperum*, which became the textbook on Roman law in England. It was thought that if a student knew Vacarius's Roman law, he knew enough to work on ecclesiastical law. Students of common law read Vacarius, and it has been postulated that the author of Glanvill may have read an early version. Leonard E. Boyle, "The Beginnings of Legal Studies at Oxford," *Viator*, The Center for Medieval and Renaissance Studies at the University of California, Los Angeles, 14 (1983): 107, 114-118, 126; Peter Stein, "Vacarius and the Civil Law," in *Church and Government in the Middle Ages: Essays presented to C. R. Cheney on his 70th Birthday*, edited by C. N. L. Brooke et al, (Cambridge: Cambridge University Press, 1976), 119-137; R. W. Southern, "Master Vacarius and the Beginning of an English Academic Tradition," in *Medieval Learning and Literature: Essays presented to Richard William Hunt*, edited by J. J. G. Alexander and M. T. Gibson, (Oxford: Clarendon Press, 1976), 257-286; Stephen Kuttner and Eleanor Rathbone, "Anglo-Norman Canonists of the Twefth Century: An Introductory Study," *Traditio, Studies in Ancient and Medieval History, Thought and Religion*, 7 (1949-51): 279-358, esp. 323; H. G. Richardson and G. O. Sayles, *Law and Legislation from Aethelberht to Magna Carta*, (Edinburgh: University Press, 1966), 79; and *The Liber Pauperum of Vacarius*, edited by F. de Zulueta, Selden Society 44 (London: Quaritch, 1927).

[8] Ralph Russel, TNA: PRO C260/2, m 30 (formerly C47/55/6/204); Maud Levying, TNA: PRO C 260/3, m 19.

[9] For example, Roger Thurl was on trial for theft, and officials determined that he did not know good from evil (*de bono et malo*) in 1232, TNA: PRO JUST 1/62, m 5. Ralph Russel in the example above was also described as *insanus* and knowing neither good nor bad.

[10] Pickett, 13. Thomas Aquinas summarized the Church's official stand on baptizing the insane by advocating baptism either while a person was lucid and could consent or as if they had consented when lucidity did not seem an eventuality. *Summa Theologiae*, 3a, 71.2.

[11] TNA: PRO C 66/70, m. 13. See also: CPR 1247-58, p. 471.

[12] See case of Drew de Henle above and note 7.

[13] TNA: PRO C 260/11, m 1A (formerly C47/82/5/136) and *CCR* Ed. I, v. 2, 143.

[14] The author of *De legibus et consuetudinibus Angliae* wrote that just as young children lacked the knowledge and understanding to judge a situation, the mentally incapacitated should be accounted as children in their lack of understanding even though outwardly they might be adults. Henry de Bracton, *De Legibus et Consuetudinibus Angliae,* edited by George E. Woodbine, edited and translated by Samuel E. Thorne, 4 vols, (Cambridge: Harvard University Press, Belknap Press; London: Selden Society, 1968-1977), f. 336 and f. 420, (Thorne translation) IV 69, 308. See also: Frederick Pollock and F.W. Maitland, *The History of English Law Before the Time of Edward I*, 2nd edition, reissued with a new introduction by S.F.C. Milsom, 2 vols. (Cambridge: Cambridge University Press, 1968) 304-305, and 477.

[15] TNA: PRO C 260/53, mem 59.

[16] CPR Ed III v. 6, p. 15.
[17] "*... non est inde culpabit de bono et malo ...*" TNA: PRO C 260/36, m. 1
[18] *CCR* Ed. III, v. 13, 165 (Oct. 30, 1370). Similar statements in the records include: A homicide by John del Marche in 1293 in TNA: PRO C 260/7, m 46b (formerly C47/60/5/151). A homicide by Walter Makepays, in 1324 or 1325 in TNA: PRO C 260/37, m 5, C 260/35, m 9, and C 260/34, m 29 (formerly C47/86/27/712). And, a double homicide by Robert Angot in 1310 in TNA: PRO C 260/20, m 27 (formerly C47/70/4/147).
[19] Select cases from the Coroners' Rolls 1265-1413, Selden society vol. 9, 49-50.
[20] "*Ricardus ... in furore tempore quo fuit lunaticus.*" Select Pleas of the Crown, Selden Society vol. 1, p 119, #187.
[21] For Thomas Corderye see: CIM v. 2 p. 13 (#47) and for William le Vineter see CIM v. 2, p. 526 (#2093).
[22] Carole Rawcliffe, *Medicine and Society in Later Medieval England*, (Frome, Somerset: Sutton Publishing, 1977), 11, 35; and Naomi D. Hurnard, *The King's Pardon for Homicide Before A.D. 1307* (Oxford: Clarendon Press, 1969), 164-6.
[23] *Bracton* f. 149b, (Thorne II. 424).
[24] TNA: PRO C 260/3, m 19.
[25] TNA: PRO JUST 1/909A, m 27.
[26] TNA: PRO C 260/2, no 41 (formerly C47/64/8/240).
[27] TNA: PRO C 260/37, m 5; C260/35, m 9; and C260/34, m 29 (formerly C47/86/27/712).
[28] This is the raw data collected for each term and its variations per year.
[29] The "other" terms include the occasional use of some of those terms for mentally incapacitated criminals—*nec bonum nec malum, lunaticus, furiosus, freneticus, infirmitas*—and other terms rare to both groups—*demens, amens, ignorans, insanus, impotens, stultus, and sine intellectum.*
[30] Each graph from 5 through 8 depicts both the percentage of the total terms that each term was used per year and the relative percent each term was used in comparison to all other terms. To calculate this latter quantity for a specific year a running "boxcar" average for ten years prior and post of the usage of each term divided by the usage of all terms during the same 21 years and converted to a percentage. These "trend" lines are in relation to all other charts in the right-hand column, and they indicate changes in use patterns over time for each term. Because of the "boxcar" calculation, these lines begin and end ten years from the edge of the plot.
[31] A 10% yearly error translates to $10\%/\sqrt{21}$ for the running average, or approximately 4.5%. So, fluctuations of less than 4.5% between each time point of the running average are insignificant. The factor of $1/\sqrt{21}$ arises in standard statistical analysis to account for the number of terms in the running average.
[32] The spelling here is one of the various spellings of *idiota* and reflects this manuscripts spelling. TNA: PRO C 135/67, m 17.1 and m 17.6. See esp. *CIPM* Ed. III, v. 8, no. 713, p. 518.
[33] Scott L. Waugh, *England in the Reign of Edward III,* (Cambridge: Cambridge University Press, 199), 3.

[34] TNA: PRO C 60/234, m 7 and CRF v. 15 p. 180. See also: TNA: PRO C 60/235, m 21 and CFR v. 15, p. 192.
[35] TNA: PRO C 66/457, m 7. See also: CPR H VI v. 4 p 236 (1443). Most of the time during the period from 1355 to 1430, *fatuus* appears in conjunction with *idiota*; generally it is difficult to find *fatuus* as a single term.
[36] For a breakdown of the "other" terms, see note above.
[37] TNA: PRO C135/141, m. 33 and CIPM Ed III v. 10, p. 382 #483.
[38] TNA: PRO C 134/13, m 1. Bartholomew is also described as "*fatuitatis*" in C 66/109, m 25.
[39] TNA: PRO C 66/49, mem. 12, referring to Savary de Boun in 1240.
[40] TNA: PRO C 66/110, m 4.
[41] TNA: PRO C 60/213, m 26.
[42] TNA: PRO C 137/51, m 57 and C 60/211, m 12.
[43] For example: William Berchaude is "*idiota et non composes mentis sue*" in TNA: PRO C 133/106, m 17 (1302).
[44] TNA: PRO C 135/141, m 32 (1360).
[45] See: Savary de Boun, in footnote 35, and in the example above of Bartholomew Sakevill.
[46] "... *ideota fatuitate nec sane memoere* [sic] *est* ..." TNA: PRO C 137/29, m 74.
[47] TNA: PRO C 133/106, m 17 and CIPM Ed. I, v. 4, p. 78. See also: *CIPM* Ed. III, v. 7, p. 171 (1336) when William died. Elsewhere William was described as "*fatuus et idiota,*" see TNA C 135/44, m. 2).
[48] William's mother, Alice, and her sister (his aunt) Margery and her daughter, Joan, would have been his heirs, but he outlived them all. His first guardian was someone from his father's family, a John Berchaud; and, at the time of William's death, William de Redmer, was listed as his heir. See note above.
[49] TNA: PRO C 260/20, m 9b (1309).
[50] TNA: PRO C 66/62, m 6 and CPR 1247-58, p. 100.
[51] TNA: PRO C 66/83, mem. 22 and CPR 1258-66 p. 407. The translator for the calendar translated *fatuus* as "idiot." The roll reads in part, "*William Pilche de Sonky fatuus pro regiam fatuitam noctantus* ..." See also: CPR 1258-66, p. 407.
[52] Ibid.
[53] TNA: PRO C 54/129, m 22; CIM v. 2 p. 13; and CCR Ed. II v. 1 p. 382. The records do not say whether the king planned to care for Thomas, only that he had taken charge of the property.
[54] TNA: PRO C 133/46, m 2 and CIPM Ed. I v. 2 #611 p. 373.
[55] TNA: PRO C 66/73, mem 2 and CPR 1258-66, p. 46.
[56] TNA: PRO C 66/74, m 14; C 66/84, m 25; and C 66/88, m 27. See also: CPR 1258-1266, p. 58 and 564, and CPR 1266-1272, p. 392.
[57] CCR H III v. 7, p. 177

Figure 1. Frequency of Terms used for Mentally Incapacitated Criminals

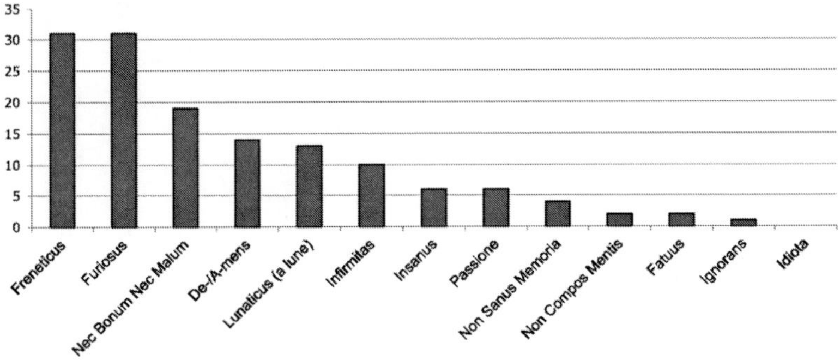

Figure 2. Frequency of Terms used for Mentally Incompetent Landholders

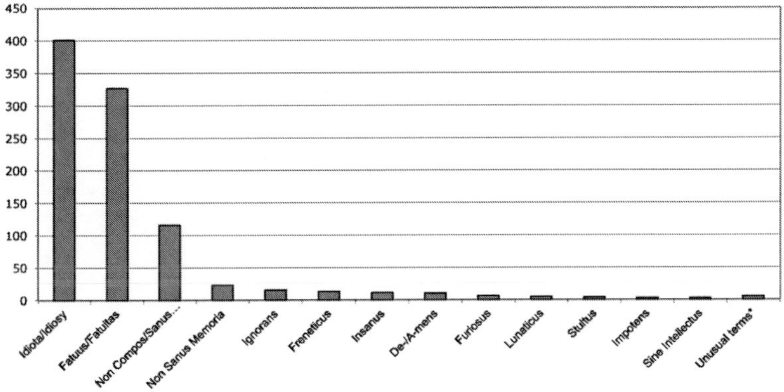

Figure 3. Documents analyzed per year from over 650 manuscripts

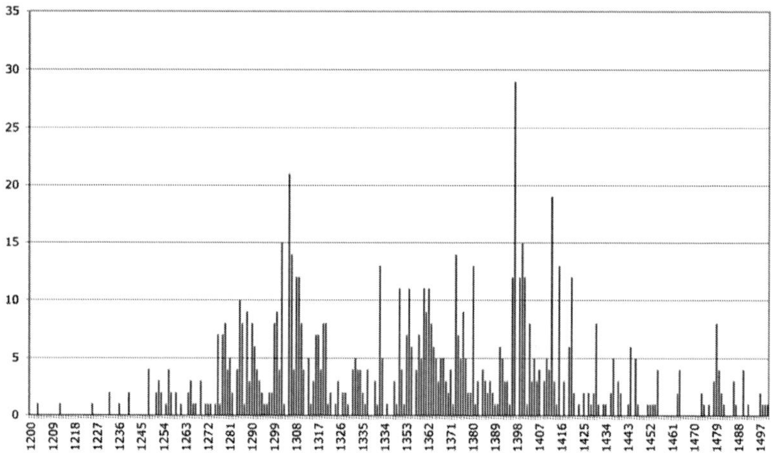

Terms taken from the records per year for a total of 1593 terms used. The average used per year is in bold.

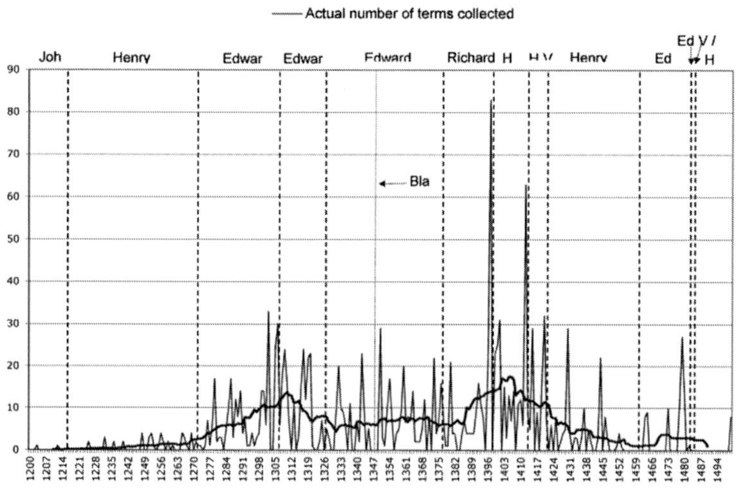

Figure 4. Data Collected for each term for mentally incapacitated landholders by year

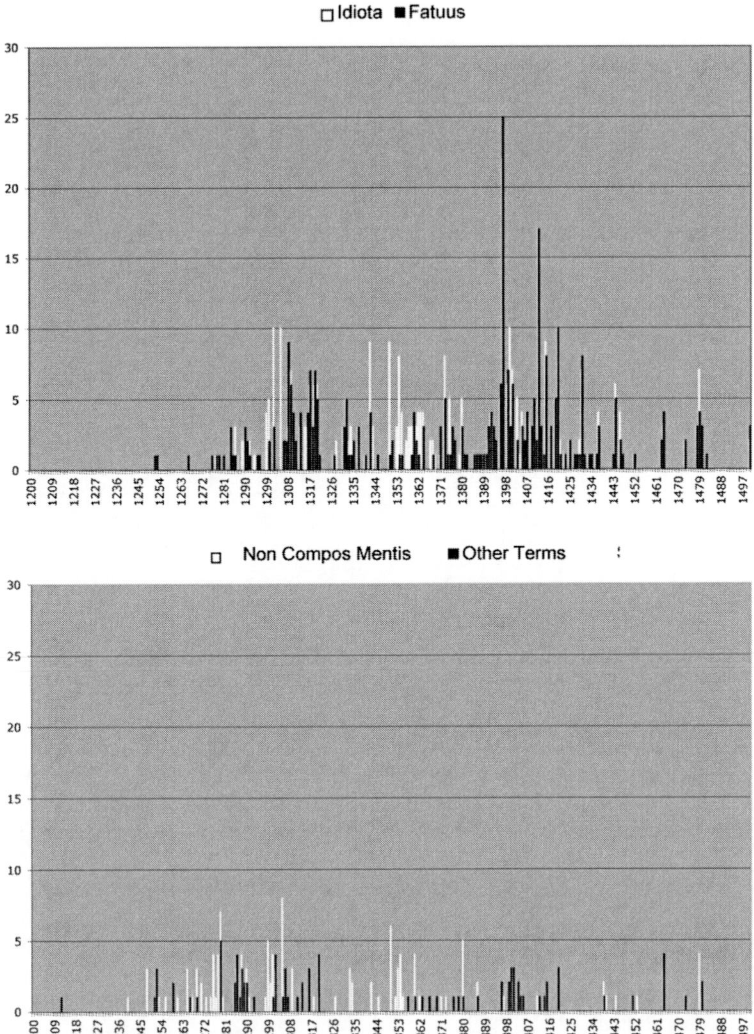

Figure 5

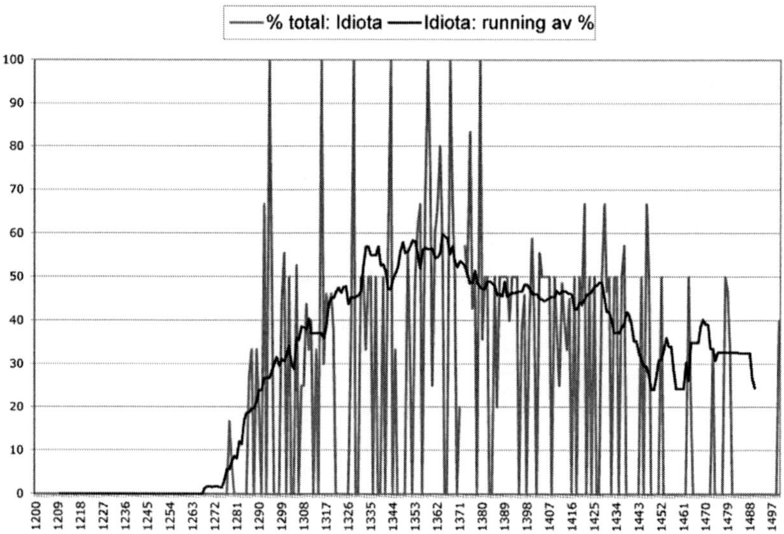

Figure 6

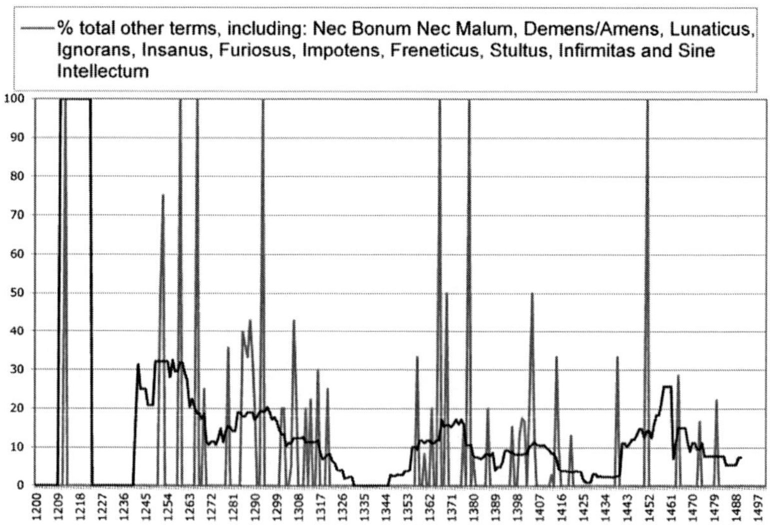

Figure 7

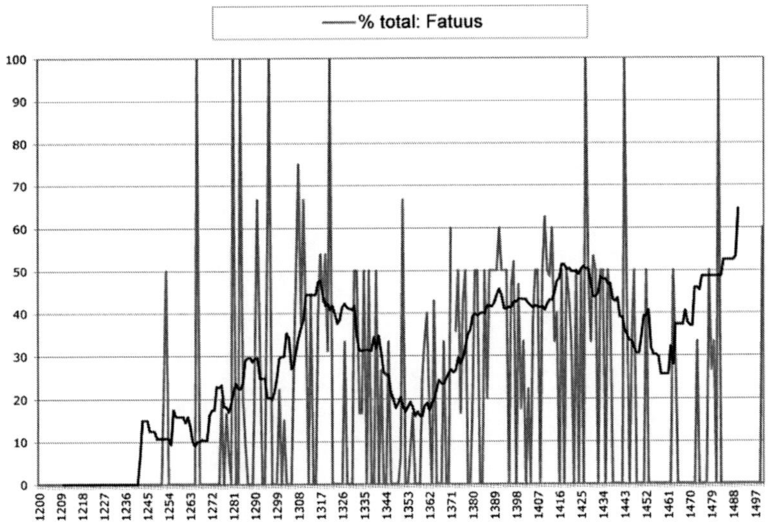

Figure 8

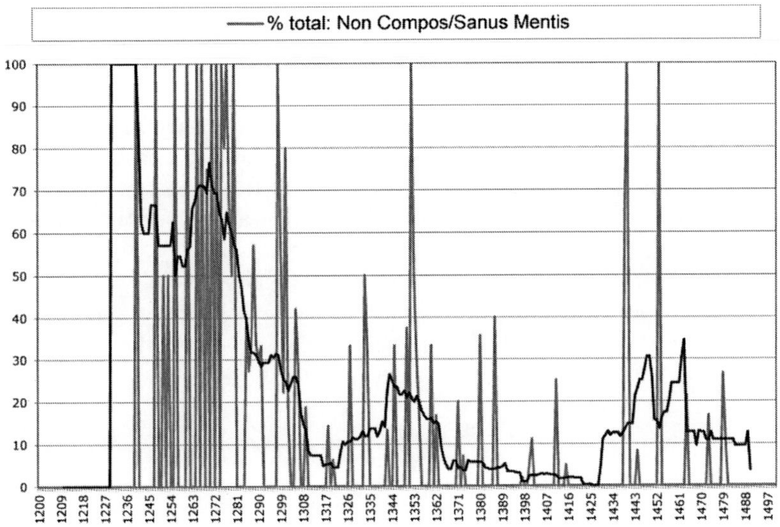

Figure 9. Comparison of percentage of use of Terms for Landholders and Criminals

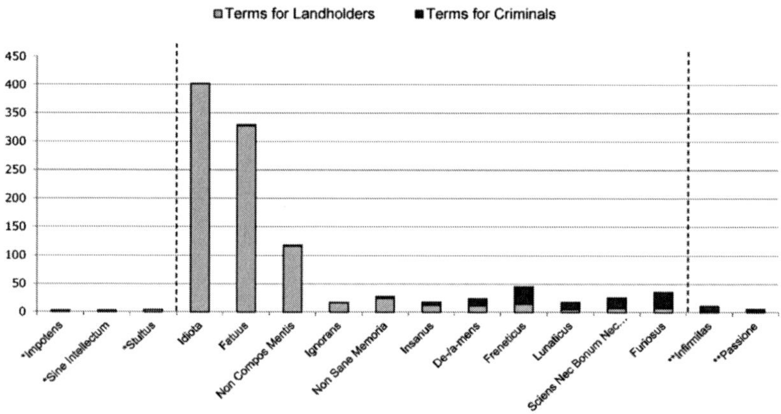

* These terms are rare and, of those found in the records, only used for landholders. This does not mean that they would never be used for criminals since the data on criminals is so much lower than that for landholders.
** These terms are only used in conjunction with other terms for criminals. They are not used for landholders in administrative records. Typically these are employed in conjunction with other terms, such as *furiosus* or *frenticus*, in descriptions of reasons criminals are being granted a pardon.

The center portion of this chart, between the two dashed lines, is the main scale by percentage from most used terms to least used for landholders, and running opposite—from right to left—most used to least used for criminals. The medieval English administration used these terms, from *idiota* to *furiosus*, on a continuum of persons lacking comprehension from passive to uncontrolled. *Freneticus* is used significantly to indicate the quality of a mentally disabled person's actions for both landholders and criminals. *Insanus*, at the midpoint and used equally for both landholders and criminals, seems to be a general term for the mentally unhealthy in the records.

PHILOMELA ACCUSES

CORY JAMES RUSHTON

Chaucer's use of the Philomela legend, in his *Legend of Good Women*, suggests that he saw a number of interconnected issues in Philomela's story. One of these, I will attest, is a previously unnoticed interest in disability, communication and accommodation involving the consequences of a criminal act. In the story, a woman is raped and mutilated by her brother-in-law, Tereus of Thrace, raising the obvious issue of male violence against women; less obviously it raises the place of pity and sympathy in medieval culture, and the problem of voice raised by that culture's deep investment in a particular gendered and hierarchical vision of authority (of who can speak and when). Chaucer's motivations for writing *The Legend of Good Women* are debated and, at the same time, probably varied. Comedic and meta-textual, unfinished either by design or because Chaucer grew bored, the *Legend* is a text that rewards a variety of approaches (further complicated by the existence of two distinct versions of the prologue).[1] Within the text itself, the poet-narrator is clearly Chaucer, who is being forced to pursue the *Legend* project as a penance for the composition of *Troilus and Criseyde*, which the God of Love Cupid has deemed offensive to women since it contains Criseyde's betrayal of her lover Troilus. In the *Legend*, Chaucer will make amends by telling the stories of women betrayed and harmed by faithless men. Philomela's story is only one of several told in the *Legend*, some of which will be discussed below, and the text is generally considered unfinished both because of and despite the ludicrous nature of the project: not only does the narrator have to tell stories "Of wommen trewe in lovyng al hire lyve" (438), the F version has the God of Love point to "twenty thousand" women whose stories should be included; with a perverse kindness, he tells the narrator to start anywhere he likes (559-62). Kara A. Doyle puts this central understanding of the text best: "…with its angry and hermeneutically challenged God of Love, its obsequious and misunderstood poet-narrator, and its generous queen Alceste, Chaucer poses the question: how did medieval audiences, particularly women, respond to representations of women in texts?"[2] I will argue that the

Philomela tale, at least, also testifies to anxieties about the spoken word, particularly in the context of a very specific "reporting": that of the witness, even the victim, of a crime. This is inextricably related to gender, but has wider implications when considered in light of Philomela's disability.

The *Legend* (henceforward *LGW*) has been seen as a series of hagiographic parodies or anti-feminist rhetoric (or both), often based on stories by the Roman poet Ovid, or an ironic meditation on courtly love. Further, the text seems to speak to anxieties about the written word and composition and about the writing of history in particular.[3] In this case, the loss of Philomela's ability to speak symbolically and simultaneously deprives her of the right to be heard. This article will attempt to bring Chaucer's multiple themes into dialogue with the idea of law, particularly the role of the witness. For Philomela is both a witness and a victim, who cannot tell her own story in a way that medieval English law perceives as legitimate and binding: her tongue is cut out so she cannot report the rape she has suffered, and can no longer voice her own pain. Instead, she weaves the story into a tapestry, a different kind of witness – in fact, something prosthetic, an aid that makes up for a perceived abnormality taking the form of a lack or an absence. In Ovid, the prosthetic tapestry leads to something like justice, in the form of revenge; in Chaucer, it leads nowhere, for his culture's attitude to and reliance upon the spoken word is very different from Ovid's (as Ovid's differed from the culture that first told Philomela's story).

Within the texts, we can dismiss what Foucault called the spectacle of the scaffold: in no version is Philomela's mutilation a proper punishment (she has done nothing wrong) nor is it meant to be perceived as an object lesson. Indeed, it is not meant to be perceived at all: here, "power" tries to hide a violation through another violation, and is over-determining things by both eliminating the possibility of speech/witness and then imprisoning the victim. As Foucault put it, torture "assured the articulation of the written on the oral, the secret on the public, the procedure of investigation on the operation of the confession; it made it possible to reproduce the crime on the visible body of the criminal; the same horror had to be manifested and annulled. It also made the body of the condemned man the place where the vengeance of the sovereign was applied, the anchoring point for a manifestation of power".[4] In the Philomela tradition, any link/correlation between the power of the sovereign and justice is inverted: power is abused, even stolen, by a man who has no real claim to Philomela. What is made semi-visible in this story (as brutal it is, a severed tongue is not as immediately manifest as a severed hand or a branded face) is a man's crime on the body of his victim; while it might be perversely comforting to suggest this is simply the wrong way around, another level of injustice, it is closer to the point to suggest that this is how power has always worked, the law of the sovereign being whatever the sovereign sees as legal and proper. Chaucer, I suggest, comes closest to acknowledging this reality in his version, which lacks any resolution which might offer closure and catharsis.

Muteness is often linked to deafness in popular discourse; in both cases, the inability to engage in oral, heard communication is imagined as crippling, given that the social norm would seem to depend on oral communication. Something like sign language, then, is seen even today as a substitute for the normal, an also-ran form of communication. Yet change is occurring rapidly. Roger J. Carver has written on the deaf community's on-going debate over whether or not it is a disabled community: many deaf persons point to their own living language, sign language, and to growing evidence of deaf culture in order to demonstrate that the deaf community is a culture like any other (henceforth the Deaf community, upper case). To this way of thinking, a speaking person would have the same problems communicating with Deaf people as they would with the citizens of a foreign country.[5] In this context, the speaking person would be the disabled one, because the Deaf community's communication system is unknown to them. While it would be a stretch to say that Sign language is as old as communication itself, there is compelling evidence that "as early as Plato's *Cratylus*, Western 'hearing' intellectuals have been aware of the manual languages of Deaf communities".[6] To qualify as a language, of course, a system of signs needs to be understood across different groups and regions. Philomela's story, especially if woven into pictures and unaccompanied by words, is fully legible only to a handful of people, none of whom share her new disability.

Muteness, as in Philomela's case, is potentially in the same category and finds the same solution: she finds a way to communicate her story non-orally, perhaps even more effectively than with mere words, but her culture cannot see past her voicelessness and thus cannot bear witness to her actual voice. Henry Bracton's opinion was that the mute could not swear any oath: "It is clear that one who is dumb can neither stipulate nor promise, since he cannot speak or utter the words appropriate to a stipulation."[7] An English court in 1224 asked William Maufre to appoint an attorney because he was ill; unable to speak, Maufre appointed his son Reynold "in so far as he could speak" through his paralysis, only to later learn that Reynold would not be admitted to the court. His father's inability to communicate extended as far as his legal ability to appoint someone to speak for him.[8] When this is the case, what hope does a tapestry have to replace the all-important tongue? Ovid imagines the possibility of communication beyond the spoken word, but Chaucer cuts that possibility off for wider textual reasons. Philomela's helplessness suits his thematic purpose in the *Legend of Good Women*, but that her mutilation can work so easily with that sense of helplessness tells us something about medieval thinking about disability, especially when the latter is linked to gender: pity first, charity second, accommodation a distant third. The trick here is to locate Philomela's story not in–or just in–the history of gender relations or the reception of Greek legend, but in the history of the written document or recording, particularly the oath which is often central to historical legal and social customs across cultures.

Clanchy's discussion of the long movement from a predominantly oral culture to a culture of the written word in a medieval English context, the written oath or contract, is relevant here. Resistance to written contract was both wide and lasted a long time: Clanchy's book tracks the period from the Norman Invasion of 1066 to 1307, and notes that the process continued after his period. He notes how books were perhaps more important as objects than they were for the specific wording recorded in them, almost magical objects, and sometimes seem to be in the same category as seals, relics, and even weapons, all of which could symbolize agreements and relationships. The English experience is indeed part of a much longer, pan-cultural European movement towards a literacy culture which Socrates, in Plato's *Phaedrus*, found disturbing: communication without a body, present and able to defend its own speech, was for him dead and inert. M. T. Clanchy remains the best discussion of this process in the context of medeval England: "Taken together, these fragmentary details help to reconstruct ways of thinking and remembering which were widespread before the coming of written records. The growth of literacy did not occur in a cultural vacuum. It replaced non-literate ways, which seemed equally natural to those who were accustomed to them. The most difficult initial problem in the history of literacy is appreciating what preceded it."[9] Philomela's tapestry, in this long context, itself shifted in meaning: the earliest legend, orally communicated, would not testify to the same anxious concern for "proper" communication. Its anxieties fully rooted in the Greek attitude to gender: the problem of proper masculine authority, and who holds it, but also the problem of the vengeful woman (or better, the problem of woman as moral agent). Philomela's ability to portray the crime that occurred would be something like a miracle; by Chaucer and Gower's time, the technologies of narrative have passed by the pictorial, and legal authority has begun to revolve around the written in ways that would horrify Socrates. Philomela's desperate plea to be "heard" becomes ever-more desperate, ever less likely to achieve anything like a satisfactory resolution, as the technologies of communication and authority change around her story.

Ovid's Philomela

The original story of Philomela ultimately comes to Chaucer from one of his favourite sources, Ovid's *Metamorphoses*, a collection of tales largely concerning the male pursuit of women and female efforts to avoid rape and seduction. King Tereus of Thrace marries Procne, the eldest daughter of King Pandion of Athens; five years later, Procne misses her sister and asks Tereus if they can visit, whether that means Philomela coming to Thrace or Procne going home to Athens. Tereus goes to bring Philonela to Thrace, and overcome with lust he rapes her on the way back; when she threatens to tell the world what he has done, he cuts out her tongue and imprisons her. She weaves the story into a tapestry (sometimes a robe), and sends it to Procne. Together, the sisters kill Itys, son of Tereus and Procne, and feed him to his father. They flee. When they fear Tereus will catch them, the sisters pray to the goods for help, and are transformed into birds: Procne becomes a swallow, Philomela a nightingale (although earlier Greek sources suggest the other way around, with Philomela becoming the silent swallow). Tereus is transformed as well, usually but not always into a hoopoe. In Ovid, the tortured body of Philomela speaks not to the justice of power but its opposite: the revelation of the torture brings down a powerful man, and leaves only birdsong in its place.

Elissa Marder provides the best articulation of the modern (feminist) response to Philomela's fate:

> The textual relationship established between these two acts (the rape and the severed tongue) interrogates the significance and readability of the term "rape" itself. The severed tongue does not merely function as a narrative consequence of the rape, but rather becomes a figurative representation of it. The act of cutting off the tongue reads that rape and gives it a figurative meaning. The rape itself does not become either fully figured or fully meaningful until it is repeated by the mutilation that ostensibly functions to cover it up. Rather than suppressing the rape, Tereus' act of cutting off Philomela's tongue both represents and repeats it.[10]

The text appears to reverse the literal and the symbolic: "The first actual rape is accompanied and preceded by a speech act that announces the crime. The act of speaking rape is supplemented by the act of "raping" speech – the cutting off of the tongue – that occurs later."[11] Interpretation of the textuality of the rape is obviously complicated by Philomela's own textualizing of the actual rape and the symbolic rape effected by the mutilation:

> Because the possibility of an immediate vocal articulation is no longer open to her, weaving becomes a medium of self-expression and a communication. In this respect, we may say that her weaving takes place in a sphere of intermediacy: in weaving she allows meaning to unfold between the spoken and the written, between the natural and the conventional, between the sensitivity of the tongue and the external rule of an objective language.[12]

As Vered Lev Kenaan notes, Ovid is concerned throughout the *Metamorphoses* with his own poetics, particularly in Books 4-6 which see a proliferation of stories which conflate women, weaving, and narrative itself.[13] This is one reason for Chaucer's interest in Ovidian narrative: he, too, is obsessed with the problem of truth and fiction, narrative and the events narrated.

The Philomela story appears elsewhere in the Ricardian era, in John Gower's Middle English *Confessio Amantis*.[14] Gower's Tereus is found in the fifth book, dedicated to Avarice, which looks odd to the modern reader but is really a reminder that, at root, rape was still a property crime: however much Chaucer and Gower are beginning to pay attention to the person we'd consider the actual victim of the crime. Gower's Tereus is overcome with a lust that seems to give him a greater strength and power than that which he normally has:

> And with the sihte he gan desire,
> And sette his oghne herte on fyre;
> And fyr, whan it to tow [straw] aprocheth,
> To him anon the stengthe acrocheth,
> Til with his hete it be devoured,
> The tow ne mai noght be socoured. (*CA* V.5621-26)

This is an old but still troubling explanation for rape: that it is motivated first by an uncontrollable lust for a physical body which then, like straw, both feeds the fire and is consumed by it. Gower emphasizes how her own body becomes a weapon used against Philomela: she is later bound by her own hair moments before he clips out her tongue with a pair of shears (*CA* V.5685-91; Chaucer's Tereus uses a sword, a more traditional symbol of masculine, phallic authority).

Gower's Philomela is allowed dialogue in which she promises to tell her story "with my speche" (*CA* V.5659-60), and after her mutilation, we hear her internal speech (5741-68) – she still has more of a voice than Chaucer's version ever has, as we will see. Gower's Philomela can apparently write: her tapestry, based on a "cloth of Selk al whyt", contains both "lettres and ymagerie" which outlines the "felonie, / Which Tereüs to hire hath do" (5770-73). (In antiquity, only the Philomela of Apollodorus can actually weave in letters rather than images.)[15] When Procne sees the cloth, she immediately concludes that "wepinge is not the bote" or remedy. Something must be done: vengeance taken, justice served. Chaucer's version ends very differently, precisely focused on the use (or lack of use) of weeping.

Pity Party: Chaucer's Version

Tereus' violent desire to eliminate Philomela's ability to speak, and thereby accuse him of rape, effectively disables her. The point seems an obvious one, although a closer attention to disability theory itself will complicate how this sense of the obvious. Philomela's voice is already ineffective even before her mutilation:

> She cryeth 'Syster!' with ful loud a stevene,
> And 'Fader dere!' and 'Help me, God in hevene!'
> Al helpeth nat; and yit this false thef
> Hath don this lady yit a more myschef,
> For fere lest she shulde his shame crye
> And don hym openly a vilenye,
> And with his swerd hire tonge of kerveth he … (*LGW* 2327-34)

Alone, Philomela finds that voice without audience is essentially no voice at all: the "al" that she performs includes injunctions to two people who are not there (Procne and Pandeon) and one who is distant (God, in fact absent because Philomela's is a pre-Christian world without access to God's grace or assistance, a thematic concern in Chaucer's work, particularly the *Knight's Tale*). Corinne Saunders has fully examined the trope of rape in medieval English literature, including in this story; she argues that Tereus's literal silencing of Philomela graphically evokes larger cultural silences concerning sexual assault, and she notes that while Ovid gives Philomela a long speech following the rape, Chaucer deletes this: "Philomela has in a sense already been silenced by the rape".[16] Scholarship has often reminded us that rape is a property crime throughout much of the Middle Ages; Saunders argues that Chaucer testifies to a new trend in the fourteenth century, in which the woman is increasingly seen as the primary victim. But the exchange of women still lurks in these stories: Philomela is in Tereus's power because Tereus is her brother-in-law, who has sought and been given permission to bring her to visit Procne, her sister and his wife.

Gia Aloni discusses a similar issue in another of the legends, that of Hypermnestra, finding in this tale a positive transition space between father and husband: when Hypermnestra is ordered by her father to kill her husband on their wedding night, she finds herself in a suspended space, not quite daughter, not yet fully a wife. Her imprisonment, following her refusal to obey her father's command, results in a "paradoxical liberation from the structure of the exchange of women."[17] If, as Aloni argues, Chaucer here "radically questions the very nature of the exchange of women", he may be doing so in the other legends as well. When Philomela's father grants Tereus his request, he and his daughter weep as though it were the last time they will ever see each other, and he specifically asks Tereus to give Procne permission to see him "oones or I deye" (*LGW* 2296-2301). Tereus's absolute ownership of Procne seems, somehow, transferred onto Philomela as well. The original story makes it clear that Tereus is given Procne as a means of averting a Thracian invasion of her father's kingdom, Athens. That Tereus clearly feels he has some kind of claim to both sisters comes through in virtually every version. Chaucer's legend, however, faintly hints that some of the blame for Philomela's mutilation lies not with the exchange itself, but with the one effective use of female voice in the legend: Procne's request that Philomela visit her. Philomela's tapestry narrates "How she was served for her suster love" (2365).

Chaucer's legend itself emphasizes the senses, preparing the reader for Philomela's loss of voice: Procne's desire to *see* her sister is repeated three times in five lines:

> … Til on a day she gan so sore longe
> To seen her suster that she saughe nat longe,
> That for desire she nyste what to sey.
> But to hir husband gan she for to prey,
> For Goddys love, that moste ones goon
> Hir suster for to seen … (2260-65)

Tereus echoes this emphasis on sight when he asks their father Pandeon if Philomela "myght / On Procne his wyf but ones have a sight" (2275-76). The text emphasizes sight so often because it is sight that will be found wanting at the conclusion: sight without the words to describe what is seen or experienced is imagined as ineffective. Procne's foreshadowing inability to speak her desire, albeit a temporary inability, as she then proceeds to pray "day be day" for a visit from her sister; Chaucer might already be hinting that it would have been better for Philomela if Procne's speechlessness had lasted, for her prayers put Philomela in harm's way – however rightly uncomfortable this hint that anyone but the rapist Tereus is responsible for his crime might make us. Chaucer may, in fact, be more alive to this discomfort than might be expected.

The problem of Tereus is a problem of inappropriate sovereignty: Tereus abrogates a power to himself that he does not really have, over a person/body he does not have the right to control. Even to imprison Philomela is to create a civilized space in the wilderness, a habitation in which Tereus can aspire to true sovereignty, the power to dispense justice and create law – to control the bodies of others. To some extent, the tale's ending, with both sisters weeping and voiceless in this prison space, would seem to imply that Tereus has succeeded. He goes unpunished (except intertextually, which is less than satisfying). Once pity becomes thre main point of the story, revenge becomes impossible if there is no way to communicate the crime to the proper authority. And in this version more than any other, Chaucer undermines the efficacy of the tapestry.

Philomela's tapestry is perhaps of greater importance for a disability reading of Chaucer's version than her horrific impairment itself. When Philomela finds a way around her injury by using other skills, the reader should admire her. Chaucer tells us that Philomela had "ylerned in yowthe" to weave and embroider, and that she "koude eke rede wel ynogh and endyte" as part of that weaving; she can write with thread, but "with a penne coulde she nat wryte" (2350-57). Saunders suggests that this means that Philomela can create letters through weaving, but the act of penmanship is beyond her.[18] At the same time, Clanchy notes that it was possible to imagine someone illiterate even if they could, as Walter Map put it, "transcribe any series of letters whatever."[19] Even before her injury, Philomela has access to an alternate (feminine) mode of communication, albeit one which must be more time-consuming than the masculine pen. Momentarily, Chaucer opens up the possibility of radically different forms of "literacy", of what can and should be read or be legible. But it is shut down again very quickly, contrary to most other versions. While Clanchy does note that other kinds of objects (knives, for example, with writing on them) could be read symbolically, that symbolism seems to preclude reading them in a documentary sense: "The unfamiliar idea of a writing being interpreted primarily as a symbolic object, rather than as documentary proof, is most clearly evident when the object written upon is not a parchment, but something else."[20]

Hypermnestra disobeyed her father's order to murder her husband because she felt that her hand was not shaped to hold a knife: "I am a mayde, and, as by my nature .... / Myne handes ben nat shapen for a knyf" (2690-92). The *Legend* consistently notes that pens and knives, phallic objects metonymically and traditionally invested with male/masculine authority, are out of place in the hands of women Chaucer is trying to make us pity. If voice is rooted in phallic authority, women are already voiceless in the sense that their communication is rootless; the physical removal of a tongue only makes real what is already symbolically true. Nevertheless, faced with a silencing injury Philomela refuses to act disabled, and instead attempts to enable herself through this alternative means: the weaving of her story in the physical form of a tapestry (2350-65). The presence of the servant who brings the tapestry to Philomela's sister does not here undermine the disabled woman's efforts (2366-72); the "knave" or man-servant is necessary because, in addition to her physical impairment, Philomela is being kept "in a prisoun everemore" for her assailant's "usage and his store" (2335-38). Hypermnestra's prison might be liberating in some limited sense, but Philomela's prison is a different and more traditional kind of stasis.

The language of pity is ubiquitous in the *Legend of Philomela*: Chaucer's "eyen waxen foule and sore" when he recalls what he is about to narrate. Philomela weeps piteously when she is brought to the cave prior to the rape, and Tereus pretends to weep piteously when he falsely relays the news of Philomela's death (2317, 2340). There is more than enough weeping to go around: Pandeon when first asked to let Philomela go at 2279, Procne when she finds her sister at 2380. Everyone already seems have some sense concerning what is about to happen beforehand, leading to perpetual lamentation. Procne finds Philomela and is at first equally speechless (again) "for sorwe and ek for rage" (2374). Chaucer leaves them lamenting in each other's arms, and further says nothing of the subsequent fate of Tereus. Laura Getty argues that "Procne's act of reading is informative ... since it is clear that the story is powerful enough" and "would be more powerful if it were told in full, truthfully", by which she means the inclusion of the fate of the son of Procne and Tereus, but she draws from this the conclusion that Chaucer is limited – even silenced – in what he can say.[21] The God of Love's commandment to tell stories in praise of women necessitates Chaucer's silence. Certainly, the revenge of Philomela and her sister can have no place in Chaucer's project; any sympathy would be lost in the time it takes for Procne to cook her son and serve him to his father, her husband. For Chaucer (or the God of Love), the power of this story must reside not in the escalation of horror as Tereus's crime tears the family apart, but in the initial reaction of the two women to that crime. In other words, the power of the story is its potential for the evocation of pity: melodramatic, emotional, and ultimately harmless.

The fate of Tereus is not the only element missing from this version of Philomela's story. Chaucer also chooses not to depict the transformation of the three main characters into birds: Tereus, a hoopoe; Philomela, a nightingale; Procne, a swallow. Saunders sees in the Ovidian legend's conclusion "a sense of pathos and loss rather than simply replacing the silencing of the woman with further violence and destruction … [and] … ends with a shift of power back towards the woman through her regaining of a voice".[22] To eliminate the birds is again to enforce silence, to eliminate voice and noise. As discussed earlier, Aloni sees the collection's final tale of Hypermnestra as concerned with the woman's refusal to participate in family violence, and ending in the peaceful stasis of a prison; the tale that comes between Philomela's and Hypermnestra's is that of Phyllis of Thrace, which argues for incomplete restoration of the female agency even more clearly. The original story reverses Philomela's geography–now the betrayer, Demophon is from Athens, and the victim from Thrace–but its original ending has the same shock value: knowing she is to be abandoned, Phyllis gives Demophon a casket which he should only open when he knows he will never return. He does so a year later, just as she herself commits suicide, and he goes mad at the sight of the mysterious contents. Chaucer's Phyllis kills herself after writing a very sad letter. In fact, as Dinshaw notes, Chaucer only gives us the parts of her letter which he thinks were good enough to report:[23]

> Hire letter was right long and therto large.
> But here and ther in rym I have it layd,
> There as me thoghte that she wel hath sayd (2515-17)

Hypermnestra may find a way out that is paradoxically a staying-in, fitting for the final legend of the collection, but if Phyllis finds a voice here, it is no more effective than Philomela's. Chaucer's beleaguered narrator takes control of her tongue, communicating only the best – because most piteous – parts. Gower's Phyllis suffers the same traditional fate, although his Demophon fails to return to her not because he is insensitive but because he procrastinates (the overarching theme of Gower's Book 4 of the *Confessio Amantis*, where the story is retold, is Sloth).

This emphasis on pitying Philomela may be perfectly understandable, particularly in light of the sexual crime committed; but that pity falters when it leads nowhere, and Chaucer very carefully ensures that it does not. Joseph Shapiro, a disability activist, called his book *No Pity*, arguing that pity is useless if not backed up with a dedication to breaking down barriers.[24] It is not enough to feel sorry for Philomela (or the others); it would be better to read her message, but alternative forms of communication are unacceptable, to some degree even unthinkable. Chaucer's evocation of pity is integral to any reading of the *Legend of Good Women*, which truncates the stories of the good women wherever necessary to maintain the reader's sympathy. The question is whether Chaucer intends us to lament not just the events, but the apparent lack of legal remedy (but also spiritual remedy, in that the pagan Philomela has no access to the Christian God she cries out to during the rape).

Hearing Philomela – Is a Tapestry Prosthetic?

The tongue is "the producer of language" which is also "the organ that most closely allies the sexual body to the speaking soul."[25] Sarah Stanbury suggests that the tongue is a metonymy for language as it is located in the body, specifying that "Chaucer's tongues serve much more often as agents of language than as agents of digestion"; she notes several instances of the linguistically disruptive tongue in Chaucer's *Canterbury Tales*, including the *Clerk's Tale* and the *Manciple's Tale* (which could be expected in the latter, a tale which gives us the observation that just as "a swerd forkutteth and forkerveth / An arm a-two … right so / A tonge kutteth freendshipe al a-two").[26] Stanbury's discussion of the Prioress' little clergeon, a young boy who is murdered for singing a Christian hymn in a Jewish neighbourhood, begins with a moment she herself admits is "very brief, a small flash in the narrative": at the end of her tale, an abbot grasps the dead child's tongue in order to remove the miraculous "greyn' which the Virgin Mary has placed there to allow the latter to tell his story, a true prosthetic device.[27] As Stanbury argues, the abbot's action "literally severs language, and by holding the tongue he masters it"; in doing so, he marks the "the moment that defines the body of the boy as sacred object":

> And if the abbot appears to violate the child's body by reaching into his mouth to grab his tongue, that action can be typologically justified or at least explained by the move of the narrative towards severance and salvation. The body is inert, dead matter signifying the split between corpus/corpse and eternal life. The abbot cannot violate the body, since

> that body, in part through the very sacramental action of the abbot himself, is now supremely unimportant. Life is elsewhere.[28]

There is much to interest us here. The abbot's severing of language through a mastery of the tongue is a metaphorical one, and furthermore an act of kindness: the boy requests that he be allowed to rest after telling his story (the prosthetic enables the boy to remain in a painful world, an ambiguous gift at best). Tereus' severing of Philomela's tongue is, obviously, a literal carving of the flesh which leaves Philomela speechless but does not leave Tereus in control: he can discard her tongue but not master it. 'Life is elsewhere' for the boy, but not for Philomela, who must live on, and the tale traditionally allows for the possibility that speech will always find a way out. Chaucer gives us only the readable or interpretable tapestry, but other than Procne's, he shows us no accompanying act of reading or interpretation (or consequence).

This is text-as-prosthetic device, text as substitute for voice. While Chaucer leaves the sisters lamenting, he nonetheless has access to their story and provides access to us: this is more than source studies, more than reception of Ovid: diegetically, the first recorded version of the story is Philomela's tapestry. All others derive from it, on the level of the narrative itself. Chaucer's iteration seems to leave them weeping and alone, but by deleting their own vengeance on Tiresias, another path opens up: juridicial, in the form of the God of Love ordering Chaucer to make restitution (ironically for another act of violence, itself textual). Philomela's tapestry is evidence which does speak, or which at least allows Chaucer to "speak." Consciously or otherwise, Chaucer provides a defense of the written document as something potentially recuperative and liberating, not silent, unchanging, or oppressive.

> Chaucer's inadequate moral makes matters worse, then:
> Ye may be war of men, if that yow liste.
> For al be it that he wol nat, for shame,
> Don as Tereus, to lese his name,
> Ne serve yow as a morderour or a knave,
> Ful lytel while shal ye trewe hym have –
> That wol I seyn, al were he now my brother –
> But it so be that he may have non other. (2387-93)

Most men might not murder you, the narrator says, but if they don't sleep with your sister, it's merely through lack of opportunity. Linked to this is the growing manuscript evidence that the *Legend of Good Women* was seen in the fifteenth century as, in Nicola McDonald's phrase, "a series of admonitory lessons in female deportment and conduct".[29] One wonders what a young woman was supposed to learn from Philomela's story, as presented by Chaucer: don't go visit your sister; don't be pretty; embroidery can be really useful in a pinch, but penmanship is better? There are surely echoes of the various historical justifications for rape here, anathema to a modern audience; add to this Procne's role in Philomela's fate, and the general passivity of the women in the *Legend* as a whole, and an equally dark alternative but entirely inadequate moral emerges: keep quiet and hope for the best. A mute woman cannot make an oath, and a tapestry cannot lead to justice. Rest easy knowing you will be pitied, for that is the only real purpose of your story: to remind women that men are awful, and it is better to keep your head down and go unnoticed.

Gower's Amans (or "the Lover"), who is listening to the stories told in the *Confessio Amantis*, draws what we would see as the proper moral from the story of Philomela and Tereus Warned that anyone who commits rape might end up like Tereus, Amans ignores bird-metamorphosis and cannibalism to draw a different conclusion:

> Me were levere be fortrode
> With wilde hors and be todrawe,
> Er I ayein love and his lawe
> Dede eny thing or loude or stille,
> Which were noght my ladi wille. (CA V.6053-58)

Amans has internalized the idea of violation: it is not that he fears any particular punishment, by wild horse or otherwise, but that such physical pain would be preferable than to have performed a rape against his lady's "wille" at all. As Saunders points out, Gower's emphasis is on "justice, on the condemnation of rape and the punishment of the rapist" as opposed to Chaucer's "sense of a woman's need for a voice within a patriarchal world that threatens silence and death." For Saunders, Philomela's tapestry is merely a "formal indictment" and not a new voice.[30] This seems to me to be both optimistic and misguided: where will that voice come from, if not from the victims themselves? If Philomela is to have a voice which might be considered efficacious and even equal, would it not need to begin with a formal indictment, a restorative act which leads to justice? To read Chaucer's silencing of Philomela as an argument for listening to women's voices is subtle, given that the narrator's moral conclusion (that men will sleep with your sister) is comically inept. It is true that Chaucer's version ends with Philomela's own version of events, a privileged narrative position, and Saunders reads this affective conclusion ("pathos and loss rather than … further violence and destruction") as a positive thing. Philomela's transformation into a bird in Gower allows her a new kind of speech, one which allows her to communicate her mingled joy and sorrow (CA V.5976-5997): "This note sche reherceth ofte / To hem whiche understonde hir tale" (V.5996-97). But perhaps speech, reduced to birdsong which only gains meaning through the words of male mythographers, is not the most reliable – certainly less so than a tapestry with the story drawn out. One leaves far less room for misinterpretation, if not for co-opting. If we refuse to choose between the two versions, we might conclude that both Chaucer and Gower make the case that true justice must be based on clear narrative combined with proper authority, and that for a variety of reasons this is impossible for Philomela. The most prominent reason is her lack of "normal" voice, the authority of the speech act in a society for which personal authority is still best expressed orally.

What emerges here is not only a matter of new emphases in the legal system, in which the written is replacing the oral to the exclusion of other kinds of oath (a binary between oral/written that excludes other kinds of testimony altogether). Chaucer's version of Philomela also witnesses a conflict between rights themselves. Saunders has made a compelling case for a new awareness of the problem of rape in Chaucer and other late medieval English writers, specifically that the victim was the woman and not her father or husband (that this was a crime against the person, not against property). We see this, rightly, as a step towards a more just approach to the crime of rape (albeit that this journey, to judge by recent political events in America and elsewhere, is by no means complete). This new understanding eventually led to increased protection for women themselves, and a strong push to place rape more firmly in the category of the taboo, the always-criminal. But this possibility arises just as the law takes another step, towards an arguably more impersonal view of what constitutes proof and witnessing: the move from oral witnessing to written, in which written evidence not only comes to take precedence, it replaces other possibilities. Clanchy tells the story of the Earl de Warenne, who when asked to produce the evidence that his family owns a piece of land, brings a rusty sword to court: the very sword, he claims, that his Norman ancestor used in 1066.[31] The story, like Philomela's, is more legend than historical event: but as Clanchy argues, it indicates the extent to which this shift, from a variety of possible proofs to a world in which written documentation was the only possibility, produced social anxieties. The adaptation decisions Chaucer makes in "Philomela" seem of a part with both a new interest in women's control over their own bodily integrity, and simultaneously an acknowledgement that this new sympathy (this pity) is ultimately unproductive when it is not matched with action. The legal system of Chaucer's era could not listen to Philomela even before she is mutilated, and her idiosyncratic form of literacy is increasingly difficult to accommodate. It would be centuries before the law would begin to properly accommodate various forms of disability, and to enforce accommodation in other social areas. Even now, that fight is not over; pity and charity still rule social responses to disability, a long legacy of Christian attitudes to the distinction between the normal, the able-bodied, and the disabled.

Notes

[1] This essay will make use of the "F" version. All quotations are from *The Riverside Chaucer*, 3rd edition, edited by Larry D. Benson (Boston: Houghton Mifflin, 1987).

[2] Kara A. Doyle, "Thisbe out of context: Chaucer's Female Readers and the Findern Manuscript," *Chaucer Review* 40.3 (2006): 231-61.

[3] See Laura J. Getty, '"Other Smale Ymaad Before": Chaucer as Historiographer in the *Legend of Good Women*', *Chaucer Review* 42.1 (2007), 48-75.

[4] Michel Foucault, *Discipline and Punish*. Trans Alan Sheridan (New York: Vintage, 1995), 55.

[5] Susan Wendell, *The Rejected Body: Feminist Philosophical Reflections on Disability* (New York: Routledge, 1996), 28-31.

[6] H-Dirksen L. Bauman, "Toward a Poetics of Vision, Space, and the Body: Sign Language and Literary Theory," in Davis 2006, 355. Indeed, the noted inventor of Sign language, the Abbé de l'Epée, had merely "discovered" that deaf-mutes were already communicating by gesture (366, n. 7).

[7] Bracton 2:286; Richard Firth Green, *A Crisis of Truth* (Philadelphia: University of Pennsylvania, 1999), 60.

[8] M. T. Clanchy, *From Memory to Written Record* (Oxford and Cambridge, Mass: Blackwell), 275.

[9] Clanchy, 41.

[10] Elissa Marder, "Disarticulated voices: Feminism and Philomela," *Hypatia* 7.2 (1992), 158.

[11] Marder, 158.

[12] Vered Lev Kenaan, *Pandora's Senses: The Feminine Character of the Ancient Text* (Madison, WI: University of Wisconsin Press, 2008), 164.

[13] Lev Kenaan, 163.

[14] John Gower, *Confessio Amantis*. Ed. Russell A. Peck. Medieval Academy Reprints for Teaching 9 (Toronto: University of Toronto Press, 1980), 308-22.

[15] M. Lynn Rose, "Deaf and Dumb in Ancient Greece", in Davis 2006), 27 n. 83.

[16] Corinne Saunders, *Rape and Ravishment in the Literature of Medieval England* (Woodbridge: D. S. Brewer, 2001), 274.

[17] Gia Aloni, "A Curious Error? Geoffrey Chaucer's Legend of Hypermnestra," *Chaucer Review* 36.1 (2001), 84.

[18] Saunders, 275.

[19] Clanchy, 230.
[20] Clanchy, 257.
[21] Getty 66.
[22] Saunders, 276.
[23] Carolyn Dinshaw, *Chaucer's Sexual Poetics* (Madison: University of Wisconsin Press, 1989), 83.
[24] Joseph P. Shapiro, *No Pity* (New York: Random House, 1994).
[25] Sarah Stanbury, *The Visual Object of Desire in Late Medieval England* (Philadelphia: University of Philadelphia, 2008), 154.
[26] Stanbury 154; Chaucer, *Manciple's Tale* 342.
[27] Stanbury, 153; Chaucer, *Prioress' Tale* 1839-52.
[28] Stanbury, 154-55.
[29] Nicola McDonald, "Chaucer's Legend of Good Women, Ladies at Court and the Female Reader," *Chaucer Review* 35.1 (2000), 39; Louise O. Fradenburg, "'Our owen wo to drynke': Loss, Gender and Chivalry in Troilus and Criseyde," in *The Norton Troilus and Criseyde*, ed. Stephen A. Barney (New York and London: Norton, 2006), 599.
[30] Saunders, 276-77.
[31] Clanchy, 41-2.

BIBLIOGRAPHY

Albrecht, Gary L., Katherine D. Seelman, and Michael Bury. *Handbook of Disability Studies*, Katherine D. Seelman, and Michael Bury. Thousand Oaks, CA: Sage, 2001.

Aloni, Gia. "A Curious Error? Geoffrey Chaucer's Legend of Hypermnestra," *Chaucer Review* 36.1 (2001): 73-86.

Althoff, Gerd. "*Ira Regis*: Prolegomena to a History of Royal Anger." In *Anger's Past: The social uses of am emotion in the Middle Ages*, ed. by Barbara Rosenwein. Ithaca and London: Cornell University Press. 59-74.

Amundsen, Darrel W. "Medieval Canon Law on Medical and Surgical Practice by the Clergy." *Bulletin of the History of Medicine* 52 (1978): 22-44.

Aers, David. *Community, Gender, and Individual Identity: English Writing, 1360-1430*. London: Routledge, 1988.

Archibald, Elizabeth. "Incest in Medieval Literature and Society." *Forum for Modern Language Studies* 25, no. 1 (1989): 1-14.

—. *Incest and the Medieval Imagination*. Oxford: Clarendon Press, 2001.

Attenborough, Frederick Levi (ed). *The Laws of the Earliest English Kings*. Cambridge: Cambridge University Press, 1922. Rpt Felinbach: Llanerch Publishers, 2000.

Barone, Giulia. "S. Francesco, S. Bonaventura e la malattia." In *San Bonaventura Francescano,* 271-278. Todi: Centro di studi sulla spiritualità medievale, 1974.

Bartlett, Robert. *Trial by Fire and Water: The Medieval Judicial Ordeal*. Oxford: Clarendon Press, 1986.

Baudrillard, Jean. "Symbolic Exchange and Death." In *Literary Theory: An Anthology*, edited by Julie Rivkin and Michael Ryan, 488-508. Oxford, UK: Blackwell, 1998.

Beckwith, Sarah. *Christ's Body: Identity, Culture and Society in Late Medieval Writings*. London: Routledge, 1993.

Bildhauer, Bettina. *Medieval Blood*. Cardiff: University of Wales, 2006.

Bliss, Jane. *Naming and Namelessness in Medieval Romance*. Cambridge: Cambridge University Press, 2008.

Bloch, R. Howard. *Etymologies and Genealogies: A Literary Anthropology of the French Middle Ages*. Chicago and London: University of Chicago Press, 1983.

Boockman, Hartmut. *Die Stadt im späten Mittelalter*. 3d ed. Munich: C. H. Beck, 1994.

Boyle, Leonard E. "The Beginnings of Legal Studies at Oxford," *Viator* 14 (1983): 107-32.

Bracton on the Laws and Customs of England, George E. Woodbine (ed) and Samuel E. Thorne (trans), 4 vols. Cambridge, MA: Harvard University Press, 1977.

Britton, Francis Morgan Nichols (ed), 2 vols. Oxford: Clarendon Press, 1865.

Brooke, Rosalind. *Early Franciscan Government: Elias to Bonaventure.* Cambridge: Cambridge University Press, 1959.

Brown-Grant, Rosalind. *French Romances of the Later Middle Ages: Gender, Morality and Desire*. Oxford: Oxford University Press, 2008.

Brundage, James. *Law, Sex, and Christian Society in Medieval Europe*. Chicago and London: University of Chicago Press, 1987.

—. "The Teaching and Study of Canon Law in the Law Schools." In *The History of Medieval Canon Law in the Classical Period,* edited by Wilfried Hartmann and Kenneth Pennington. Washington, DC: Catholic University of America Press, 2008. 98-120.

Butler, Judith. *Bodies that Matter: On the Discursive Limits of "Sex."* New York: Routledge, 1993.

Butler, Sara M. *The Language of Abuse: Marital Violence in Later Medieval England*. Leiden and Boston: Brill, 2007.

—. "Medicine on Trial: Regulating the Health Professions in Later Medieval England." *Florilegium* 28 (2011): 71-94.

Bynum, Caroline Walker. *Holy Feast, Holy Fast: The Religious Significance of Food to Medieval Women*. Berkeley: University of California Press, 1987.

Cadden, Joan. *The Meanings of Sex: Difference in the Middle Ages: Medicine, Science, and Culture*. Cambridge: Cambridge University Press, 1995.

Chaucer, Geoffrey. *The Riverside Chaucer*. Ed by Larry D. Benson. 3rd ed. Boston: Houghton Mifflin, 1987.

Christine de Pizan, *The Book of the Body Politic*. Ed. and trans. by Kate Langdon Forhan (Cambridge: Cambridge University Press, 1994).

Citrome, Jeremy J. *The Surgeon in Medieval English Literature*. New York: Palgrave MacMillan, 2006.

Clanchy, M. T. *From Memory to Written Record.* 2nd ed. Oxford and Cambridge, Mass: Blackwell, 1993.

Clarke, Basil. *Mental Disorder in Earlier Britain: Exploratory Studies.* Cardiff: University of Wales Press, 1975.

Codex Justinianus, Gottfried Härtel and Frank-Michael Kaufmann (eds). Leipzig: Reclam Verlag, 1991.

Cohen, Esther. *The Crossroads of Justice: Law and Culture in Late Medieval France*. Leiden, New York, and Cologne: Brill, 1993.

Cohen, Jerome Jeffrey (ed.) *Monster Theory*. Minneapolis: University of Minnesota Press, 1997.

—. *Of Giants*. Minneapolis: University of Minnesota Press, 1999.

Cohen, Yehudi A. "Ends and Means in Political Control: State Organization and the Punishment of Adultery, Incest, and Violation of Celibacy." *American Anthropologist*, n.s. 71 (1969): 658-87.

Coldewey, John C. (ed). *Early English Drama: An Anthology*. New York: Garland, 1993.

Compilatio assisiensis. In *Fontes Franciscani*, 1471-1690.

Connolly, Seán (ed). *Bede: On Tobit and on the Canticle of Habakkuk.* Dublin: Four Courts Press, 1997.

Crawford, Catherine. "Medicine and the Law". In *The Companion Encyclopedia of the History of Medicine*, edited by W. F. Bynum and Roy Porter (eds), 2 vols., 1619-40. London and New York: Routledge, 1997.

Critchlow, F. L. "On the Forms of Betrothal and Wedding Ceremonies in the Old French 'Romans D'Aventure'." *Modern Philology* 2, no 4 (1905): 497-537.

Crook, J. A. *Law and Life of Rome, 90 B.C. – A. D. 212*. Ithaca: Cornell University Press, 1967, rpt 1987).

Cusato, Michael. "Talking About Ourselves: The Shift in Franciscan Writing from Hagiography to History (1235-1247)." *Franciscan Studies* 58, (2000): 37-75.

Cusato, Michael. "Towards a Resolution of the Franciscan Question: Introduction to the Roundtable." *Franciscan Studies* 66 (2008): 479-481.

Cuttler, S. H. *The Law of Treason and Treason Trials in Later Medieval France*. Cambridge: Cambridge University Press, 2003.

Dalarun, Jacques. *Francis and the Feminine.* Translated by Paula Pierce and Mary Sutphin. St. Bonaventure, NY: Franciscan Institute Press, 2006.

—. *Francis and the Question of Power.* St. Bonaventure, NY: Franciscan Institute, 2007.

—. *The Misadventure of Francis of Assisi: Towards a Historical Use of the Franciscan Legends.* Translated by Edward Hagman. St. Bonaventure, NY: Franciscan Institute Publications, 2002.

—. *Vers une résolution de la question franciscaine: La légende ombrienne de Thomas de Celano.* Paris: Fayard, 2007.

Davis, Lennard J. *Bending Over Backwards: Disability, Dismodernism & Other Difficult Positions*. New York: New York University Press, 2002.

—. ed. *The Disability Studies Reader*. New York and London: Routledge, 1997.

—. ed. *The Disability Studies Reader*. 2nd edition. New York and London: Routledge, 2006.

De Beaumanoir, Philippe. *The Coutumes de Beauvaisis of Philippe de Beaumanoir*, translated by F. R. P. Akehurst. Philadelphia: University of Pennsylvania, 1992.

De Remi, Philippe. *Roman de la Manekine, par Philippe de Reimes, trouvère du triezième siècle*. Edited by Francisque Michel. Paris: Maulde et Renou for the Bannatyne Club, 1840. http://www.archive.org/details/romandelamaneki6800philuoft.

—. *Le Roman de la Manekine*. Edited and translated by Barbara N. Sargent-Baur. Amsterdam: Rodopi, 1999.

De Zulueta, F. (ed). *The Liber Pauperum of Vacarius*. Selden Society 46. London: Quaritch, 1927.

Dean, Trevor. *Crime in Medieval Europe, 1200-1500*. Harlow: Longman, 2001.

Debozy, Maria (trans). *The Saxon Mirror: A Sachsenspiegel of the Fourteenth Century*. Philadelphia: University of Pennsylvania Press, 1999.

Decrees of the Ecumenical Councils: Nicaea to Lateran V. Edited by N. Tanner. 2 vols. Washington DC: Georgetown University Press, 1990.

Delorme, Ferdinand. "La 'legenda antiqua s. Francisci' du MS 1046 de la Bibliothèque communale de Pérouse."*Archivum franciscanum historicum* 15 (1922): 23-70.

Dinshaw, Carolyn. *Chaucer's Sexual Poetics*. Madison: University of Wisconsin Press, 1989.

Doyle, Kara A. "Thisbe out of context: Chaucer's Female Readers and the Findern Manuscript," *Chaucer Review* 40.3 (2006): 231-61.

Drew, Karen Fisher (ed). *The Lombard Laws*. Philadelphia: University of Pennyslvania Press, 1973.

—. *The Laws of the Salian Franks*. Philadelphia: University of Pennsylvania Press, 1991.

Duby, Georges. *Love and Marriage in the Middle Ages*. Translated by Jane Dunnett. Cambridge: Polity Press, 1994.

Dunbabin, Jean. *Captivity and Imprisonment in Medieval Europe, 1000-1300*. Basingstoke and New York: Palgrave Macmillan, 2002.

Ebel, Friedrich (ed). *Sachsenspiegel. Landrecht und Lehnrecht*. Stuttgart: Reclam, 1999.

Ehrenreich, Barbara. *Bright-Sided: How Positive Thinking is Undermining America*. New York: Picador, 2010.

Elliott, Dyan. "Seeing Double: John Gerson, the Discernment of Spirits, and Joan of Arc." *The American Historical Review* 107, no.1 (Feb. 2002): 26-54.

Engel, Evamaria and Frank-Dietrich Jacob, *Städtisches Leben im Mittelalter: Schriftquellen und Bildzeugnisse*. Cologne: Böhlau Verlag, 2006.

Epperlein, Siegfried. *Bäuerliches Leben im Mittelalter. Schriftquellen und Bildzeugnisse*. Cologne: Böhlau Verlag, 2003.

Farley, Mary Hardiman. "Her Own Creature: Religion, Feminist Criticism, and the Functional Eccentricity of Margery Kempe." *Exemplaria* 11, no. 1 (1999): 1-21.

Favazza, Armando R. *Bodies Under Siege: Self-mutilation and Body Modification in Culture and Psychiatry*, 2nd ed. Baltimore, MD: Johns Hopkins University Press, 1996.

Feldmann, H. "Die forensische Bewertung von Körperschäden im frühen Mittelalter – ein Vergleich mit heutigen MdE-Sätzen." *Laryngo-Rhino-Otologie* 69 (1990): 166-70.

Fenster, Thelma. "Beaumanoir's *La Manekine*: Kin D(r)ead: Incest, Doubling & Death." *American Imago* 39, no. 1 (1982): 41-58.

Flint, Valerie. *The Rise of Magic in Early Medieval Europe* (Oxford: Oxford University Press, 1991.

Fontes Franciscani. Edited by E. Menesto and S. Brufani. Assisi: Edizioni Porziuncola, 1995.

Foucault, Michel. *History of Madness*. Edited by Jean Khalfa and translated by Jonathan Murphy and Jean Khalfa. London and New York: Routledge, 2009. 1961.

—. *Discipline and Punish*. Trans by W. Sayers. Ann Arbor: University of Michigan Press, 1977.

—. *History of Sexuality: An Introduction*. Trans. by Robert Hurley. New York: Vintage Books, 1990.

Fradenburg, Louise O. "'Our owen wo to drynke': Loss, Gender and Chivalry in *Troilus and Criseyde*," in *The Norton Troilus and*

Criseyde, ed. Stephen A. Barney. New York and London: Norton, 2006. 589-606.

Francis of Assisi: Early Documents. Edited by R. J. Armstrong, J. A. W. Hellmann, and W. J. Short. 3 vols. New York: New City Press, 2002.

Francis of Assisi. *Regula non bullata.* In *Fontes Franciscani,* 184-213.

Francomano, Emily C. "The Hands of Phillipe de Remi's *Manekine.*" Mediterranean Studies 15 (2006): 1-20.

Frugoni, Chiara. *A Day in a Medieval City*. Trans by William McCuaig. Chicago and London: University of Chicago Press, 2005.

Geary, Patrick J. (ed). *Readings in Medieval History, Vol 1: The Early Middle Ages*. Orchard Park, NY: Broadview Press, 1992.

Geltner, Guy. "Medieval Prisons: Between Myth and Reality, Hell and Purgatory." *History Compass* 4 (2006): 1-14.

—. *The Medieval Prison: A Social History*. Princeton: Princeton University Press, 2008.

Getty, Laura J. "'Other Smale Ymaad Before': Chaucer as Historiographer in *The Legend of Good Women*," *Chaucer Review* 42.1 (2007): 48-75.

Gibson, Gail McMurray. *The Theater of Devotion: East Anglian Drama and Society in the Late Middle Ages*. Chicago: University of Chicago P, 1989.

Godot-Calogeras, Jean François. "Francis of Assisi's Resignation: An Historical and Philological Probe." In *Charisma und religiöse Gemeinschaften in Mittelalter*. Edited by G. Andenna, M. Breitensten and G. Melville, 281-300. Berlin, Hamburg and Münster: LIT Verlag, 2005.

Goffman, Erving. *Stigma: Notes on the management of spoiled identity*. Harmondsworth: Penguin, 1990. 1963.

Gonthier, Nicole. *Le Châtiment du crime au Moyen Âge, XIIe-XIVe siècles*. Rennes: Presses Universitaires de Rennes, 1998.

Goodman, Anthony. "The Piety of John Brunham's Daughter, of Lynn." In *Medieval Women*, edited by Derek Baker, 347-58. Oxford, UK: Basil Blackwell, 1978.

Gower, John. *Confessio Amantis*. Ed. by Russell A. Peck. Toronto: University of Toronto Press, 1980.

Gratian. *Decretum*. Edited by A. L. Richter. Graz: Verlagsanstaldt, 1959.

Gravdal, Kathryn. *Ravishing Maidens: Writing Rape in Medieval French Literature and Law*. Philadelphia: University of Pennsylvania Press, 1991.

Green, Richard Firth. *A Crisis of Truth*. Philadelphia: University of Pennsylvania Press, 1999.

Grimm, Jacob. *Deutsche Rechtsaltertümer*. Darmstadt: Wissenschaftliche Buchgesellschaft, 1994.
H-Dirksen, L. Bauman. "Towards a Poetics of Vision, Space, and the Body: Sign Language and Literary Theory," in Davis 2006. 355-56.
Haldon, John. "Humour and the Everyday in Byzantium." In *Humour, History and Politics in Late Antiquity and the Early Middle Ages*, edited by Guy Halsall, 48-74. Cambridge: Cambridge University Press, 2002).
Hanawalt, Barbara A., and David Wallace. "Introduction". In *Medieval Crime and Social Control*, edited by Barbara A. Hanawalt and David Wallace. Minneapolis and London: University of Minnesota Press, 1999.
Harvey, Ruth E. *The Inward Wits: Psychological Theory in the Middle Ages and the Renaissance*. London: Warburg Institute, University of London, 1975.
Hebdige, Dick. "Subculture: The Meaning of Style." In *Literary Theory: An Anthology*, edited by Julie Rivkin and Michael Ryan, 1065-75. Oxford, UK: Blackwell, 1998.
Heene, Katrien. "'Ad sanguinis effusionem': Automutilatie en gender in middeleeuwse heiligenlevens." *Queeste: Tijdschrift over middeleeuwse letterkunde in de Nederlanden* 6 (1999): 1-22.
Hellemann, J. A. Wayne. "Francis of Assisi: Saint, Founder, Prophet." In *Francis of Assisi: History, Hagiography and Hermeneutics in the Early Documents*. Edited by J. A. Hammond, 15-38. New York: New York City Press, 2004.
Henry d'Avranches. *Legenda sancti Francisci versificata*. In *Fontes Franciscani*, 1131-1242.
Henslow, George. *Medical Works of the Fourteenth Century*. London: Chapman and Hall, 1899; New York: Burt Franklin, 1972.
History of Medieval Canon Law in the Classical Period (The): From Gratian to the Decretals of Pope Gregory IX. Edited by Wilfried Hartmann and Kenneth Pennington. Washington: Catholic University of America Press, 2008.
Hollenbach, Paul W. "Jesus, Demoniacs, and Public Authorities: A Socio-Historical Study." *Journal of the American Academy of Religion* 49, no. 4 (1981): 567-88.
Huet, Gédéon. "Les Sources de la *Manekine* de Philippe de Beaumanoir." *Romania* 45 (1918-19): 94-9.
Hurnard, Naomi D. *The King's Pardon for Homocide before A.D. 1307*. Oxford: Clarendon Press, 1969.

Ives, George. *History of Penal Methods*. London: Stanley Paul and Company, 1914.

James, R. R. *Studies in the History of Ophthalmology in England prior to the Year 1800*. Cambridge: Cambridge University Press, 1933.

Jansen, Katherine Ludwig. *The Making of the Magdalen: Preaching and Popular Devotion in the Later Middle Ages*. Princeton, NJ: Princeton University Press, 2000.

John of Salisbury, *Policraticus*. Trans. and ed. Cary J. Nederman. Cambridge: Cambridge University Press, 1990.

Julian of Speyer. *Vita sancti Francisci.* In *Fontes Franciscani,* 1025-1095.

Jurasinski, Stefan. *Ancient Privileges: Beowulf, Law, and the Making of Germanic Antiquity.* Morgantown: West Virginia University Press, 2006.

Justinian's Institutes. Peter Birks and Grant McLeod (trans and intro). Ithaca: Cornell University Press, 1987.

Kagay, Donald L. Kagay (trans). *The Usages of Barcelona: The Fundamental Law of Catalonia.* Philadelphia: University of Pennsylvania, 1994.

Kan, Steven S. "Corporal Punishment and Optimal Incapacitation." *Journal of Legal Studies* 25 (1996): 121-30.

King, David S. "The Meaning of Amputation in the *chansons de geste*." *Symposium: A quarterly journal in modern literatures* 62 (2008): 35-51.

—. "A Motif Transformed: The Meaning of Lost Limbs in Arthurian Romance." *Arthuriana* 18, no. 2 (2008): 31-41.

Kleinberg, Aviad. *Flesh Made Word: Saints' Stories and the Western Imagination.* Cambridge, Mass: Belknap Press, 2008.

Kolve, V. A. *The Play Called Corpus Christi.* Stanford: Stanford University Press, 1966.

Kuttner, Stephen, and Eleanor Rathbone, "Anglo-Norman Canonists of the Twelfth Century: An Introductory Study." *Traditio* 7 (1949-51): 279-358.

Lambert, Malcolm. *Medieval Heresy: Popular Movements from the Gregorian Reform to the Reformation*, 3rd edition. Oxford: Blackwell, 2002.

Landau, Peter. "Gratian and the Decretum Gratiani." In *The History of Medieval Canon Law in the Classical Period: From Gratian to the Decretals of Pope Gregory IX,* 22-54.

Langland, William. *Piers Plowman: An Annotated Edition of the C-Text.* Ed. Derek Pearsall. Exeter: University of Exeter Press, 2008.

Laqueur, Thomas W. *Making Sex: Body and Gender from the Greeks to Freud*. Cambridge, Mass: Harvard University Press, 1990.

Lawes, Richard. "Psychological Disorder and the Autobiographical Impulse in Julian of Norwich, Margery Kempe, and Thomas Hoccleve." In *Writing Religious Women: Female Spiritual and Textual Practices in Late Medieval England*, edited by Denis Renevey and Christiania Whitehead, 217-43 Toronto, ON: University of Toronto Press, 2000.

Lee, R. W. *The Elements of Roman Law with a translation of the Institutes of Justinian*. 4th ed. London: Sweet and Maxwell, 1956, 1986.

Legenda trium sociorum. In *Fontes Franciscani,* 1373-1445.

Leges Alamannorum, MGH, Leges I: Leges Nationum Germanicarum V.1, Hanover: Hahn, 1888.

Leges Burgundionum, MGH, Leges I: Leges Nationum Germanicarum II.1, Hanover: Hahn, 1892.

Leges Henrici Primi, L. J. Downer (ed. & trans.), Oxford: Clarendon Press, 1972.

Leges Saxonum, MGH, Fontes Iuris Germanici Antiqui, Hanover: Hahn, 1918.

LeGoff, Jacques. *Saint Francis of Assisi.* Translated by Christine Rhone. London and New York: Routledge, 1999.

Lev Kanaan. *Pandora's Senses: The Feminine Character of the Ancient Text*. Madison, WI: University of Wisconsin Press, 2008.

Lex Baiwariorum, MGH, Leges I: Leges Nationum Germanicarum V.2, Hanover: Hahn, 1926.

Lex Ribuaria, MGH, Leges I: Leges Nationum Germanicarum III.2, Hanover: Hahn, 1954.

Lieberman, Felix. *Die Gesetze der Angelsachsen*. 3 vols. Halle: Niemeyer, 1898-1916.

Linton, Simi. "Reassigning Meaning", in Davis 2006. 161-72.

List of the General Ministers dating from the 1260s (A). In *Francis of Assisi: The Early Documents,* 3.824.

Lockett, Leslie. "The Role of Grendel's Arm in Feud, Law and the Narrative Strategy of *Beowulf*." In *Latin Learning and English Lore: Studies in Anglo-Saxon Literature for Michael Lapidge, Vol. 1*, edited by Katherine O'Brien O'Keeffe and Andy Orchard, 368-88. Toronto: University of Toronto Press, 2005.

MacBain, William. "The Outside at Court, or What is so Strange about the Stranger?" In *The Court and Cultural Diversity: Selected Papers from the Eighth Triennial Congress of the International Courtly Literature*

Society, edited by Evelyn Mullally and John Thompson, 357-65. Cambridge: D. S. Brewer, 1997.

Magdaliano, Paul. *The Empire of Manuel I Komnenos, 1143-1180*. Cambridge: Cambridge University Press, 1993.

Manestò, E. "Introduzione." In *Fontes Franciscani,* 1449-1471.

Mann, William E. "Augustine on evil and original sin," in *The Cambridge Companion to Augustine*, ed. by Eleonore Stump and Norman Kretzman. Cambridge: Cambridge University Press, 2001. 40-48.

Mardar, Elissa. "Disarticulated voices: Feminism and Philomela," *Hypatia* 7.2 (1992): 148-66.

Markus, R. A. "Two Conceptions of Political Authority: Augustine, *De Civitate Dei* 19.14-15, and Some Thirteenth Century Interpretations," *Journal of Theological Studies*, n.s. 16 (1965): 68-100.

McDonald, Nicola. "Chaucer's *Legend of Good Women*, Ladies at Court and the Fenale Reader," *Chaucer Review* 35.1 (2000): 22-42.

McLaughlin, Terence P. "Introduction." In *The* Summa parisiensis *on the Decretum gratiani,* XVII-XX. Toronto: PIMS, 1952.

McRuer, Robert. *Crip Theory: Cultural Signs of Queerness and Disability*. New York and London: New York University Press, 2006.

Metzler, Irina. *Disability in Medieval Europe: Thinking about physical impairment during the High Middle Ages, c. 1100-1400*. London and New York: Routledge, 2006.

Mills, Robert. *Suspended Animation: Pain, Pleasure and Punishment in Medieval Culture*. London: Reaktion Books, 2005.

Mitchell, David T. and Sharon L. Snyder. "Representation and Its Discontents: The Uneasy Home of Disability in Literature and Film." In Albrecht et al., 195-218.

Mitchell, Piers D. *Medicine in the Crusades: Warfare, Wounds and the Medieval Surgeon*. Cambridge: Cambridge University Press, 2004.

Montford, Angela. *Health, Sickness, Medicine and the Friars in the Thirteenth and Fourteenth Centuries.* Aldershot: Ashgate, 2004.

Moorman, John. *A History of the Franciscan Order from its Origins to the Year 1517*. Chicago: Franciscan Herald Press, 1968.

Nederman, Cary J. *Lineages of European Political Thought: Explorations along the Medieval/Modern Divide from John of Salisbury to Hegel*. Washington, DC: The Catholic University Press of America, 2009.

Newman, Barbara. "Possessed by the Spirit: Devout Women, Demoniacs, and the Apostolic Life in the Thirteenth Century." *Speculum* 73, no. 3 (July 1998): 733-70.

Nicholas, David. *The Domestic Life of a Medieval City: Women, Children and the Family in Fourteenth-Century Ghent*. Lincoln: University of Nebraska Press, 1985.

Ogden, Amy V. "The Centrality of the Margins: Medieval French Genders and Genres Reconfigured." *French Forum* 30 (2005): 1-23.

Ohler, Norbert. *The Medieval Traveller*. Translated by Caroline Hillier. Woodbridge: Boydell, 1989.

Oliver, Lisi. *The Body Legal in Barbarian Law*. Toronto, Buffalo and London: University of Toronto Press, 2011.

Oliver, Michael. *The Politics of Disablement*. Basingstoke, UK: Palgrave Macmillan, 1990.

O'Neill, Ynez Violé. *Speech and Speech Disorders in Western Thought Before 1600*. Westport, CT, and London: Greenwood Press, 1980.

Parsons, Kelly. "The Red Ink Annotator of *The Book of Margery Kempe* and His Lay Audience." In *The Medieval Professional Reader at Work: Evidence from Manuscripts of Chaucer, Langland, Kempe, and Gower*, edited by Kathryn Kerby Fulton and Maidie Hilmo, 129-72. Victoria, B.C.: English Literary Studies, University of Victoria Press, 2001.

Patrologia Latina. Edited by. J. P . Migne. 217 vols. Paris: Garnier fratres, 1866-1882.

Pearman, Tory Vandeventer. Women and Disability in Medieval Literature. New York: Palgrave MacMillan, 2010.

Pelligrini, Luigi. "A Century of Reading the Sources for the Life of St. Francis of Assisi." *Greyfriars Review* 7:3 (1993): 323-346.

Perkins, Judith. *The Suffering Self: Pain and Narrative Representation in the Early Christian Era*. London and New York: Routledge, 1995.

Peters, Edward M. "Prison before the Prison: The Ancient and Medieval Worlds." In *The Oxford History of the Prison: The Practice of Punishment in Western Society*, edited by Norval Morris and David J. Rothman. New York: Oxford University Press, 1995.

Pickett, R. Colin. *Mental Affliction and Church Law: An Historical Synopsis of Roman and Ecclesiastical Law and a Canonical Commentary*. Ottawa: University of Ottawa Press, 1952.

Pollock, Frederick, and F. W. Maitland. *The History of English Law Before the Time of Edward I*. 2nd ed. Introduction by S. F. C. Milsom. 2 vols. (Cambridge: Cambridge University Press, 1968).

Powicke, F. M. "The Murder of Henry Clement and the Pirates of Lundy Island," *History* 25 (1941): 285-310.

Prioreschi, Plinio. *A History of Medicine, vol. IV: Byzantine and Islamic Medicine*. Omaha: Horatius Press, 2001.

Rawcliffe, Carole. *Medicine and Society in Later Medieval England.* Frome, Somerset: Sutton Publishing, 1977.

—. *Leprosy in Medieval England.* Woodbridge: Boydell, 2006.

Raymond of Peñafort, *Decretalium gregorii.* In *Decretalium collections.* Edited by A. L. Richter. Graz: U. Verlagsanstalt, 1959.

Renna, Thomas. "St. Francis as Prophet in Celano and Bonaventure." *Michigan Academician* 33.4 (2000): 321-332. General OneFile Web. (accessed 1 Mar 2010).

Richardson, H. G. and G. O. Sayles. *Law and Legislation from Aethelbert to Magna Carta.* Edinburgh: Edindburgh University Press, 1966.

Robinson, Daniel N. *Wild Beasts and Idle Humours: The Insanity Defense from Antiquity to the Present.* Harvard University Press, 1996.

Roffe, David and Christine Roffe. "Madness and care in the community: a medieval perspective," *British Medical Journal* 311 (1995): 1708-12.

Rose, M. Lynn. "Deaf and Dumb in Ancient Greece," in Davis 2006. 17-31.

Rubin, Stanley. *Medieval English Medicine.* New York: Barnes and Noble, 1974.

Rushton, Cory James. "The King's Stupor: Dealing with Royal Paralysis in Late Medieval England'. In Turner, *Madness*, 147-76.

Rushton, Peter. "Idiocy, the family and the community in early modern north-east England.' In *From Idiocy to Mental Deficiency: Historical Perspectives on People with Learning Disabilities.* London and New York: Routledge, 1996.

Sabatier, Paul. *Life of Saint Francis of Assisi.* Translated by Louise Seymour Houghton. New York: Charles Scribner's Sons, 1894, 1930.

Sachsenspiegel. Ein Rechtsbuch speigelt seine Zeit (Der). Exhibition Catalogue. Oldenburg, 1996.

Sargent-Baur, Barbara N. "Introduction." In de Remi (Sargent-Baur), 69-128.

Saunders, Corinne. *Rape and Ravishment in the Literature of Medieval England.* Woodbridge: D. S. Brewer, 2001.

Scarry, Elaine. *The Body in Pain: The making and unmaking of the world.* Oxford and New York: Oxford University Press, 1985.

Schatzlein Joanne and Daniel P. Sulmasy. "The Diagnosis of St. Francis: Evidence for Leprosy."*Franciscan Studies* 47 (1987): 181-217.

Schleusener-Eichholz, Gudrun. *Das Auge im Mittelalter.* 2 vols. Munich: W. Fink Press, 1984.

Schroeder, H. J. *Disciplinary Decrees of the General Councils: Text, Translation and Commentary.* St. Louis: B. Herder, 1937.

Schuld, J. Joyce. "Augustine, Foucault, and the Politics of Imperfection," Journal of Religion 80.1 (2000): 1-22.

Schulenburg, Jane Tibbetts. *Forgetful of Their Sex: Female Sanctity and Society, ca. 500-1100*. Chicago and London: University of Chicago Press, 1998.

Sedlar, Jean W. *East Central Europe in the Middle Ages, 1000-1500*. Washington: University of Washington Press, 1994.

Shahar, Shulamith. *The Fourth Estate: A History of Women in the Middle Ages*. London and New York: Routledge, 1991. 1983.

—. *Growing Old in the Middle Ages: 'Winter clothes us in shadows and pain.'* Translated by Yael Lotan. London and New York: Routledge, 1997.

—. "The Middle Ages and Renaissance." In *The Long History of Old Age*, edited by Pat Thane, 71-111. London: Thames and Hudson, 2005.

Shapiro, Joseph P. *No Pity*. New York: Random House, 1994.

Shepherd, M. *Tradition and Re-creation in the Thirteenth-century Romance: 'La Manekine' and 'Jehan et Blonde' by Philippe de Remi*. Amsterdam and Athens, GA: Rodopi, 1990.

Shklar, Ruth. "Cobham's Daughter: The Book of Margery Kempe and the Power of Heterodox Thinking." *Modern Language Quarterly* 56, no. 3 (1995): 277-304.

Siebers, Tobin. "Disability in Theory: From Social Construction to the New Realism of the Body," in Davis 2006. 173-84.

Silence (*Roman de*). Ed. by Sarah Roche-Mahdi. East Lansing: Michigan State University Press, 1992.

Singer, Julie. "Toward a transhuman model of medieval disability," *postmedieval* 1 (2010): 1-7.

Smith, Julia M. H. *Europe After Rome: A New Cultural History 500-1000*. Oxford: Oxford University Press, 2005.

Snyder, Sharon L., and David T. Mitchell. *Narrative Prosthesis*. Ann Arbor: University of Michigan, 2000.

—. *Cultural Locations of Disability*. Chicago and London: University of Chicago Press, 2006.

Sontag, Susan. *Illness as Metaphor and AIDS and Its Metaphors*. New York: Picador, 1988.

Southern. R. W. *Western Society and the Church in the Middle Ages*. Harmondsworth: Penguin, 1970.

—. "Master Vacarius and the Beginning of an English Academic Tradition," *Medieval Learning and Literature: Essays presented to Richard William Hunt*. Ed. by J. J. G. Alexander and M. T. Gibson. Oxford: Clarendon Press, 1976. 257-86.

Stainton, Tim. "Reason, grace and charity: Augustine and the impact of church doctrine on the construction of intellectual disability," *Disability and Society* 23:5 (2008): 485-96.

Staley, Lynn, ed. *The Book of Margery Kempe*. Kalamazoo, MI: Medieval Institute Publications, 1996.

—. ed. and trans. *The Book of Margery Kempe*. New York: Norton, 2001.

—. *Margery Kempe's Dissenting Fictions*. University Park, PA: Pennsyvlania State University Press, 1994.

Stanbury, Sarah. *The Visual Object of Desire in Late Medieval England*. Philadelphia: University of Pennsylvania Press, 2008.

Stein, Peter. "Vacarius and the Civil Law," in *Church and Government in the Middle Ages: Essays presented to C. R. Cheney on his 70th Birthday*, ed. by C. N. L. Brooke at al. Cambridge: Cambridge University Press, 1976. 119-37.

Stiker, Henri-Jacques. *A History of Disability*. Translated by William Sayers. Ann Arbor, MI: University of Michigan Press, 2002.

Stones, Alison. "The Manuscript, Paris BNF Fr. 1588, and its Illustrations." In de Remi (Sargent-Baur), 1-39 plus plates.

Stork, Nancy P. "Did Margery Kempe Suffer from Tourette's Syndrome?" *Mediaeval Studies* 59 (1997): 261-300.

Strohm, Paul. *England's Empty Throne: Usurpation and the Language of Legitimation, 1399-1422*. New Haven, Conn.: Yale University Press, 1998.

Suchier, Hermann. *Oeuvres Poétiques de Philippe de Remi*. 2 vols. Paris: Librairie de Fermin Didot et Cie, 1884-85.

Tanner, Norman P., ed. and intro. *Heresy Trials in the Diocese of Norwich, 1428-31*. London: Offices of the Royal Historical Society, 1977.

Thomas of Celano. *Vita prima sancti Francisci.* In *Fontes Franciscani*, 273-424.

—. *Vita secunda sancti Francisci.* In *Fontes Franciscani,* 441-649.

Thomas, J. A. C. (ed). *The Institutes of Justinian: Text, Translation and Commentary*. Amsterdam and Oxford: North Holland Publishers, 1975).

Tierney, Brian. *Medieval Poor Law: A Sketch of Canonical Theory and Its Application in England*. Berkeley and Los Angeles: University of California Press, 1959.

Titchkosky, Tanya. *Reading and Writing Disability Differently: The Textured Embodiment of Life*. Toronto, Buffalo, and New York: University of Toronto Press, 2007.

Turner, Ralph V. *The English Judiciary in the Age of Glanville and Bracton, c. 1176-1239*. Cambridge: Cambridge University Press, 1985.

Turner, Wendy J. "'Afflicted with Insanity': The Care and Custody of the Feeble Minded in Late Medieval England." Dissertation, UCLA (2000).

—. "Mental Incapacity and Financing War in Medieval England," in *The Hundred Years War: A Wider Focus*. Ed. by L. J. Andrew Villalon and Donald Kagay. Vol. 2. Leiden and Boston: Brill, 2008.

—. (ed). *Madness in Medieval Law and Custom* (Leiden and Boston: Brill, 2010).

Velay-Vellantin, Catherine. *L'Histoire des contes*. Paris: Arthème Fayard, 1992.

Vincent of Beauvais. *Speculum naturale.* B. Belleri, 1624. Reprinted, Graz: Akademischen Druck-u. Verlagsanstalt, 1967.

Voaden, Rosalynn. *God's Words, Women's Voices: The Discernment of Spirits in the Writing of Late-Medieval Women Visionaries*. Woodbridge, Suffolk, UK: York Medieval Press, 1999.

Von Bar, Ludwig, et al. *A History of Continental Criminal Law*. Translated by Thomas S. Bell et al. South Hackensack, NJ, and New York: Rothman Reprints and Augustus M. Kelley, 1968. 1916.

Watson, Nicholas. "Censorship and Cultural Change in Late-Medieval England: Vernacular Theology, the Oxford Translation Debate, and Arundel's Constitutions of 1409." *Speculum* 70, no. 4 (Oct. 1995): 822-64.

Waugh, Scott L. *England in the Reign of Edward III*. Cambridge: Cambridge University Press, 1991.

Wendell, Susan. *The Rejected Body: Feminist Philosophical Reflections on Disability*. New York: Routledge, 1996.

Werner, Hans. *Geschichte des Taubstummen-problems bis ins 17. Jahrhundert*. Jena: Gustav Fischer, 1932.

Whitelock, Dorothy (ed). *English Historical Documents, Vol. 1.* 2nd ed. London: Eyre Methuen, 1979.

Whittaker, William Joseph (ed). *The Mirror of Justices*. London: Selden Society, 1895.

Williams, David. *Deformed Discourse*. Exeter: University of Exeter Press, 1996.

Wilson, Janet. "Communities of Dissent: The Secular and Ecclesiastical Communities of Margery Kempe's Book." In *Medieval Women in their Communities*, edited by Diane Watt, 155-85. Toronto: University of Toronto Press, 1997.

Winroth, Anders. *The Making of Gratian's* Decretum. Cambridge: University of Cambridge Press, 2000.

Winstead, Karen A., ed. *The Life of Saint Katherine by John Capgrave*. Kalamazoo, MI: Medieval Institute Publications, 1999.

Winzer, Margaret A. "Disability and Society Before the Eighteenth Century", in Davis 1997. 75-109.

Zeppa, Rosario. "San Francesco's Blindness." *The Journal of Paleopathology*. 3:3 (1991):133-135.

Ziegler, Joseph. *Medicine and Religion c. 1300: The Case of Arnau da Vilanova.* Oxford: Oxford Historical Monographs, 1998.

LIST OF CONTRIBUTORS

Irina Metzler is Wellcome Trust Research Fellow, MEMO Centre/Department of History of University of Swansea and Associate Member, Homo-debilis-Projekt, Institut für Geschichtswissenschaft, Universität Bremen. She is thr author of *Disability in Medieval Europe: Thinking about physical impairment during the High Middle Ages, c. 1100-1400* (Routledge, 2006) and *A Social History of Disability in the Middle Ages: Cultural Considerations of Physical Impairment* (Routledge, 2013). She has published eleven other articles on various aspects of medieval disability, as well as articles on travel, dansomania, and animals.

Amanda Hopkins is Tutor in the Department of English and Comparative Literary Studies, University of Warwick. She is co-editor, with Cory Rushton, of *The Erotic in the Literature of Medieval Britain* (D. S. Brewer, 2007), and has published articles on the Breton lay in *Arthurian Literature*, *Nottingham Medieval Studies*, and several collections. She edited *Melion* and *Biclarel* for the Critical Editions of French Texts in the Liverpool Online Series, and contributed *Melion* to *French Arthurian Literature IV: Eleven Old French Narrative Lays* (ed. and trans Glyn S. Burgess and Leslie C. Brook, D. S. Brewer, 2007).

Marian E. Lupo, J.D., Ph.D., is Research Fellow, Graduate Interdisciplinary Specialization in Disability Studies, The Ohio State University, Columbus, Ohio. Recent publication: "Bringing Back the Baby Lion: Reflections on the Conference on Disability, Culture, and Human Rights," in *Disability in Kenya: The Nairobi Workshop: Personal Narratives and Reactions to the Workshop, Disability Studies Quarterly* 29.4 (2009).

Donna Trembinski is Associate Professor of history at St. Francis Xavier University in Antigonish, Nova Scotia. Her research focuses on the intersections of medicine, disability, religion and theology. Her most recent publications include "Comparing premodern melancholy/mania and modern trauma: An argument in favor of historical experiences of trauma", published in History of Psychology and "[Pro]passio doloris: Early Dominican Perceptions of Christ's Physical Pain", published in the

Journal of Ecclesiastical History. She is pleased to be returning to a study of St. Francis' disabilities, a topic she explored in her thesis work at the University and Toronto and about whom she wrote her first academic article "Non Alter Christus, Early Dominican Lives of St. Francis" published in *Franciscan Studies*.

Wendy J. Turner is Professor of History in the History, Anthropology, and Philosophy Department at Georgia Regents University. She is editor of *Madness in Medieval Law and Custom* (Brill), and co-editor of *The Treatment of Disabled Persons in Medieval Europe: Examining Disability in the Historical, Legal, Literary, Medical, and Religious Discourses of the Middle Ages* (with Kevin Corrigan and Tory Vandeventer Pearman, Edwin Mellen, 2011).

Cory James Rushton is Associate Professor of English at St. Francis Xavier University in Nova Scotia. He is the co-editor of *A Companion to Medieval Popular Romance* (with Raluca Radulescu, D. S. Brewer, 2009), *The Erotic in the Literature of Medieval Britain* (with Amanda Hopkins, D. S. Brewer, 2007), and two volumes on zombies and popular culture (with Christopher Moreman, McFarland, 2011).

INDEX